Costume Designing

Costume Designing

Parul Gupta

MD Publications Pvt Ltd
New Delhi

Published by
MD Publications Pvt Ltd
"MD House", 11, Darya Ganj
New Delhi-110002
Tel. : +91-11-41563325, 41562846
E-mail : contact@mdppl.com
Website : www.mdppl.com

ISBN: 978-81-7533-105-1

PRICE: Rs. 1195.00

Published and Printed by **MD Publications Pvt Ltd** at Times Press, 910, Jatwara Street, Darya Ganj, New Delhi.

Contents

Preface

Costume design is the design of the appearance of the characters in a theater or cinema performance. This usually involves designing or choosing clothing, footwear, hats and head dresses for the actors to wear, but it may also include designing masks, makeup or other unusual forms, such as the full body animal suits worn in the musical Cats.

The Costume designer is the person whose responsibility is to design costumes for a film or stage production. He or she is considered part of the "production team," alongside the director, scenic and lighting designers. The costume designer might also collaborate with a hair/wig master or a makeup designer, with the latter two operating on a subordinate level. In European theatre the role is somewhat different as the theatre designer will design both costume and scenic elements.

Costume designers will typically seek to enhance a character's persona, within the framework of the director's vision, through the way that character is dressed. At the same time, the designer must ensure that the designs allow the actor to move in a manner consistent with the historical period and enables the actor to execute the director's blocking of the production without damage to the garments. Additional considerations include the durability and washability of garments, particularly in extended runs. The designer must work in consultation with not only the director, but the set and lighting designers to ensure that the overall design of the production works together. The designer needs to possess strong artistic capabilities as well as a thorough knowledge of pattern development, draping, drafting, textiles and costume/ fashion history.

Professional costume designers generally fall into three types: freelance, residential, and academic. A freelance designer is hired for a specific production by a theatre, dance or opera company, and the decorative were combined in costume as may be noted in people of wealth and nobility down to the present time. Leaders of religious orders also adapted this combination in order to distinguish them and their office.

The types of garments for all periods from the most remote down to the present time may be divided into four classifications: The tunic, the loin cloth, the cloak, and fitted garments.

The tunic was the first and simplest form of body covering. It was made of a straight piece of material with an opening cut in the middle, large enough for the garment to pass over the head, and the selvedge sewed together at the sides, leaving a space for the arms to pass through the top. From this simple garment was developed the different types of tunics worn by the Egyptians, the Greeks, the Assyrians, the Romans and many other early nations. Also the waist, shirt, blouse, bodice, smock and all other similar garments which hang from the shoulders.

From the loin cloth, which consisted of a piece of material wrapped around the waist and falling down over the hips and thighs, developed the skirt, apron, trousers, tights, breeches, bloomers and all other garments which hang from the waist.

The cloak, which was an outer garment and used chiefly for protection, developed many different forms; the peplum of the Greeks, the toga and stola of the Romans, the surplice of the church, the cape, shawl, poncho, and other developments of this kind used as outer garments.

Aside from these, there is only one important division to be made in the types of garments: the fitted garments. These include the bodice, tights, fitted coat, and all garments which are cut to conform to the contour of the body and differ from the other types in that they do not depend on draperies and folds. The headdresses which form a very essential part of certain costumes, although they are not garments, must be designed as part of the costume. In the theater, anything that is worn by a character or a group of people having the same characteristics must be considered as part of the costume whether it is a garment, a headdress, jewelry, shoes, gloves, objects which are carried, such as, fans, scepters, wands, or any other accessory which is relative to the character of the person carrying or wearing it. The personality of the character in the drama should be interpreted through the costume as well as the acting. The relation of one character to another and the scenes which two or more characters play together should be taken into consideration by the designer in planning the costumes, as well as line, color and silhouette. This method of planning may be carried out to such a fine degree that one costume will not be complete without the color and design of one or more additional costumes.

The period in which the action is placed must be carefully considered. The characteristics which distinguish one character from the other should be accented and the color scheme which is distinctive of the period must be adhered to. For example, the yellows, reds, yellow greens, turquoise blues, ultramarine blues, black and white of the Egyptians should be the colors used throughout a drama placed in some period of Egyptian history. In addition to an accurate historic knowledge, it is very important for the designer of costumes for dramatic performances to conceive of the individual characteristics of a person as expressed through his clothes. For example, the costume to be designed might be that of an Egyptian princess. It must be Egyptian in line, color and decorations, but it also must express the individual type of that particular princess. Perhaps she was dainty, elusive, or spiritual, or possibly, she was pompous, regal and sensuous.

The designer must remember that his task is to design costumes for a theatrical performance through which a truth, a story or a characteristic is to be shown by the aid of his designs, which must be more than just designs for dress. There are four general types of costumes which are used in theatrical designs: the historical, the fantastic (which includes the symbolical costume), the dance costume, and the modern dress. The designer concerns himself more with line, color and decorations according to accurate historical knowledge when he attempts period costume, and with color and expressive line in connection with fantastic costume. If he is designing dance costume, in addition to line and color, the weight of textiles employed is important. With modern dress, the style is fixed, but the designer must plan the color scheme and the dramatic fitness of each costume to the character as interpreted by the playwright. Certain phases of this interpretation are to be emphasized by costume.

For the theater, it is necessary to exaggerate and over-accent the important points in costume design, because of the artificial lighting and the distance between the audience and the players. In the little theater, this is not carried out to the extent that is necessary in large theaters or in pageantry where a still greater exaggeration is necessary. All unnecessary detail should be eliminated. Single costumes may consist of one or two colors to be effective, and rarely can more than three colors be used to any advantage. The general line of a costume should be accented to the greatest degree possible, and for characters of importance this is absolutely essential in order to give them precedence over minor characters.

In planning designs for costumes, the designer must also consider the materials to be used, the amount required and the construction of the garment. A design to be practical must be something more than an attractive drawing. Unless the effect produced in the drawing can be carried out in the actual garments, the drawing is useless. Therefore, it is necessary for the designer to have some knowledge of cutting and fitting as well as the materials which give the desired effect. He must also understand the relation of the figure to clothes, and how the figure can be helped or hindered by costumes. The comfort of the person wearing the clothes must be considered as well as the beauty of the garment.

Each person who is to be costumed should be carefully measured. The measurements which are to be taken are shown in the diagram. They are as follows: the circumference of the neck and chest, the width of the shoulders, the bust measurement taken with a tape passing well up under the arms, the normal waist line, the hips at the widest part, the distance from the waist to the hip, the distance from the waist over the hip to the edge of the skirt or trousers, the thickness of the thigh, the thickness of the knee, the thickness of the calf, the thickness of the ankle, the arm measurement for the armhole from the point of the shoulder under the armpit, the biceps, the elbow and the wrists, also the length of the sleeve, measuring from the point of the shoulder down the back of the arm to the point where it is to terminate. These measurements are all which are required in any type of garment, and in most garments only the measurements which are necessary need to be taken. In fitting the garments it is important to determine whether or not they are tight in the right places and the fullness is left where it is required. If these points are not accented, the garments do not fit and lose all character unless they depend entirely on draped lines for their character.

In costuming a group which is to present a uniform appearance, certain points or lines such as the length of a skirt or cloak, the position of a waist line and the silhouette, should be considered and emphasized. In making several costumes of the same design, the costume and not the figure of the person who is wearing it should be accented. The measurement for the length of the skirt should be measured from the floor to the edge of the skirt, instead of from the waist line to the edge of the skirt. The same rule applies to measuring cloaks and capes. The waist lines should all be kept as near the same levels as possible. In costumes which require hoopskirts or full sleeves, the fullness or slenderness of the figures should be taken into consideration, so as to correct any noticeable difference between them. Narrow shoulders can be broadened by lengthening the shoulder seams and setting the sleeves farther out. Broad shoulders can be narrowed by shortening the shoulder seams and setting the sleeves in. The hoops which are worn with crinoline dresses should be measured in circumference instead of in proportion to the figure when a number of costumes are to present a similar appearance, such as in the chorus of a musical comedy. Successful and pleasing costuming can be done even by persons who are not specialized designers if they will plan the costumes with regard to emphasizing the vital principles underlying costume design, carefully considering æsthetic, historic and dramatic fitness.

Difference in material for the same design will make the difference, for instance, between the costume of the Puritan and the King, a Cromwell or a James. A correct basis upon which to work would be the mastery of the principles of color and design. A chosen design of the example of a certain period is the simplest thing to carry out if a designer is not very experienced. Such a design must be dramatically good even though very simple. The massing of color, the successful breaking away from the conventional, the effective exaggeration of line, the artist touch, no book on costume can give.

Colour

The colour of costumes is one of the two most important factors in a finished production of the visual side of a play. Colour must be as carefully considered as any other aspect of costuming. A color scheme is not chosen from the viewpoint of what the individual designer likes or what the individual player fancies is becoming. It must be worked out according to the dramatic requirements of the play, the laws of harmony, the action of certain color in material under certain color used in lighting, and the historic accuracy in regard to the kind of dyes existing at certain periods of the world's history.

The designer must have the knowledge of the simple combinations of color at least. He should know that the combinations of the three primary colors—red, blue and yellow *in paint or dyes,* make gray or black; and that the combination of the three primary colors orange, violet and green, or red, blue and green *in light*—make white. He must understand that amber light used alone will gray or kill the value of a scene with blues or greens in it. He must know that a red light will destroy all color except the red values. He must understand that in order to emphasize colors in a stage picture, the color of the light with which he illuminates his scene must be obtained by the use of the three primary colors, as each color will emphasize itself and its variations.

In addition to a knowledge of what colored light will do to color in materials, it is important to consider the use of one color in masses against other colors in masses and how light will affect the appearance of the stage picture. It is also necessary to realize that one color may be used in its various degrees of strength and intensity and give the effect of variety without the use of any other color in a scene. A color scheme in costumes must be planned systematically. The designer should first read the play which is to be presented, noting the colors mentioned in the text, and which colors were used in the period of history during which the action takes place. For example, if the play should be incident of Indian Life, the color would necessarily be influenced by the fact that the Indians in primitive times had only a few vegetable dyes with which to color their dress or themselves, and the color scheme would be confined to these colors. Having noted the limitation of his color chart historically, the designer then plans his color scheme according to what is most suited personally and dramatically to the characters in the play. For a play like "Tantagiles," which has no element of joy or gaiety in the whole action and is built up around the theme which is based on struggle, it would be extremely inappropriate to introduce brilliant light colors. Even rich coloring would not be suitable. A heavy somber treatment would be more effective. That does not mean that all the characters should be costumed in black. Grays, white, purple and neutral shades should be also used. For plays like "Prunella" or "The Wonder Hat," which suggest youth and fantasy, brilliant colors should be used. For a color scheme of this kind, apple green, Nile green, citron, cerise, majenta, mauve, lemon yellow, yellow orange, buff or putty color, or a combination such as black, white, cornflower blue, turquoise blue, jade green, American Beauty red, tangerine and pale yellow would be interesting. These colors all have brilliancy and are light in key without suggesting what is known as pastel shades. For costumes like those of "The Ren naisance," which were made of heavy damask, brocades and other rich materials, a richer color scheme is required.

For these use maroon, rich blues, purples, gold, silver, darker greens, golden brown and bright yellows. In planning costumes for a certain period, always try to discover the colors which predominated at that time. Certain colors at different periods were very popular while others were most unpopular and perhaps not used at all. The best sources of information on any period are the paintings, fabrics and ceramics of that period. These give authentic information as to colors preferred at the time.

The colors for the different characters should be considered in relation to the importance of the characters. An unimportant character should not be costumed in a way that would give it more attention than is due. Neither should a leading character be costumed to subordinate the character. On the other hand, it is possible to overdress the part and subordinate the character and the acting to the clothes.

Scenery is the background against which the actors move and the color of the scenery and the color of the costumes should be planned together by the costume designer and the scenic designer if the same person does not do both. When the costume designer and the scenic designer are the same, this can be carried out much more easily. If blue is used in costume, blue must be used in some of the lights also, even if the scene itself does not require blue lighting. The blue in the costume will in this manner be intensified. Under a white light or an amber light, blue loses its intensity and unless very brilliant takes on a grayish appearance. All warm colors, the reds and the yellows, are brought out by either white or amber light.

In plays for children, as much brilliant color as can be used consistently should be employed, as children are particularly attracted by color. Although brilliant colors are used for children's plays, it should not be as crude as color which is required for primitive periods.

If color is used symbolically as, for example, a specific character representing Grief is dressed in gray, then no other gray should be used in the scene. If there is a figure to be dressed in scarlet symbolizing Sin, in order to point this costume no other figure should wear this shade of red. This manner of emphasizing by color is important, and may be done by using a certain color to isolate a figure against a massed group of another color. Suppose there is a massed group costumed in shades of green, one figure or several, if the group is large, may be costumed in gold or black or scarlet to give character to the whole mass.

The designer should have a standard color chart showing color in three dimensions. *The color combinations must be mixed carefully and pure color used as much as possible. Working up and down the chart, the value gradations can be used from light to dark and white to black. Colors become cooler as they descend the scale and warmer as they ascend; colors increase in luminosity or intensity as they become higher or brighter. Yellow has the highest pure intensity and will light up a scene like a flood of sunlight. It is important to remember in connection with a color scheme that dark strong colors must be shown against a light background, and light colors against a dark background. Light color used in backgrounds gives a sense of space and distance, while dark backgrounds often make a stage space seem much smaller than it actually is. In costuming, brilliant colors give brilliancy and movement to a scene while dark colors give strength and dignity.

In order to plan a color scheme, it is absolutely necessary that the person who is doing it should have a correct color sense. Everyone is not so endowed and if a designer, however clever he may be with his line, has not the gift of color, then he had best solicit the assistance of someone who has. Color illuminates the drama emotionally as well as symbolically. A stage set and costumed in tones of cool colors has a distinctly calming effect on an audience, so much so that if a spiritual significance is planned in such a setting, the most successful way to obtain it is to confine the colors to blues, greens, violets and lavenders. On the other hand, a group of dancers costumed in flame and crimson will elicit a round of applause for no other reason than that of the effect of the color itself. It must be remembered in dealing with color, that black and white are not colors but only values. There is too much white used in most big spectacles. It is a great mistake and a very common one to costume great groups of Greek maidens or Roman youths in white. The designer who does this has not looked up his period. Black is exceedingly depressing but tremendously effective if used sparingly. Grays and purples have the same emotional value as black and are much more interesting under light. A designer of costumes cannot make too careful a study of the science of color and color combinations.

❑❑❑

2

Scenographer and the Physical Stage in Costume Designing

Introduction

It is not possible to design for any theater without first examining the various physical forms the stage within it can assume. It is, perhaps, the first—in some ways most important—duty of scenographers to reconsider the possibilities that lie open to them when given a production to design. This is true for the smallest and simplest of theaters, as it is for the largest and most complicated of theater plants. Few scenographers have the opportunity (or need) to completely remake the stage and auditorium for one particular production, as did Norman Bel Geddes for Max Reinhardt production of The Miracle or as John Napier has for the musicals Cats, Starlight Express, and *Les Miserables*. Still, most scenographers are more and more not content to accept as inviolate the flat floor and proscenium picture frame that still characterize most theaters today. They feel less inhibited about extending their settings (in many instances conceived of as scenic environments rather than static settings) into an area that for the past three hundred years has been given over exclusively to audience seating in new and radical relationships. It would be well to examine briefly, therefore, just what basic relationships between the acting area and the audience's viewing area are possible in theater today. For the most part, however, we will restrict our attention to the two kinds of theater structures the scenographer of today is apt to encounter: the open stage and the proscenium stage.

Open Stage

The historical aspects of the open stage (although the scenographer should be aware of this form's development and of those open stage theaters built in this century like the Tyrone Guthrie Theater in Minneapolis or the newer Swan Theater in Stratford-upon-Avon in England) as we are with the role the scenographer plays when working for the stage. Additionally, we should be aware how actors move through the space on such stages as well as how directors guide that movement. Established in the Greek countryside hundreds of years before the fifth-century B.C. theater we usually focus upon, it was then and remains still the most powerful of all actor-audience relationships. The lines of communication between the viewer and the actor are as direct as is possible in any theater form. It is little wonder that this relationship has been the prevalent one for many thousands of years, since it results from two very basic human traits: curiosity to know and desire to show. In this form of relationship all viewers have equal access to what is to be seen; the distance between actor and audience is also equidistant to the greatest degree possible, and the locus of the action is always as near to the individual viewer as is feasible. The immense popularity of the cinema has as its basis this fact: *The camera eye always places the individual viewer at precisely the point where experience of an event is at its optimum and moves that view as the event changes.*

Basically, movement on any form of open stage (and this includes theaters where audiences completely surround the acting areas) tends to be circular in nature. Directors find, because of the audience-actor relationship, that they must cause the actor to move in such a way that (1) she does not spend any appreciable time with her back to any one section of the surrounding audience, so that (2) when she is speaking, she is generally in a position that allows her to face both her partner and the greatest number of the audience at the same time.

The basic action that puts the actors in a favorable position to be seen and heard (although actors in this form of theater must often deliver lines with their backs to a large portion of the audience) is known as an "exchange." This movement (again basically circular) allows the actor on whom the focus has been placed, because he has lines to speak or actions to perform, to give over his position when the focus changes from him to another. Directors for the open stage find that they must also continually keep the actors moving in order to keep the audience's attention properly focused; the amount of physical action, therefore, in the average open stage production would be at least two-thirds as much again as in the average proscenium production.

At the same time, space on the open stage is almost always more restricted; that is, there just is not as much of it as there would be on the average proscenium stage, nor does the scenographer have access to the traditional offstage space most proscenium stages possess. The director and scenographer, therefore, must be expert in the use of this limited space. A director, for example, will often require the scenographer to provide sitting arrangements around the periphery of the acting area so that the speaking actor (or the one with the focus on him) can gain dominance through (1) height he is standing, the one to whom he speaks is sitting, and (2) position on the platform he faces the larger number of the audience, the one to whom he speaks faces up to him. We have already noted that the scenographer can and does affect the actor by restricting and channeling his movement; on the open stage it is imperative that the director and scenographer work closely together so that the available space is used most effectively.

Many actors like the open stage generally for several reasons. Being closer to the audience and being among them, not separated and isolated to one side as they are in the proscenium theater, actors need not work as hard to secure proper effects, either vocal or physical. Their characterizations can be more natural, more subtle in interpretation when they do not have to project their words and actions over great distances as is the case in proscenium arch theaters with large auditoriums. At the same time, they are able to establish better relationships and more deeply motivated involvements with their acting partners, since they do not have to "cheat" toward the audience while trying to maintain the illusion they are relating to other actors on the stage. One of Stanislavsky's most desired reforms was to bring the attention of the actor more to the stage, to the objects on it as well as to other actors, and less to the audience. (It was a hallmark of nineteenth-century theater that the actor, no matter how realistic the intent of the play he was performing, almost always was more aware of the audience he was playing for than of the other performers on the stage. Stanislavsky did not want the actor to discount or ignore the audience, as he has often been accused; he merely felt that an audience would be more deeply engrossed in the drama if the actors themselves were.)

Even though the pendulum has swung from a naturalistic theater (the direction it was taking at the end of the nineteenth century) to a more theatrical one today, much of the open stage technique of acting and directing has now found its way onto the proscenium stage. More and more settings, for this reason, are "violating" conventions of the proscenium arch—that is, acting areas are being built across the curtain line and into the auditorium so that the performance of the actor can be more immediate than if it were contained wholly on the stage behind the arch line.

From the beginning of this century there has been a renewed interest in the open stage form. During the past four decades a number of theaters dedicated to this kind of stage have been built and most continue to draw audiences to them. The most successful new theaters built in this hemisphere have been, perhaps, those that exhibit the basic features of such a theater, even though there has been little attempt to reproduce exactly any historical open stage in detail. (The new open stage theater built on the south bank of the Thames in London will probably come closest to reproducing the kind of theater we think Shakespeare knew. At this writing it is still being de- signed.) The Stratford Theatre in Ontario, Canada, and the Tyrone Guthrie Theater in Minneapolis, Minnesota, are only two of the outstanding examples of new theaters built primarily to present works from the various ages of the theater and yet have been highly successful in accommodating modern plays as well. Some of the Guthrie's most popular presentations have been works by Chekhov, who wrote during his lifetime exclusively for a theater whose form and style are all but diametrically opposed to that of the open stage theaters of the past. Nevertheless, his plays not only have withstood the transfer from one form to the other but in many cases have greatly benefited from the advantages the open stage has to offer.

If one man were to be singled out as having popularized this type of theater in our own time, it would probably have to be Tyrone Guthrie; for a number of years he was one of the most successful directors working in the theater and many of his best productions were done on the open stage. Here is an article, "A Director Views the Stage," written by him in which he explains why the Minneapolis theater the one named in his honor-was designed as it was.

In designing an auditorium, the prime consideration should be the relation of performer to audience. Since the middle of the seventeenth century when Italian opera took Europe by storm theatres have been designed almost exclusively in the manner best suited to operatic performances. Such designs have a raised platform in front of which is a horseshoeshaped auditorium, usually in several tiers of seating. Between stage and auditorium a great gulf is fixed, literally a pit, in which the orchestra plays. The stage of the opera house is further removed from the audience by a partition with a large hole through which the spectators view the performance. This proscenium opening is often decorated as a picture frame to enhance the illusion that the performance is a picture in which the figures magically move, dance, or sing. When the performance demands that the picture be changed a curtain falls and appropriate pulling and hauling prepares the stage for further surprises to delight the audience. When all is ready, the stagehands are replaced by painted mummers in fine raiment, and the curtain is raised. For many years I have worked in such theatres, and it never crossed my mind that a theater could or should be otherwise. When I was in my early thirties, I was hired to direct the Old Vic Shakespeare Company. Gradually it became clear to me that trying to put Shakespeare's plays into the conventional framework for opera was wrong. The plays had been written by a master craftsman for a theatre of altogether different design. It was certainly possible to adapt them to the requirements of conventionally planned theatres. It seemed more desirable, however, to adapt some common-place building than to adjust a masterpiece. As is often the case, the obviously sensible building plan was too expensive to execute. Yet, I realized that a more logical and easy way to stage these plays existed. It led to an examination of the whole premise of illusion which is the basis for the proscenium stage.

It has always seemed to me that people do not submit to illusion in the theatre much after the age of ten or eleven. They are perfectly aware that the middle-aged lady uncomfortably suspended on a wire is not Peter Pan but an actress pretending to be Peter Pan. In planning the Tyrone Guthrie Theatre, it was necessary to decide whether the stage should be the conventional platform separated from the audience by a proscenium arch or whether it should be an open stage such as the Elizabethan theatre and the ancient Greek and Roman theatres. A third alternative was available. We might have asked our architect to create a flexible design which could adjust to both types. We rejected this, however, on the ground, that an all-purpose hall is a no-purpose hall—that insofar as a purpose is flexible, it is not wholehearted; that it was better to be firmly and uncompromisingly on one kind than to attempt to compromise between opposites which we considered to be theatrically and architecturally, theoretically and practically irreconcilable. We argued for the open stage for the following reasons: first, our intended program is of a classical nature, and we believe that the classics are better suited to an open stage than to a proscenium one. Second, the aim of our performances is not to create an illusion, but to present a ritual of sufficient interest to hold the attention of, even to delight, an adult audience. Third, an auditorium grouped *around* a stage rather than placed in front of a stage enables a larger number of people to be closer to the actors. Fourth, in an age when movies and TV are offering dramatic entertainment from breakfast to supper, from cradle to grave, it seemed important to stress the *difference* between their offering and ours. Theirs is two-dimensional and is viewed upon a rectangular screen. The proscenium is analogous to such a screen by forcing a two-dimensional choreography upon the director. But the open stage is essentially three-dimensional with no resemblance to the rectangular postcard shape which has become the symbol of the canned drama.

No claim is made that the open stage is better than the proscenium stage for every type of play. But, in our opinion, the open stage is more desirable for the kind of plays we propose to perform and the kind of project we propose to execute.

What Guthrie omits in the discussion of the reasons why his theater chose as it did is that not only are plays of the past best suited to the open stage but that almost all proscenium arch plays benefit from this form as well. For example, the Guthrie Theater is as famous for its Chekhov productions as it is for its Greek and Elizabethan works. Many works of the present-day theater, in fact, adapt well to the open stage. It is a design for the Harold Pinter play The Caretaker, a work that takes well to open stage production. One cannot, however, use the same kind of thinking for both. Having different actor-audience relationships between the two forms means that the scenographer must conceive of the acting areas attuned to those differences. Notice, for instance, that the furniture is not arranged, as it would be in the proscenium theater, so as to favor any one direction. And yet there is in this arrangement, casual though it may seem, a certain amount of planned orientation imposed on the actors working in this setting; when one sits on the bed, or in the chair, or at the table, he naturally would be forced to face toward anyone in the general area of the center of the stage, the area where most movement is possible. Actor-to-actor relationships are thus strengthened (almost forced, one might say, upon the actors) by the placement of the furniture and the layout of the playing area.

As it has been pointed out, there is probably a great deal more movement occasioned by open stage productions than on the proscenium stage; the better the director, however, and the more skilled the actor, the less likely the audience will be able to perceive or be aware of the fact that the life they are seeing on this type of stage is much more active than that outside the theater or in the proscenium theater. For this and other reasons, then, the scenographer's task is often more difficult—if not more extensive—than when working in other stage forms.

The Proscenium Theater

In proscenium theaters, the audience is almost entirely isolated on one side from the action on the stage. The performance is therefore viewed two-dimensionally; that is, primarily as a picture. This analogy to paintings and drawings is often heightened in older theaters by the ornate frame often placed around the proscenium arch opening. This kind of relationship cannot help but force the scenographers to compose settings more pictorially than spatially. But what is even more detrimental is that this relationship cannot avoid separating an audience and the performers into two distinct groups. Lines of communication are, for the most part, in one direction: from the stage to the auditorium, from the actor to the audience. During the past century, moreover, the practice of turning down the lighting in the auditorium and increasing it on the stage has done much to make audiences more passive than during past periods of theater. In this form of theater, the members of the audience feel less called upon to participate as actively as they might in the arena situation or while attending the open stage form of theater. There seems to be a willingness on the part of an audience to extend its attention more actively to the open or arena stage than in the proscenium arch theater. In any case, the proscenium arch does often act as a barrier to audience involvement and there can be little doubt that integration of audience and performer is at a minimum.

For some time now, and especially during the last half of this century, there has been a growing dissatisfaction with the proscenium arch theater. And if there is one trend apparent in present-day production practice, it lies in the abolition of strict barriers rather than in their construction. As a result, newer proscenium arch theaters are now built that allow the possibility of modifying the arch to differing types of production as well as making it possible to extend the stage areas more into audience areas. Much of the growing dissatisfaction with picture-frame stages stems from, and is in reaction to, the playwrights and producers who made a conscious attempt, starting in the late nineteenth century, to keep the stage and audience apart in separate units. What we observe during this period is a reaction of the more progressive playwrights (most of whom were championing a new wave of writing called *naturalism*) against what they felt was too much audience-performer fraternization. August Strindberg, one of the most vocal of this new generation, had distinct views on the subject and was instrumental in making the separation between stage and audience as complete as possible. He along with Stanislavsky in Russia, Antoine in France, and the Duke of Saxe-Meiningen in Germany eventually won out over the more theatrical approaches to producing plays, with the result that most of the dramas written since Ibsen have sought to present on the stage an illusion of life much as it appears outside the theater.

Even today the average audience member considers the proscenium arch theater as the true theater form; that other stage forms are simply quaint places where less important stage works are done. The serious consideration of theater buildings that departed from this "true" form began to emerge. The Ford Foundation Program for Theater Design initiated a program to study theater structures: what they were during the present time, and what they might be in the future. The American Federation of Arts issued a catalog showing the results of scenographers working in close relationship with architects to formulate many of the new ideas in theater design that had been considered during the previous three years. This book, *The Ideal Theater: Eight Concepts,* represents the thoughts of a number of the best scenographers and architects of the time. Even though it has been almost thirty years since that book, much of what is presented there still has the power to provoke thought, even to stir controversy. One of the more interesting portions of the book is a number of statements by Arthur Miller concerning the proscenium theater. What he said then deserves our attention still and repays the time to review his remarks:

> *I have no doubt that plays are not being written just because of the limitations of New York's theaters. You just can't write for these "shoe boxes" with the same ideas, with the same emotional scope, as you would for a (more adaptable) theater. The New York theater is a limitation to the playwright at least to the degree that it is no inspiration to him – he is dragging it around on his back half the time.*
>
> *In some kinds of plays, the actors have to come and say, well here I am; but the proscenium says, here I am not. In fact, here you aren't.*

The proscenium is a limitation for a hell of a lot of plays. You see, the drama has become more and more a first person thing. Even such a really traditional writer as O'Neill started talking biographically as he grew older. There's subconscious analogy, I think, between the proscenium theater and the third person; here, the play is pretending to take place without any author; these people are supposed to be really talking to each other, and we are overhearing them. You see, it's all a question of how much you're pretending that this isn't a play, or that this is a play – whether the emphasis is on the author or the actor – presentational or representational. The proscenium favors the latter.

What we are trying to do now is make a theater of essences. That is, where an Ibsen would create the surrounding documentation of social existence (a new discovery – people weren't aware of themselves in society to the degree that they are now) – well, we take for granted that kind of documentation. So, when Ibsen would get to the essences at about the last third of each act—the first two-thirds being the setup for the social situation—we share an awareness of our situation to the degree that numerous plays can simply deal in essences.

You know, every flight from one form is always the attempt to fly into the most direct confrontation with the essence. You break up a form because its appurtenances keep you further and further away from the center. But then when you get into the center, it gradually begins to move out into the periphery again—and somehow you've got to get back into the center again. Time after time, scientists believe that they have reached the ultimate understanding of some process—then it turns out that there is a smaller world inside of the one discovered, a new path into a more recessed center always requires new kinds of documentation if the vision is to be proved to others.

What Miller would like to escape is the kind of theater that was during his period increasingly devoted to the use of literal scenery manipulated by highly complicated, antiquated, often cumbersome mechanisms. And yet since he spoke, many theaters have been built with mechanical abilities that far outstrip the possibilities of the theaters he knew. Whether we like it or not, the age of large elaborately equipped stages will be with us for some time to come. American theaters continue to rely less heavily on built-in stage mechanisms than do their European counterparts. Still, the most completely mechanized theater in the world today is the Metropolitan Opera House in New York City. It is interesting to note the reviews given the productions done in this house during the past twenty years. Critics have increasingly found that production (overproduction, in the view of many) has all but usurped the place performers used to occupy. Consider these strong comments:

> *At one time, Franco Zeffirelli was an opera director of artistic significance. His productions for Maria Callas and for Joan Sutherland showed off their great if dissimilar talents to advantage. His "Falstaff" at the old Metropolitan Opera House raised staging standards there. For the last couple of decades, however, Mr. Zeffirelli's interest in opera has centered around the superficial and the trivial. As his new Metropolitan production of "La Traviata" showed conclusively on Monday evening, he is most charitably thought of nowadays as a fashion designer and interior decorator rather than as an opera director.*

> *Throughout the party scene at Violetta's place, scenery rose and fell, slid in and out, and doggedly followed the plot with distracting literalness. At least four complex scene changes took place in the first act alone (I may have lost count while absorbed in the watching the salon and bedroom come and go). Perhaps to take advantage of the turntables and other stage machinery of the Met, Mr. Zeffirelli allowed Alfredo to accost Violetta in her bedroom, thereby establishing her as an extraordinarily permissive hostess.*
>
> *In such a furbelowed, tasseled and bedizened production, the greatest singers would have a difficult time making an impression. Wendy White, making her Met debut as Flora, disappeared in the scenery. No surprise: so did "Traviata."*

And yet no scenographer can avoid knowing well the machinery of the proscenium arch theater, or how one designs for it. Let us therefore, look more closely into what is involved in designing for this form of stage.

Regardless of the complexity of the stage mechanisms, the relationship of the audience to stage in proscenium theaters is approximately. Partly through necessity, but mostly from habit and practice, performers generally orient themselves directly toward the audience; this is also true for many scenographers who, often unthinkingly, orient furniture, important entrances, and scenic effects directly facing the arch opening. Although there is at times an attempt to disguise the practice, more today than in the past, movement—confined by the horizontality of the scenic elements of the stage tend to be forced into corresponding patterns. This horizontal relationship to the audience causes a certain strain on the performers, since they must orient both to the audience (to be seen and heard) and to each other (to maintain the necessary involvement with one another) at the same time. The three-quarter down position seems to be about the best compromise possible. During the past thirty years, however, directors and actors have become more bold and begun using the three-quarter up and full back positions as well.

In this regard it is interesting to remember that when, in 1893, Strindberg wrote *Miss Julie*, he slyly complained about some of the restrictions we have just been discussing. In a preface to that play, he gave some of his views on current stage practices. Here are a few things with which he found fault: "Of course, I have no illusions about getting the actors to play for the public and not at it, although such a change would be highly desirable. I dare not even dream of beholding an actor's back throughout an important scene, but I wish with all my heart that crucial scenes might not be played in the centre of the proscenium, like duets meant to bring forth applause. Instead, I should like to have them laid in the place indicated by the situation. Thus I ask for no revolutions, but only for a few minor modifications. To make a real room of the stage, with the fourth wall missing, and a part of the furniture placed back toward the audience, would probably produce a disturbing effect at present."

Until recently the scenographer rarely (if ever) bothered himself with the problems and incongruities the box setting presented. Furniture was usually lined up so that the audience could reasonably see the actors use it, and in such a way that the actors could easily speak to the audience as directly as possible. Although few in the audience ever thought to question this arrangement, the characters in most plays, musicals, or operas spent most of their lives facing one direction in rooms with one wall missing.

It is more the common practice in today's production to rethink these arrangements of objects and the movement of performers; the theater has made some progress in this regard since Strindberg. We do see furniture with its back to the audience, or at least not lined up as it was in the traditional arrangements common to his time. Since the legacy of Stanislavsky and other naturalists is still a strong influence in our theater, both the director and the scenographer are trying to make the actor's environment appear more natural even if they often "cheat" furniture relationships toward the general view of the proscenium arch. In fact, there has been, on the part of directors and actors, a sometimes radical orientation of movement techniques used for the proscenium stage. (To cite only one example in this regard, when Charles Laughton directed a revival of Shaw *Major Barbara*, during some of the longer "set" speeches in the first act, he seated two of his actors on a low bench directly downstage center with their backs to the audience; these actors became themselves, in a real sense, an extension of the audience. Later in the arsenal scene, at least five actors at times more performed most of the scene facing up toward the rear of the stage.) Before leaving the subject of the proscenium theater let us review the standard elements one will encounter on such a stage: Elements of the Proscenium Arch Stage

1. Proscenium arch

2. Stage floor—(A) trap in stage floor (Opened here, closed when not in use.)
3. Apron (Wider in older theaters, increasingly narrower during second half of nineteenth century and during most of twentieth century.)
4. Offstage space (Often called the wings.)
5. Orchestra pit (In some theaters, slightly recessed under stage. In some theaters, such as Richard Wagner Bayreuth, pit almost entirely under apron of stage.)
6. Back wall of theater (Usually contains loading doors.)
7. Grand drape (Often decorative, especially in theaters of the seventeenth, eighteenth, and nineteenth century. In addition to being lowered to make changes of scene, the grand drape can be lowered to change arch opening height.)
8. Main curtain (In many theaters this curtain can be either lowered from above or opened laterally from the side of the arch. Some curtains-such as that at the Metropolitan Opera in New York City—has the additional feature of being opened in a decorative arch fashion. This is accomplished by an elaborate set of lines sewn directly into the curtain itself.)
9. Second portal (This arch, usually black velvet or some light-absorbing fabric, comes after the main curtain; its purpose is to help mask off backstage and sidelighting arrangements.)
10. Gridiron (A number of supports suspended from the ceiling of the stage house, which allow scenery to be flown up and out of sight. Other features necessary to production-such as lighting instrument battens, curtain tracks—are also suspended from this gridiron.)
11. Fly gallery (Usually suspended some distance from the stage floor and where the lines attached to the flown scenery or other suspended units are manipulated after they have been counterweighted.)
12. A back drop (A large piece of material usually made of cloth or other flexible material. These units are temporarily attached to battens suspended from the gridiron and can be flown into sight or out of sight into the area immediately over the stage. Cloth drops usually have rigid battens at top and bottom, sometimes wooden but more often metal pipe.)

13. A cut drop (A piece of material like the back drop but cut to some decorative profile. If the pattern of the cut is extensive, netting or other transparent materials are put on the rear to keep the profiles from sagging out of shape. These units are also temporarily attached to battens suspended from the gridiron and can be flown into sight or out of sight.)
14. Cyclorama (Sometimes called a "horizont" —surrounds most of the stage area, unlike a sky drop, which is usually flat. The cyclorama is often part of a theater's permanent installment, not part of a temporary production's scenery.)
15. Scenic unit (Composed of flats, platforms, steps, etc. Temporary structures built for a particular production. Scenic units must be capable of being removed from the stage in short periods of time. Sometimes this is accomplished by building an entire setting on a platform wagon that can remove the setting to an offstage position while another setting takes its place. The Metropolitan Opera theater is equipped with a wagon stage on each side, one in the rear, and one on an elevator that allows an entire scene to be stored below the stage. All these wagon stages are controlled electrically. In addition to these, the theater has a large revolving stage built into the permanent floor.)
16. Groundrow (Scenic unit cut and painted to simulate a distant view: hills, houses, etc. Sometimes these groundrows are built as are cycloramas, semicircular rather than flat. At times they are constructed three-dimensionally in smaller than actual scale in order to give the illusion of distance.)
17. Footlights (Rarely found in most recently built theaters but a feature of most theaters built in the last two hundred years. When they are included in modern-day theaters, they are usually recessed and are able to be covered over when not in use.)
18. Light batten suspended from gridiron (These battens most often have attached to them permanent lighting connections that feed into known circuits and are not used for anything else but lighting equipment. In some recent theater installations these battens have units that, when connected to lighting instruments, allows positioning and focusing by remote control, a feature that alleviates intensive manual labor while

saving time. By coupling this technology to that of the computer the Metropolitan Opera theater is able to change a lighting plot from one production in their repertory to another in a short amount of time.)

19. Front of house lighting portals and positions (Usually built into the ceiling of the auditorium, although older theaters do not have them. They are in most cases self-masking and have protective wire mesh over the front openings to ensure the safety of the audience seated below. Generally there is more than one portal, and often there are portals built into or attached to the auditorium sides nearest the stage.)

New Stage Forms

The nature of theater art have challenged the old ideas as to what the theater art is and where it should be performed. While Richard Wagner was one of the first of those who questioned traditional theater forms and their systems of belief, many others were close behind. By the start of the twentieth century there were literally hundreds of theater artists clamoring to change the directions theater had pursued during the seventeenth, eighteenth, and for most of the nineteenth century. This was true for every country. A common desire infected the thought of countless playwrights, directors, actors, and especially visual artists who worked for the "old style" of theater: to abolish the standard forms of the stage, along with the accepted audience-actor relationships that existed in order to render the stage a more flexible instrument capable of confronting the spectator in a much more direct manner and with a greater impact than heretofore. Newer kinds of theaters were necessary, it was postulated, to express newer forms of theater. It was not possible for playwrights and their interpreters, it was felt, to involve audiences in theater forms of the past. While many of those, such as Stanislavsky, still relied on production techniques left over from earlier times, there were some who wished to break completely with practically all theater after that of archaic Greece. Perhaps the most articulate of this new breed was Antonin Artaud, a French poet and actor who left us a highly provocative document saying what he thought the theater of the future should be. In his book *The Theater and Its Double*, Artaud describes how the theater he envisions should be realized. Here are some of the basic requirements he proposes:

> *The Stage – The Auditorium: We abolish the stage and the auditorium and replace them by a single site, without partition or barrier of any kind, which will become the theater of action. A direct communication will be reestablished between the spectator and the spectacle, between the actor and the spectator, from the fact that the spectator, placed in the middle of the action, is engulfed and physically affected by it. This envelopment results, in part from the very configuration of the room itself.*

Thus, abandoning the architecture of present-day theaters, we shall take some hangar or barn, which we shall have reconstructed according to processes which have culminated in the architecture of certain churches and holy places, and of certain temples in Tibet.

In the interior of this construction special proportions of height and depth will prevail. The hall will be enclosed by four walls, without any kind of ornament, and the public will be seated in the middle of the room, on the ground floor, on mobile chairs which will allow them to follow the spectacle which will take place around them. The scenes will be played in front of whitewashed wall-backgrounds designed to absorb light. In addition, galleries overhead will run around the periphery of the hall as in certain primitive paintings. These galleries will permit the actors, whenever the action makes it necessary, to be pursued from one point in the room to another, and the action to be deployed on all levels and in all perspective of height and depth.

However, a central position will be reserved which, without serving, properly speaking, as a stage, will permit the bulk of the action to be concentrated and brought to a climax whenever necessary.

Artaud's theories have been widely accepted and put into practice in numerous instances especially during the past three decades. Peter Brook is only one of many directors who have been influenced by Artaud and at least one major critic, Jan Kott, has written extensively on his influences in present-day theater practice. Probably the most famous group to make use of Artaud's visions has been the Laboratory Theater of Jerzy Grotowski in Poland, who after becoming increasingly dissatisfied with the conventional theater its purposes as well as its form decided to create a theater of his own that, as Artaud did, broke with most theater practices established after fifth-century Greek theater. (In fact, Artaud decided to go back even further to archaic forms of ritual and spectacle that predate that period of theater.) While the theater of Grotowski has been essentially dormant from beginning of the 1980s, it has had a distinct influence on theater both in America as well as in Europe. The reason for this influence is that, unlike Artaud, Grotowski was one of the very first directors to successfully realize many of the ideas that Artaud had only theorized about.

Along with implementing new concepts of acting, Grotowski also abandoned traditional theater structures. Many of his productions take place in locations selected specifically for individual project. A stage can be as small as a large table around which no more than a few dozen spectators are placed. In fact, each project is allowed to determine the number of people able to see it at any one time. In many of Grotowski's productions, the audience is fragmented into small unequal groups and placed in spacial combinations in a larger space that has also been broken into smaller acting areas of unequal size. It shows just such an arrangement for Kordian, one of the productions in the Laboratory Theater's repertory. In Towards a Poor Theatre, Grotowski gives his reasons for completely disavowing all stage forms and relationships as they exist today. In the following passage taken from that book, he gives the rationale for the position he holds:

> *By gradually eliminating whatever proved superfluous, we found that theatre can exist without makeup, without autonomic costume and scenography, without a separate performance area (stage), without lighting and sound effects, etc. It cannot exist without the actor-spectator relationships of perceptual, direct, "live" communion. This is an ancient theoretical truth, of course, but when rigorously tested in practice it undermines most of our usual ideas about theatre. It challenges the notion of theatre as a synthesis of disparate creative disciplines – literature, sculpture, painting, architecture, lighting, acting (under the direction of a* metteur-en-scene*). This "synthetic theatre" is the contemporary theatre, which we readily call the " Rich Theatre" – rich in flaws.*

The Rich Theatre depends on artistic kleptomania, drawing from other disciplines, constructing hybridspectacles, conglomerates without backbone or integrity, yet presented as an organic art-work. By multiplying assimilated elements, the Rich Theatre tries to escape the impasse presented by movies and television. Since film and TV excel in the area of mechanical functions (montage, instantaneous change of place, etc.), the Rich Theatre countered with a blatantly compensatory call for "total theatre." The integration of borrowed mechanisms (movie screens onstage, for example) means a sophisticated technical plant, permitting great mobility and dynamism. And if the stage and/or auditorium were mobile, constantly changing perspective would be possible. This is all nonsense.

No matter how much theatre expands and exploits its mechanical resources, it will remain technologically inferior to film and television. Consequently, I propose poverty in theater. We have resigned from the stage-and-auditorium plant: for each production, a new space is designed for the actors and spectators. Thus, infinite variation of performer-audience relationships is possible.

Actually Grotowski has not created a new theater so much as he has returned to that very first relationship that began theater, jettisoning everything accumulated to that relationship between then and now. His theories (which, if we accept his words at face value, are more rediscoveries than original inventions) and his experiments will undoubtedly continue to affect the theater of the future. Few who have seen and studied his work and his words doubt the depth of accomplishment or his sincerity of purpose. Still, it is probable that the inherent disciplines he demands and the methods he imposes on both actors and production-not to mention the smallness and specific kinds of audience he requires – will keep Grotowski's work always in the avant garde of theater and will prevent his theories and practices from ever being assimilated into the mainstream of the modern theater. There are many, in fact, who do accept the idea of a synthetic theater as a defensible aesthetic of theater, which, of course, Grotowski does not. One cannot escape or totally discount the traditions of the past one-hundred-fifty-odd years. This book is tacitly based on the supposition that synthetic theater (meaning here a theater that depends on putting together concepts and practices from a wide range of resources) is a defensible and viable attitude that will be with us for the near future at least, if not longer. But Grotowski has been of great service to those who do not fully espouse his philosophies; if nothing else, it causes us who work in the so-called Rich Theater occasionally to stop and take stock of what we think is important to our theater and what should be changed, what is necessary and what should be abandoned. Reading and thinking about how Grotowski views the theater could even send us back to reevaluate our most basic (usually unconsidered) beliefs. Perhaps it will cause us to once again consider Henry David Thoreau's great principle for all human activity: *Simplify, simplify, simplify.* It could even make us look through the complicated technologies of a Starlight Express to see the essential hollowness of its conception and purpose as well as the vapidity of its music and story.

If one salient point can be derived from the investigation of theater forms and actor relationships, it would probably be that no single point can be made. Quite possibly there is, for every single person who works in the theater, a single form as well as an accompanying philosophy that he or she feels most comfortable working in and with. We should always recognize that "best" for A may be acceptable (not first) for B and totally unacceptable for C. Who has the ultimate right to make a final judgment that will decide this question of the "right theater form" once and for all? Perhaps each age gets—s Thomas Jefferson said of government—the theaters it deserves (a blessing in good times, a curse in bad). It is certain that scenographers training today will during their career encounter frequently and be confronted by the ever-changing virtues and shortcomings of many stage forms. One mode of thought should be avoided at all costs, however: that one kind of theater or that one stage form is inherently superior to another. Perhaps the only real point we should make here is that no single stage and auditorium could ever be expected to satisfy all the philosophies that exist concerning the physical theater. But we should hold as well the idea that it is the individual scenographer who can assist in the making of the best use of a particular theater form for a specific production.

The Scenographer's Areas of Influence

Few members of a viewing audience are critical of a production's scenery. When the curtain rises on a sumptiously decorated or highly detailed realistic setting, almost without exception audiences react with surprise and pleasure, following which spontaneous applause erupts. Even seeing scenic elements move—walls opening, platforms shifting position, solid objects mysteriously appearing or disappearing into the floor or into the space above the stage; almost magical accomplishments—give an audience visual delights akin to those encountered in childhood tales of magic and of adventure. Few of us are so jaded that we do not take pleasure in such spectacles; few who do not delight in having our eye dazzled and our minds teased by the visual transformations made possible by modern stage technology. And yet the scenographer of today must approach such possibilities with a firm understanding as to when spectacle is needed and when it is inappropriate. We need a means to assess when a production demands spectacle. More important, we need some principles that will tell us when we need to forego that formidable arsenal of technical machinery today's theater possesses. The natural curiosity most theater people have often tempts us to test the limits of a new technology rather than to seek out what real use it might have. For many years now we have had a safe way to fly Hamlet in for his first entrance. Few would deny this would be spectacular. Fewer still would ever consider this a reasonable thing to do even though the possibility exists. To confuse the entrance of Hamlet with that of Peter Pan, despite the gasps of delight that any audience would doubtless give, would be totally inappropriate to Shakespeare's intent.

It is not an unreasonable observation to make that a strong current trend in the producing theater can be summed up thus: *if it can be done, it should be done*. (And all too often this philosophy is followed with an unspoken caveat: It *will* be done.) For the truth of the matter is that during the past century the producing theater has found the electrical and hydraulic means of shifting large masses of scenery so quickly and silently that there is virtually nothing that a modern scenographer can design that cannot be built or moved easily in to or out of an audience's view. We have, it seems, all but forgotten Robert Edmond Jones's thoughtful warning that *machines are not a substitute for imagination*. He took issue with the use of mechanistic scenic change simply to please an audience's desire for spectacle. Shakespeare, as you will recall from Chorus speech in *Henry V*, had challenged his audience with the exhortation, *On your imaginary forces work*. Jones also believed that imagination should aggressively be pursued on both sides of the curtain. In *The Dramatic Imagination*, he devotes an entire chapter to considerations young scenographers should address. An important part of that advice is a warning concerning the unrestrained use of scenic technology.

A stage setting has no independent life of its own. Its emphasis is directed toward the performance. In the absence of the actor it does not exist. Strange as it may see, this simple and fundamental principle of stage design still seems to be widely misunderstood. How often in critics' reviews one comes across the phrase "the settings were gorgeous!" Such a statement, of course, can mean only one thing, that no one concerned with producing the drama has thought of it as an organic whole. I quote from a review recently published in one of our leading newspapers, "Of all the sets of the season, the only true scenic surprise was." The only true scenic surprise, indeed! Every stage designer worth his salt outgrew the idea of scenic surprises years ago. If the critics only knew how easy it is to make a scenic surprise in the Theatre. Take two turntables, a great deal of – But, no. Why give away the formula? It is not surprise that is wanted from the audience; it is delighted and trusting acceptance. *The surprise inherent in a stage setting is only part of the greater surprise inherent in the event itself.*

Probably both Shakespeare and Robert Edmond Jones would be morbidly fascinated by the technological developments that our modern theater has at its current disposal: Cats, Phantom of the Opera, and Les Miserables would not fail to capture their attention. Certainly they would take notice of vehicles such as Starlight Express. It would be interesting to know how they assessed the underlying material of these pieces. Would they, I wonder, attach any great merit to a work that consisted largely of a mindless plot filled out by thoughtless movement all accompanied by an overpowering assault on visual and auditory nerve endings?

It is well, therefore, that we consider as an important part of a scenographer's education the investigation of not only how a scenographer influences the visual aspects of a production but how those visual elements affect the others theater artists. The question has two parts: (1) *What are the basic categories into which the scenographer's work falls,* and (2) *in what ways do each of these contribute to the visual aspect of a production?*

As we attempt to analyze these influences into separate categories, we should also keep in mind that most scenographers do not approach a production in the manner we will here. How the scenographer does approach a production will be the subject matter of later chapters in the book. Here we are concerned with the *building blocks*, as it were, the scenographer uses, not the way they are assembled. Perhaps we should keep in mind Chekhov's advice to his friend Suvorin, when he sought to defend himself from Suvorin's complaint that Chekhov was remiss in his duties as an artist to be able to explain all that he did. Chekhov very wisely pointed out to him that "you confuse two things; *solving a problem* and *stating a problem correctly*. It is only the second that is obligatory for the artist. In Anna Karenina and Yevgeny Onegin not a single problem is solved, but they satisfy you completely because the problems are correctly stated in them."

We can profit by this advice as well; when working in the theater and when analyzing the production requirements of a particular play, we should be, as scenographers, first concerned with stating the problem correctly than solving the problem whose basis has not been thoughtfully considered. We should never think of *how* to fly Hamlet in before we have stated the *why*; that is, the need to do so in the first place. When we are at the point that we begin to consider what is needed for the production at hand (and assuming that we have stated and understood our premise correctly) only then can we begin to ask the question *what do we really need*. Unless we have a firm understanding of the basic categories of ways we can influence a production, we cannot fully understand which elements we need chose to solve our problems. Like good cooks, we not only need an ability to read a recipe but must have knowledge and feeling for the ingredients we use in our craft. For now, however, the ingredients of a design is our concern.

The Stage Floor

There is a great deal of soundness in the proverbial basic requirement for theater – three boards and a passion. When Peter Brook, in his book *The Empty Space*, states that "I can take any empty space and call it a bare stage," he is simply reaffirming that aphoristic definition of the theater. In the past, few designers for the stage gave much thought to this most important subjects. In this century we have come to understand that there is no better way in which the scenographer can serve the actor (and through him the playwright) than to provide an appropriately designed area on which he can perform.

Once, the stage floor was nothing more than just a floor, something to be walked upon but not to be considered to any great extent by itself. It was merely a neutral area with no definite shape or boundaries except those of the back and side walls of the theater. This total space was almost always rendered somewhat smaller by the placement of scenic units and masking units to hide those back and side walls as well as the mechanisms used to move the scenic units from backstage storage to audience view. As the scenographer became more involved with not only visual backgrounds for performers to be seen against but also the performer's possible actions on the stage, more attention was paid to this heretofore unregarded subject. Treatment of this area began to receive attention if not equal to that of the background, at least much more than in the past. Now, for many in the theater, this area has become the single most important element in the total design. The emphasis of scenography, once almost totally confined to the periphery of the stage area, has now all but given way to the treatment of the stage floor. Once only a simple horizontal plane (slightly tipped toward the rear wall in older theaters to facilitate the sight lines of an audience then seated on a flat floor), this area is now being fractured, extended, raised, lowered, and angled in literally every possible combination. To resolve the stage floor into appropriate acting areas is now for many scenographers (as well as directors) the first major step (some consider the most important step in the whole process of design) in planning a production.

The General Background

After the stage floor, the next area of design generally considered in that of the general background. This includes walls, backdrops, overhead units such as arches, foliage borders, ceiling. In one way, this is the least most important area, since performers cannot often relate directly to the general background; in another way it is an extremely important area, since items in this category tend to be the largest visual elements an audience sees. Because nothing can be seen without relationship to some sort of background, the scenographer must always carefully consider what the impact of the background will be on the performer standing before it.

Until the nineteenth century all theatrical performances were treated in an identical fashion; plays, operas, and ballet used settings that had been designed only as pictorial accompaniment, much the same way, in fact, as incidental music for a production was written. Even today in the ballet we can see settings not unlike those used for all productions in the theaters of the seventeenth and eighteenth centuries. Here we see a large expanse of floor virtually unencumbered to facilitate the movement of the dancers. Even today scenery for the ballet is largely a matter of producing oversized paintings. Painters who have made their reputations elsewhere than on the stage are still routinely engaged to design works for this form of theater. During the heyday of Diaghilev Ballets Russes all the major painters working in France were commissioned to design for the company. Nor were any of these artists required to think or create works in a manner contrary to their already established styles. This means that they do not really attempt to work as the scenographer almost always does. All scenographers take it for granted that their function is to integrate what they design into the total production. The famous painter, on the other hand, is simply expected to present his persona as forcefully as possible; the success of such designs is largely measured on the ability of the audience to identify the painter from what is seen on the stage. Picasso was expected to remain Picasso. And it is a rare critic that ever complains of the situation as did Richard Buckle when he reported on the design of Salvador Dali for the ballet Salome: "It must be quite clear to anyone looking at. Dali's curtain and decor that the celebrated Catalan illusionist does not design ballets—he allows dancers to take part in his painting."

The general background can be, therefore, at one and the same time, the least important part of the design to the performer (in terms of real use) and the most potent visual element in terms of what the audience sees. Performers simply cannot compete with a general background that is too bright or distracting. This area of design is potentially the most dangerous if not carefully considered. Adjustment of the general background in terms of color, light, and disposition of forms is critical in the scenographic process.

Specific Units of Scenery

These units may be part of the general background, but what separates them into a different category is that they may be, in fact often are, used directly by the actors and therefore become much more important to them. Doors, windows, platforms, steps, rocks, trees, and the like, can be used by themselves, that is, separated from their surrounding background, to create the sense of a particular place without the connecting material—such as a wall—that would be found if the scene were completely realistic in conception. No walls connect the various units yet the room's form and period are easily comprehended.

Actors have an instinctive desire to relate to units of scenery in emotional as well as practical terms. For similar reasons playwrights have an equally instinctive urge to provide them for the actor to use. Windows and doors especially have always had a special symbolic fascination for both the playwright and the actor; it is a poor actor or an unimaginative playwright who does not seek out metaphorical possibilities in the physical elements of a play's scenic environment. These units provide, in fact, an invaluable means by which the actor can physically externalize hidden thoughts or motives. But in what way can the dramatic use of these elements be assured by the scenographer? A clue as to how this can be accomplished is furnished by these remarks of Katharine Kuh, an art critic and historian:

> *A window is to look through, both into and out of. Though often the symbol of an eye, it is not an eye, but a vehicle for light and for that volatile mirage we call atmosphere. A window is selective; it can frame nature in sweeping panoramas or in magnified close-ups. It provides access to inner visions more vivid than real ones. It can be nothing more than a blank, a vacant opening, or it can reproduce the unedited reflection of one's own image. Because windows imply secret revelations, because they are outlets to both the inside and outside world but, unlike doors, are rarely tangible passageways, they take on a variety of guises. Frequently exploited in art as compositional devices, they have come into their own only recently since Freudian discoveries infused them with new meaning.*

Let us now see how these thoughts might aid the scenographer in work on an actual production using Chekhov Cherry Orchard as our focus.

In the last moments of the fourth act, Madame Ranevsky is leaving the home she has known and loved all her life. The room where she is the nursery has been stripped of most of its possessions; only a few items of luggage remain and these too will soon be gone. Outside the windows of this room her beloved cherry orchard is being cut down, a sacrifice to progress and a signal that the old life she has lived heretofore is past, all its outward manifestations—the cherry orchard being the symbol of these things—vanishing. Soon even the house itself will be torn down to make way to a new cheap housing development. In a few moments she must walk out the door of this room never to enter again. What does she *feel* about the empty room once filled with life and promise, a place where so many happy times were spent? More important still, just what does she *see* as she looks out the windows overlooking the place where the orchard once stood? Most important of all, how can the scenographer aid the actress playing Madame Ranevsky to reinforce the un- derlying emotions of these moments? How does the scenographer approach the design of those specific architectural elements so that an audience can perceive Madame Ranevsky's relationship to this place so dear to her heart? She has few words to show these feelings and those provided are relatively banal and insignificant. Of course, most of these problems must be left to the skill and art of the actor and the director. But the scenographer is not exempt from thinking in the same way as they do; the scenographer must be as much a part of the interpretation of these last moments as the actor or director. An indifferent scenographer could fulfill much of his obligation by searching out and reproducing on the stage a Russian nineteenth-century countryhouse window; this is a relatively easy thing to do. More is expected of the scenographer working in the theater of today. Directors expect the visual artists with which they work to also see the world through the eyes of the play's characters; scenographers should demand that of themselves. Moreover, not only must they see what is before them at that moment, but they must see with the eyes of their memory as well. In the first act of the play Madame Ranevsky's windows looked out on a happy contented life, while now they present a bleak and dying world. How does the scenographer make these things we have been discussing clear? Or can they be? Can a window or a door be designed that somehow helps both the actor and the audience to understand *something* about what is happening in the play's development? The questions we have posed have no definitive solutions. Still, they must be asked. Somehow they must be answered. Moreover, it is the asking of such questions (not necessarily the quick solutions to them) that separates the artist-scenographer from the scenic craftsman.

Let us take another instance in which a door becomes greatly important to the progress of the play and to the actor who must use it. In this case we are considering the design for the center portal (always in the Greek theater the entry to the protagonist's place of dwelling) in Oedipus. What size should the doors in this portal be, how big and how heavy? Of what materials should they seem to be? What physical effort should it cause the actor to open these doors? How, for that matter, does the door open; with what speed or what sound, if any? Do they open in or out? These are all practical questions and must be solved in technological terms. But there are other questions, questions such as those that occurred in The Cherry Orchard. Careful research will provide much of the information needed to satisfy the historical aspects of these questions. Consultation with shops and technical personnel will help the scenographer to implement his research findings. Yet after all the necessary research and technical data have been assembled, we are left with other questions, and these can be answered only by an understanding of the play. What are some of those considerations?

The doors we need to design have a practical use; but they also have another important function. While this portal is the entryway to the house of Oedipus, it is also, symbolically, the final door to the mystery of the plague that besieges Athens, and it is behind these doors – the doors to his own house – that Oedipus finds the answer he seeks. How can these considerations affect the function of these doors or their appearance?

We can, for instance, make some artistic judgments in relation to the width and height of the arch that contains these doors; not only does it determine how big these doors will be, it will also have an effect on the spectator watching Oedipus, when he is seen in juxtaposition to it. We might ask in that regard, how large or high or thick this arch should be to be most effective, and what the relationship of the width to the height should be. While these are architectural considerations that can be addressed by period research, they are also visual considerations that influence the emotional response of the viewer. Once these decisions are made, we still have another problem to resolve-the quality of the doors themselves. For, like those considerations just mentioned, the treatment of the doors will also *say something* to an audience. What we have just been discussing needs some explanation. Let me use an example from my own past experience.

Several years ago a director of this play and I found ourselves discussing these very questions. At that time all he could tell me was that he wanted the door to Oedipus's house to be "the entrance to an 'unclean place,' that it it should be majestic, and "that hidden power lay behind the doors, but that dark and unclean things were also hidden there from the sight of men." He also spoke of the doors moving like "heavy oil in a dirty machine slow and sluggishly not lubricating the machine but clogging it." This is what he wanted the doors to show: *unclean, majestic, slow moving*. But at the end of the play, he went on, "this quality must be mitigated, in some way refined, made clear the doors still majestic but now cleansed and bright." This, we both agreed, was a tall order. Since the doors could not be changed (it would not be desirable even if possible), they must be initially designed to incorporate the features of both desires, of both images dark and corrupt, light and cleansed. And it was my job to make his verbal images concrete realities. The first step for any scenographer is having a clear statement of the problem at hand; that, I felt we had. Now it was time to go deeper into the play itself and find there some clues as to how the director's wishes might be accomplished. Knowing some history of the Greek theater and its traditional practices became the next level of investigation. In the first part of the play these doors are seen in a dark world full of shadows and in the mists of early morning fires set around various parts of the pestilent-ridden city. As the morning light progressively brightens, the deepest shadows dispel. Greek plays actually did start, we are reasonably certain, during the first light of dawn and progressed into the light of full day. Audiences were in their seats before the sun rose, and the actual effects of sunrise were incorporated into the dramatic structures of many of the plays that have come down to us, Oedipus being one of those. There is, in fact, a similar progress from *darkness into light* in this play. The solving of the play's central mystery is fundamental to this dynamic image. Light, as all visual artists know, radically alters what it strikes if its source and tonality are also altered. Perhaps, we thought, this is the clue to fulfilling the director's images suggested to him in the text; the emerging strength of the light was also integral to the proper interpretation of the text, to the solving of the mysteries embedded there. After much discussion, thought, research, experimentation, and more discussion, research, and further experimentation, we were able to arrive at a workable solution. The doors were designed that relied heavily on the properties of light (its ability, as we mentioned, to change color, direction, and intensity). The ornamentation of these doors consisted of massively carved entwined serpents in simulated antiqued bronze. At the beginning of the play these doors were lighted to capitalize on the three-dimensional qualities of the high relief, the side that the light predominantly struck was also more heavily "corroded" finished to resemble the green oxide colors and textures of old weathered bronze. The other side, which showed up during the later part of the play, was finished with brighter metallic colors. By changing the direction, color, and intensity of the light, it was possible to change both the tonality of the door and also to affect its dramatic qualities as well. The undulating movements inherent in the carving of the coiling snake forms, as the source and intensity of the light changed, were forced back and flattened more into the background design of the doors. As these forms became flatter, they lost much of their dramatic power. As they changed tonality, they lost much of the feeling of corruption (unclean things) and the feeling of decay that had permeated the early moments of the play. We had been able to make the doors progressively match the progress of the play itself. That progress followed this pattern:

1. First part of the play—dark and heavily shadowed stage (Oedipus, literally and figuratively, "in the dark").
2. Middle part of the play—with the coming of the light (both physical and intellectual), the mysteries begin to resolve; the heavy snake forms lose their hard definition; their power lessens.
3. Last part of the play—the light intensifies, all things become exposed to *the clear light of day* (the main purpose of all Greek philosophy); the palace of Oedipus, formerly an unclean place has been purged and, by Oedipus's understanding and subsequent actions, cleansed of the defiler.

When the final moment comes for Oedipus to emerge from the palace to announce the catastrophe within and to disclose the action he has taken upon himself (his blinding of himself and his decision to leave the city forever), what should we, the audience outside the door, feel? What emotions should we experience as the doors open?

Does what we see on the stage at this moment (still carrying with us the memories of what we saw when the play began) in any way heighten our involvement with Oedipus and his plight? Modern production theories are based on the assumption that we are very much influenced by those visual things that although they may work on us subliminally do in great part affect how we feel. The question has been, can scenographers in their work design specific units of scenery that not only have the necessary functional qualities to satisfy the technical demands of the production but can actually intensify the drama itself? For myself and I am certain I speak for most professional scenographers working today the answer is yes. Robert Edmond Jones observes in his book *The Dramatic Imagination* that it is only when the designer *thinks as a poet* that he truly serves the theater. This is the reason we must never dismiss the idea that while a door may be just a door or a window just a window, they might both be hidden accesses to something else; in the theater they usually are.

Furniture and Set Properties

These elements are one step nearer the actor, both in physical proximity and usefulness to him as an artist. Although there are only a few major categories of furniture that man has devised, there are innumerable variations and permutations on these basic forms:

1. Things to sit on
2. Things to lie on
3. Things to put other things on
4. Things to put other things in

Beds, sofas, tables, stools, chests, end tables, settees, desks, estageries, benches, book shelves, hallstands, bureaus, commodes, are but a few names in a long list that fall within these basic categories. But one should not overlook the point that in giving a particular name to a certain type of chair or a specific function to any piece of furniture, one is helping to establish the relationships these objects have to those who use them. Moreover, these differing names often help to establish the differing relationships between individual people or classes; the cultural as well as financial status of a person is often signaled by his possessions, and acquiring or retaining certain pieces of furniture ranks high in determining that status. Much can be told about the individual lives of people and how they view their positions in the world through a study of the objects we see around them. The scenographer needs to foster a continuing interest in the ways human beings relate to their immediate environment as defined by their immediate surroundings. But this will not furnish a complete understanding without a working knowledge of the history of furniture. To be precise, this knowledge should include the following information:

1. Awareness of individual periods of furnishing as well as the relationship of one particular period to another
2. Styles that fall within individual periods as well as an interest in how that style was created or how it evolved within the period and into any periods that followed
3. Basic forms of construction and technologies used in the manufacture of individual pieces
4. Materials used during any one period as well as consideration of why particular materials were used or favored over others
5. Finishing materials (paints, varnishes, lacquers, gold-leaf, etc.) or specific treatments individual to a particular age (kinds and uses of waxes or specific techniques of buffing, etc.) or to a specific locale, along with consideration as to how these finishes or techniques influenced subsequent periods
6. An understanding as to how time and use affect both object and its finish is of particular concern to the scenographer, since often the effects of age and individual use are specifically detailed in a text's explicit directions or implicit needs
7. History of a particular piece of furniture or of its kind often reveals clues to the age in which it existed; quite often the spirit of an age lies in an understanding as to how those living in it related to the objects they selected

While contemplating the emotional impact or dramatic possibilities of furniture may seem far afield to an interior decorator, it is precisely this kind of speculation that points to the real difference between the scenographer and the interior decorator, who, while he needs an expert knowledge of furnishing as the basis of his work, can satisfy the demands of his profession only considering the categories just listed. On the other hand, the scenographer not only needs the information given there but must extend that information into many areas of human behavior-that specifically outlined by the playwright in his text—which the interior designer would find of no possible use. A key to the way in which the scenographer makes use of his knowledge of furniture can be found in *An Illustrated History of Furnishing* by Mario Praz. There he gives a significant clue as to how the close relationship that develops between man and those objects he makes or selects is used by the scenographer.

Dickens and Gogol have written about the capacity that objects have for expressing their owner. Podsnap's silver (in Our Mutual Friend) was characterized by a "hideous solidity." "Everything was made up to look as heavy as it could, and to take up as much room as possible." Twenty years before, in *Dead Souls,* Gogol described Sobakevitch's house: "Tchitchikov looked around the room again and everything in it, everything was solid and clumsy to the last degree and had a strange resemblance to the master of the house. In a corner of the room stood a paunchy walnut bureau on four very absurd legs looking exactly like a bear. The table, the armchairs, the chairs were all of the heaviest and most uncomfortable shape; in short, every chair, every object seemed to be saying 'I am a Sobakevitch too!' or 'I too am very much like SobaKevitch!'"

This is the house in its deepest essence: a projection of the ego. And furnishing is nothing but an indirect form of ego-worship.

Praz's musings as to the interrelationship of furnishing to the lives of those who exist within the confines of particular places, then, is almost identical to the way in which a scenographer must think. The selection of a text's physical needs among which furnishings play a significant role becomes of crucial importance to the practice of scenography. There are at least three distinct steps in the process of providing furnishings for the stage. These are:

1. Determining the needs of a scene: that is, analyzing the text to find the list of objects absolutely necessary to the action of the scene. But at this stage Gertrude bed in Hamlet is no more concrete than is Maggie bed in Cat On a Hot Tin Roof; it is generic in nature and we know little more than that a bed of some kind is required in both plays.
2. Seeking images from our outside research so that differences between Gertrude's bed and Maggie's bed can be determined: not only are these differences matters of historical period or geographical location alone, but also they require an

understanding of how the characters use these beds as well as the playwright's hidden reasons his *dramatic purpose* for including them in the scene. In both instances the playwright had very different reasons for requiring such an object. In Cat On a Hot Tin Roof, the bed is crucial to the meaning of Williams's play; it is a battlefield where Maggie the Cat would like to vanquish her rival, the ghost of her husband's best friend. In Hamlet the bed is, not involved in the action as much as in Williams's play; it is, rather, more a visual reminder of Gertrude's hastening too quickly to "incestuous sheets." In the Laurence Olivier cinema version of the play, however, the bed is used as the focus of the scene, its design carefully considered in relation to Olivier's interpretation of the scene. (Kevin Klein production of Hamlet, no bed at all was present in Gertrude's closet; the only furnishing in the room was a blood-red carpet. Much of the action that Olivier used in his production required the use of a bed; much of the action in the Klein production was performed by the actors kneeling, sitting, and rolling about on the the carpet.)

3. The scenographer must now do one of two things: (1) find the items needed or (2) make working drawings from research information. In either case, it is imperative that all the considerations mentioned above have an active part in the search for an existing bed or in the designing of the item to be made in the scenic shop.

No scenographer should ever take lightly this area of influence. We should constantly keep in mind another good piece of advice included in Praz's book, which is: "perhaps even more than painting or sculpture, perhaps even more than architecture itself, furniture reveals the spirit of an age." All scenographers might be well advised to follow this simple principle in their research into period interiors: Whenever seeking information concerning furniture or set properties, do not just try to find isolated pieces and objects but, whenever possible, find these items in images where they are shown being used.

The scenographer and the director than a single object removed from its living context. As with a work of art, a good research picture is more than the sum of its parts. Furniture and set properties are far more necessary to the actor than either the general background (which he cannot use directly) or specific units of scenic architecture. But, as with this later category, it is possible to create a sense of place and period its characteristic form and atmosphere by careful selection and placement of furniture and set properties. In the arena theater and on the open stage, creating this sense becomes critically important to the scenographer's design, since furniture and set properties literally become the scenery.

It was said of Molière that he could place chairs on the stage so effectively that "they could almost speak." What does such a statement really mean? How can furniture "speak?" Does the placement of the chair in figure 46 *say* something to an audience? If one reads The Physicists, the play from which this image is taken, it will become immediately apparent what the placement of the chair means to the end of the play, the moment shown in the photograph. To the imaginative person this is not such a difficult concept to embrace. In the Collected Stories of Tennessee Williams, the playwright gives us an insight into how the creative mind often perceives the world of supposedly inanimate things:

> *This overstuffed chair, I don't remember just when we got it. I suspect it was in the furnished apartment that we took when we first came to Saint Louis. To take the apartment we had to buy the furniture that was in it, and through this circumstance we acquired a number of furniture that would be intriguing to set designers of films about lower-middleclass life. Some of these pieces have been gradually weeded out through successive changes of address, but my father was never willing to part with the overstuffed chair. It really doesn't look like it could be removed. It seems too fat to get through a doorway. Its color was originally blue, plain blue, but time has altered the blue to something sadder than blue, as if it had absorbed in its fabric and stuffing all the sorrows and anxieties of our family life and these emotions had become its stuffing and its pigmentation (if chairs can be said to have a pigmentation). It doesn't really seem like a chair, though.* It seems more like a fat, silent person, not silent by choice but simply unable to speak because if it spoke it would not get through a sentence without bursting into a self-pitying wail.

Over this chair still stands another veteran piece of furniture, a floor lamp that must have come with it. It rises from its round metal base on the floor to half a foot higher than a tall man sitting. Then it curves over his head one of the most ludicrous things a man has ever sat under, a sort of Chinesey-looking silk lamp shade with a fringe about it, so that it suggests a weeping willow. Which is presumably weeping for the occupant of the chair.

I have never known whether Mother was afraid to deprive my father of his overstuffed chair and weeping-willow floor lamp or if it simply amused her to see him with them. There was a time, in her younger years, when she looked like a fairy-tale princess and had a sense of style that exceeded by far her power to indulge it. But now she's tired, she's about sixty now, and she lets things go. And the house is now filled not only with its original furnishings but with the things inherited from my grandparent's house in Memphis. In fact, the living room is so full of furniture that you have to be quite sober to move through it without a collision and still there is the overstuffed chair.

The vision Williams demonstrates here is almost identical to that Praz reported earlier. For anyone working on a production of The Glass Menagerie, such factual information is helpful. But far more valuable is the kind of imagination that imbues that so-called dead world with such a feeling of life. It is also this kind of imagination that triggers the imagination of other visual artists such as Edward Keinholz and causes him (in a strikingly theatrical way) to create an assemblage such as this in the collection of the Whitney Museum of American Art. We who re-create the worlds playwrights outline in words would do well to emulate the kind of vision that Keinholz exhibits and that Williams writes of in his eulogy to an overstuffed chair. Nor can the decisions we make in regard to furniture and set properties be underestimated in importance to the performer who, in many instances, has an instinctive desire to relate to his immediate environment in a highly personal manner. Jean Cocteau, although a man of letters, was, like Molière, keenly aware of the importance of furniture placement on the stage. "A chair," he once wrote, "badly placed on the stage is almost as dangerous as a trapeze insecurely suspended from the roof." While it has often been observed that young actors often blithely disregard their material surroundings (and in so doing give an audience the feeling that they don't really belong there), mature actors almost always take advantage of these surroundings to extend the scope of their characters. The veteran actor (or director) realizes that these objects can, as the French Dauphin of Eisenstein Ivan the Terrible demonstrates, show something of what he is feeling and a great deal of what he is simply by the physical attitude he adopts toward the throne he sits in.

The scenographer should never forget that past ages had ways of seeing and ways of thinking that we living today do not share. These differences show up not only in the ways people think and act but in the ways they use things in the world about them. When scenographers use objects from past ages, such as furniture or other house furnishings, they, as well as the directors with whom they collaborate, must understand that our present-day attitudes toward these objects are not likely to be that of a distant time. Furniture, like all other artifacts from past times, exists in a context, a context that often has principles—often strict rules—concerning use. Moreover, these contexts, like all other human activities, change greatly as time passes. In *Home*, by Witold Rybezynski (a book that should be in the permanent libraries of all scenographers and directors), some of these important changes are discussed. Here is a brief passage from the book:

During the Middle Ages the prime function of the chair was ceremonial. The man who sat down was important—whence the term "chairman" and his upright, dignified posture reflected his social stature. This association of the seat itself with authority has remained an integral part of European and American culture: we still refer to a judge's bench, or to being in the driver's seat. The movie director continues to have his name on a chair, even if it is printed only on canvas. There are even imaginary seats, like Chairs in Art History, or seats on the boards of corporations.

Although chairs began to service more mundane activities such as eating or writing, the sitting position changed slowly. Throughout the Renaissance and the Baroque period, European sitting furniture, although it increased in quantity, accommodated what was essentially the erect posture encouraged by the earliest chairs. Even the domesticated seventeenth-century Dutch continued to sit stolidly in their straight-backed chairs, both feet planted firmly on the ground.

These thrones are used only for high occasions. They were not built for comfort but for state functions. What is interesting to note here, however, is the manner in which their height conforms to the dictates of royal protocol. Queen Elizabeth is the ruler of the British Isles. Prince Philip, sitting beside her, is only a consort; his rank is below that of hers. Those responsible for the protocol which governs this ceremony have made certain Prince Philip does not sit higher than Queen Elizabeth. The actual variation between these thrones is quite small: to be precise the difference is approximately three-quarters of an inch. To accomplish this minute but all-important difference, a small block raises her throne to the higher level. We can also see the difference if we draw a horizontal line across the tops of the two thrones. While we are apt to encounter few situations on the stage that reflect such precise thinking, we should be aware that those in the past or in different cultures do make distinctions we should be aware of.

The atmosphere of this room depends less on surrounding scenic units—with an audience seated on three of the four sides, actual walls could not, as in a proscenium arch theater, be used to reveal the nature of the locale—and more on the selection and arrangement of appropriate furniture and set properties. Casual as this arrangement appears the scenographer must use especial care in working out such an environment. Practically every moment of the play's dramatic action must be minutely considered and throughly understood if this room is to fulfill the playwright's internal demands or to accommodate the director's patterns of movement. Stanislavsky, both as an actor and as a director, considered the relationships of furniture and set properties to performing so important that he always put in his production notebooks many small sketches of proposed arrangements, which he later took care to realize on the stage.

Set properties, like furniture, can play important roles in a scenographic design. While in most instances these objects are selected to reinforce the period feel of the design, a particular item of set decoration can serve a greater function. The National Theatre of Great Britain produced Chekhov Three Sisters, directed by Laurence Olivier and designed by Josef Svoboda. Later the entire production was filmed in a studio version that duplicated the setting as it was seen on stage. While the basic settings were not realistic, the furniture and set properties were in period; these, although few, were carefully considered, both as to their placement and their dramatic purpose. One set property used in the setting for acts 1 and 2 (the same locale), was given a special function to perform. This piece was an ornate clock made in the likeness of a city cathedral; a building one might expect to find in some great Russian city. Ostensibly the clock was simply a highly decorative but essential utilitarian item; no one ever actually wound it, called attention to it directly, or even acknowledged its presence in the room. To the casual observer, this clock would appear to be nothing more nor less than what it was: something that most drawing rooms of the period might have had and something any scenographer decorating this setting might use. Yet as the play progressed, this clock became an important "actor" in the drama. At one point it helped in a distinctly positive way to underscore one of the underlying themes in this play; that life passes most people by, that if there is any excitement or gaiety to be had out of it, it is always in some other place. For the characters of The Three Sisters, this better existence can only be had in a large city; in this case, Moscow. By combining the element of time (and consequently making it a constant reminder of its passage) with an image that also reminded this group of the glittering life they were missing, Svoboda created a potent symbol that made its point without intruding on the action of the play. One does not become aware of the clock's message directly; only at a certain moment in the play, in fact, is the audience required to take notice of this item of decoration, which occurs during a long pause when the clock slowly chimes out the hour. Isolated on its own high pedestal, this symbol of time passing and lives wasted communicated to the audience a subtle but clear message, one that reenforced the scene's moody atmosphere of purposeless lethargy. In the film version, this image became stronger than in the stage version. This moment happened when the camera slowly panned across the room and came to rest on the clock as it began to strike the late afternoon hour. When the camera stopped, the image was slightly out of focus. As the clock chimes continued, the image cleared to give the spectator a closeup view of this time-passing city-life symbol. There as no mistaking the message being sent to the audience; the point was clear and entirely communicated. Objects, as we have pointed out in our other examples, can speak, and what they say is often more eloquent and powerful than any words could ever be. In A Sense of Direction, William Ball warns how easily such messages can go awry when those who direct productions do not take care in their selection. Speaking of another production of The Three Sisters he gives this advice:

> *One of the greatest errors directors make is what I call "breaking systems." This means that having established a pattern of systems, the director foolishly introduces a single detail that violates his own systems. Here is an example. I once saw a production of The Three Sisters. A great deal of effort was made to give it systems of authenticity. Nineteenth-*

century costumes, oil lamps, genuine military uniform, authentic crystal decanters, and period cameras were used. At the end of the first act, one of the actors presented a contemporary toy, a top, to Irina. By the chromium design and computerized buzz, the audience could easily see that the top was a creation. By using one contemporary toy, the director had violated his own systems authenticity, and all his work to achieve integrated naturalism in the first act was destroyed. That one moment of disbelief suddenly brought the entire act crashing to the floor. It is astounding how frequently, and with what apparent casualness, directors destroy their own systems.

It is possible for the scenographer as well-by careless selection or unthinking design of furniture and set properties to affect a performer's function adversely. He can, for instance, cause the actor to sit in markedly different attitudes simply by varying the height of a chair a small amount in either direction from its normal dimension; a little too high or too large, the character may be perceived as insignificant or helpless. Of course, there are many times when such alteration is done on purpose to produce just such effects. This is the case in the two examples just shown. Still, there is a vast difference between the purposeful intention and the accidental result. It is not uncommon for actors to have strong opinions concerning the furniture they must use directly; it is doubtful if there is one working scenographer who has not had many confrontations with performers on this particular issue. Although some might just be difficult to work with and hard to please—perhaps because they have been subjected to years of having to cope with uncooperative pieces of furniture that other scenographers selected or designed for visual effect rather than usefulness to the actor-most realize that it can affect their performance to such a degree and so directly that they feel it their prerogative to ensure the scenographer does not thoughtlessly hamper them.

Hand and Personal Properties

In the professional theater, properties are most always classified into two rough categories: set properties and hand properties. Responsibility for design or procurement of these items usually falls between two kinds of workers; set properties are almost always the direct responsibility of the scenographer (working with a properties master), while hand properties are sometimes selected by the scenographer only in part, the greater part being assembled by the property master. There are even times when a hand property falls within the province of the costume designer. In a large production that requires numerous objects, the overlapping of these categories must be carefully sorted out, or else important things can fall between the cracks of mutually exclusive responsibility.

In the amateur theater, properties are not often given the attention they deserve. Too often the making or procurement of them is relegated to a person who, rather than considering each item needed as a separate and integral objective, tends to think of them only as a list of things to be gotten as quickly and effortlessly as possible. In theaters such as the Stratford, Ontario, Festival Company or the Royal Shakespeare Company and National Theatre in London, the properties are not only carefully designed (usually in direct consultation with the scenographers of a production) but are beautifully executed by numbers of highly trained artisans. The conscientious property master finds out not only what is needed, but how those things were used in the past and will be used in the present.

It would be hard to overemphasize the importance of the role that objects play in human communication. Use of things to reenforce verbal language is as old as mankind itself. The practice is so ingrained in our daily lives that we often point to, touch, or pick up objects that lie near to hand in order to clarify those things we cannot elucidate in words alone. Using objects in this way can be a powerful means of persuasion. In many instances the thing used has little value or meaning in itself. For those who watched the televised hearings on Un-American activities, few will forget Senator Joe McCarthy's repeated waving of papers before witnesses and television cameras, papers he reported to be detailed lists of Communists who had infiltrated the U.S. state department. Later it was discovered that no such lists existed, that those papers were nothing but paper. Still, at the moment he made use of them, the effects were far-reaching and damaging to scores of persons, many of whom lost their job and reputations simply on the information they were reputed to contain. Playwrights no less than unscrupulous politicians know well the power of objects; in countless instances they use them in similar ways.

Robert Edmond Jones had a keen appreciation of the importance of properties. Jo Mielziner, another distinguished scenographer, recalls an incident that illustrates the care with which Jones approached the selection of objects to be used on the stage. In an article he wrote for the book of Jones's designs and drawings, *The Theatre of Robert Edmond Jones*, Mielziner relates the following story:

> *I recall that Arthur Hopkins' business manager very hesitantly and politely inquired of Bobby one day, "Is it necessary to have those eighteenth-century quills and sand shakers on the desk up-stage in the comer of the set? You must realize, Mr. Jones, that even the first row of the orchestra can't appreciate an object so small at that distance." Bobby turned and glared. "Do you think," he said, 'that only people on the other side of the footlights need exaltation? What about the actor? Surely he should* feel the sense of period *when working in this set?"*

Unfortunately, all too few scenographers think as Robert Edmond Jones and far too many as the business manager. Not only is this attention to detail a quality most of the great scenographers do share, it is also a mode of thought that certainly should be cultivated rather than denied, as it often is even in the professional theater.

Just what is a hand or personal property? And just how does it get its power to move those who witness acts involving them? The simplest answer although not all that easy to comprehend – is that a property included or implied in a dramatic text is the external focus of the actor's attention. In other words, the actor uses physical objects to expose what he is thinking about at the moment when the playwright provides no words to express the emotion or thought engendered by the scene. Often the most important moments of a play are those that take place in the silences between lines of written dialogue. In countless instances objects – a "prop," to use the more common term is employed to make clear what no amount of words could. This is often a difficult concept for those who think that the only way a playwright communicates with an audience is by the use of words, and that by words alone the actors can convey the full meaning of the playwright's intent. But the concept is not as hard to understand if we see how actual properties are used in actual instances. Let us examine a few illustrations to show how this works.

CBS Television produced a televised version of Death of a Salesman, using many of the original Broadway cast. In his subsequent review of the telecast Robert Lewis Shayon took especial note of one scene:

Television rarely sees exciting bits of acting, but there was one recently that could make a viewer start with a sharp intake of breath. It happened during Act Two of the two-hour color production of Arthur Miller's Death of a Salesman.

Willy Loman has been fired by his young boss. The aging salesman comes pounding hysterically into the office of Charley, his friend. Lee J. Cobb, playing Willy, finds Bernard, Charley's son, in the office. This is the school-grind, the anemic worm that Willy and his popular, athletic sons once scorned. Now Bernard is a successful lawyer on his way to Washington, carrying tennis racquet to play on the private courts of affluent friends.

Willy desperately tries to maintain the old razzledazzle about his own son Biffs "big deal." Bernard offers him a cigarette from a large, gold cigarette case. Willy stops talking, stares at the case, takes it, holds it, closes it and posses it back – in a silent passage of torment, despair, and envy.

The cigarette case is a symbol of everything Bernard has won in life – success, status, wealth – and a mocking sign of all that Willy and his two boys have failed to win. The pain on Mr. Cobb's face as his emotions overwhelmed him, the wordless eloquence of his baffled regard for that shining piece of rail that crushed his ego and pierced his boasting – were utterly communicated and shared. I think it was the production's finest moment.

Yet afterward, scanning a reading edition of the play, I found no mention of the cigarette case and this bit of stage business. Seventeen years ago I saw Death of a Salesman during its original run on Broadway at the Morosco Theater. Perhaps the bit was done on the stage but I don't recall it.

Had Mr. Shayon gone to a book called *A Theatre in Your Head*, by Kenneth Thorpe Rowe, he would have had his question answered. Included in the text is a section written by Elia Kazan, the play's original director, called "Notebook Made in Preparation for Directing Death of a Salesman." Among those notes is this: ". It is interesting to observe the economy with which the director puts down his thoughts about this particular moment. One can clearly see what the director had in mind. Did the playwright actually envision this moment played in this way as he wrote? Quite probably not.

It is interesting to note that many playwrights have taken particular care to specify exactly what the actor needs in the way of properties to make his motive clear. These are not always specified in formal stage directions (and for that reason are missed by those—such as the general reader or the literary student of a playwright's work-who are not expert in reading plays for the hidden clues to action they contain). Shakespeare, time after time, weaves into the fabric of a speech an object that would externalize a character's inner and deepest thoughts: the mirror Richard II dashes to the ground after reflecting on the image in it (and seeing there the folly of his own past life) is far more dramatic than anything he might say at that point; Yorick's skull in which Hamlet finally sees the ultimate observation that can be made on life, not the philosophical speculation of ceasing to exist expressed in words (he certainly does that up to this point) but in an actual piece of a human being he once knew and loved. Even Hamlet, who has a sentiment or word on practically every possible situation or event, is reduced to near speechlessness when confronted with this object that shows what death really means; the only word Shakespeare gives him at this moment is a barely whispered, "This?"

And yet while many playwrights do include directions in their texts (or by dialogue imply the use of objects not mentioned), directors often interpolate objects into the plays not specifically or implicitly called for by the playwright. To a certain extent, the director sometimes becomes the co-writer with the playwright. This is a condition that is often crucial to the process of interpretation, a condition most playwrights accept.

At times hand and personal properties cannot be strictly categorized; the more personal they are and the more integrated into the action of a scene they become, the more difficult it is to determine who is responsible for their introduction into a particular production. Another illustration that demonstrates this point can be found in Olivier's National Theatre cinema version of the Othello.

In the final scene of the play, Othello murders Desdemona. He believes his action justified but finds out that he has been duped by the treacherous Iago. After Othello realizes his error, he decides that death by his own hand is his only option. The play ends with Othello's suicide. The text's internal evidence reveals that his death is accomplished with a bladed implement of some sort. The exact size of the instrument is not specified: only that those around him did not know he had any kind of knife or dagger on him (Cassio says immediately after the act, "This did I fear, but thought he had no weapon"). There was a large sword in the room – it is with this that Othello wounds Iago but this is taken from him after he strikes Iago. In this production concealment of any other knife would have been difficult, since Othello's robe was made of a light, almost transparent material. Nor would he have had any real reason to be armed when he comes to the room. It is clear from the text that Othello does not mean to disfigure her; his words specifically rule out disfiguring Desdemona in any way: "Yet I'll not shed her blood / Nor scar that whiter skin of hers than snow / And smooth as monumental alabaster." How, then, does he kill himself? Even those who are familiar with this play and have seen many productions of it were shocked at the method Olivier chose. Olivier was famous during his career for the inventive ways he used the props given him. In this instance he employed a weapon that had been in full view of the audience from the first moments of the play. Why it was not seen was that it was concealed in an item of Othello's costume: a heavy metallic bracelet he wore on his right wrist. What the audience did not know was this was Othello's assurance that he would never be taken alive in battle; that he would always have near to hand (literally) a means by which he could dispatch himself although disarmed of every other weapon. This solution has, admittedly, worked well on the screen, but it was also an effective piece of business on the stage. I do not know if the decision to use this property was that of Olivier or someone else. This illustration does, however, demonstrate just how effective new solutions to old problems can be and how important properties are to even the greatest of actors.

Let us close this subject with an unusual tribute to the power of these frequently underestimated stage objects by reading a poem of an important twentieth-century writer, Bertolt Brecht. As a playwright, Brecht so thoroughly understood the dramatic power personal properties possessed that he felt compelled to record in poetic form the manner with which the famous Berliner Ensemble actress Helen Weigel went about their selection.

Weigel's Props

Just as the millet farmer picks out for his trial plot.
The trickiest seeds and the poet.

The exact words for his verse so.
She selects the objects to accompany.
Her characters across the stage.
The pewter spoon.
Which Courage sticks. In the lapel of her Mongolian jacket, the party card. For warm-hearted Vlassova and the fishing net.
For the other, Spanish mother or the pottery basin.
For dust-gathering Antigone. Impossible to confuse.
The split bag which the working woman carries.
For her son's leaflets, with the moneybag.
Of the keen tradeswoman. Each item.
In her stock is hand-picked: straps and belts.
Pewter boxes and ammunition pouches; handpicked too.
The chicken and the stick which at the end.
The old woman twists through the draw-rope.
The Basque woman's board where she bakes her bread.
And the Greek woman's board of shame, strapped to her back.
With holes for her hands to stick through, the Russian's.
Jar of lard, so small in the policeman's hand; all.
Selected for age, purpose and beauty.
By the eyes of the knowing.
The hands of the bread-baking, net-weaving.
Soup-cooking comprehender.
Of reality.

Costume

The most desirable situation is for one person to control all visual elements of a production. Costumes, like properties, are all-important to the actor, since on the stage the way a character is dressed in large part tells an audience what that character is like. Every scenographer should be able to design costumes for a production as well as know the fundamental practices of costume construction.

Robert Edmond Jones, a scenographer who always took responsibility for the entire visual design of a production, makes several excellent points about the kind of vision one needs to design costumes. Here are few of his remarks:

In learning how a costume for the stage is designed and made, we have to go through a certain amount of routine training. We must learn about patterns, and about periods. We have to know what farthingales are, and wimples, and patches and caleches and parures and godets and appliques and passementerie. We have to know the instant we see and touch a fabric what it will look like on the stage both in movement and in repose. We have to develop the brains that are in our fingers. We have to experiment endlessly until our work is as nearly perfect as we can make it, until we are, so to speak, released from it.

A stage costume is a creation of the theatre. Its quality is purely theatrical and taken outside of the theatre, it loses its magic at once. It dies as a plant dies when uprooted. Each separate costume we create for a play must be exactly suited both to the character it helps to express and to the occasion it graces. We shall not array Lady Macbeth in pale blue organdie or Ariel in purple velvet. Mephistopheles will wear his scarlet and Hamlet his solemn black as long as the theatre continues to exist. A Hamlet in real life may possess a wardrobe of various styles and colors. But in the theatre, it is simply not possible for Mr. John Gielgud or Mr. Maurice Evans to say, "Tis not alone my tawny cloak, good mother, nor customary suits of tender green."

While there is much good advice in these words, Jones's point of view is essentially a romantic conception of costume. But, then, so was his entire philosophy of theatrical design.

There have been in recent years, however, newer philosophies in theater that take a markedly different point of view as to what the role of costume is in on the stage. It would probably be more accurate to say that there are more points of view than were expressed in Jones's most creative period that spanned the early part of this century until almost the middle of it. Many of these trends have veered away from the romantic conception of costume design. More and more, dress for the stage is "elected" rather than designed, assembled rather than constructed, and many costumes are made from materials not invented until the second half of the twentieth century. It is now common practice to use clothes and accessories found in secondhand stores and attics rather than to construct costumes from new fabric that must be artificially aged and distressed. In some instances designers who are responsible for costumes that show the effects of great use and age will find their materials in old ready-made garments. These are then taken apart, recut into new patterns, and assembled into entirely new styles and periods. The shirt for the character of the Marquis de Sade was recut from a water-stained crepe de chine ballroom gown, while the rest of his costume was constructed from sunbleached velvet rescued from the vaults of a theatrical warehouse.

Another noticeable trend in the design of costume during the past four decades has been the decreasing use of brightly colored and excessively elaborate costumes for period productions. Simplification in cut and profile as well as the use of heavily textured fabrics and other materials owes a great deal to the influence of Bertolt Brecht and the designers who worked for his theater, the Berliner Ensemble. Costume designers today often work within more limited color ranges; many of their tonalities are grayer in tone when compared with the technicolorlike hues of most productions during the early part of this century. It is possible, in fact, to trace this progressive muting of color by looking at films made from various time periods. There is a marked change in how color is used. Even between the stage version of Camelot and its cinematic remaking only a few years later, noticeable differences in costume philosophy are strikingly evident.

Along with newer concepts of tonality, there has also been a corresponding interest in synthetic materials, not only fabrics but plastics, metals, artificial fur, and both real and synthetic leathers. The introduction of fiber-glass cloth and strands, as well as other plastic impregnated materials that harden when exposed to chemical treatment, have opened up whole new vistas of possibilities in costume construction not feasible, not even dreamed of, even thirty years ago.

Costume designers routinely use paintings and drawings as visual guides for gaining information on a dramatic character's dress and outward appearance. It is not as widely known that they also use the work of other graphic artists as source materials for their work, obtaining their ideas as to character traits and behavior. Working with the director, the designer also influenced the actual performance of the play by bringing to the attention of the director the stylistic possibilities inherent in the original source materials. There have even been instances when a playwright will model his characters directly from graphic images encountered in previous viewing experiences.

Along with all the technical advances in costume there has also been another development that we should note before leaving this category. This relates to the manner in which conceptual imagery most notably metaphor is used in the design of stage costume. In many instances a designer will base a character's look on images that lie beyond period detail verisimilitude. The reason for this approach is to incorporate into the dress of the character hidden clues to personality, purpose, or condition. One example should suffice to demonstrate how metaphor can be used in costume design.

In Romeo and Juliet there is a short but important scene late in the play when Romeo, banished to Mantua, is brought the news that Juliet is dead (she is not, of course, but he has no way to know the truth). Before returning to Verona where he intends to die beside Juliet, Romeo seeks out an apothecary he hopes will provide him the poison needed. Within a short while, Romeo locates the shop of the apothecary. This character appears only once in the play; the scene in which he appears is short. Nevertheless, it is a crucial one to the play. The design problem here is to create a costume for the apothecary that provides clues to who the character is and how he fits in the action of the play at this point; to show clearly those three things mentioned above: *personality, purpose, and condition*. To better understand what these are, let us read what Romeo himself says about the man (the only information we have, in fact, that gives us the necessary clues to guide the designer):

ROMEO: Well, Juliet, I will lie with thee tonight.
Lets' see for means. O mischief, thou art swift
To enter in the thoughts of desperate men!
I do remember an apothecary,
And hereabouts 'a dwells, which late I noted
In tattered weeds, with overwhelming brows,
Culling of simples; meagre were his looks,
Sharp misery had worn him to the bones;
Noting this penury, to myself I said,
"An' if a man did need a poison now,
Whose sale is present death in Mantua
Here lives a caitiff wretch would sell it him."
O this same though did but forerun my need,

And this same needy man must sell it me.
As I remember, this should be the house.
Being holiday, the beggar's shop is shut.
What ho, apothecary!
APOTHECARY: Who calls so loud?
ROMEO: Come hither, man. I see that thou are poor.
Hold, there is forty ducats; let me have
A dram of poison.
APOTHECARY: Such mortal drugs I have, but Mantuas's law
Is death to any he that utters them.
ROMEO: Art thou so bare and full of wretchedness,
And fearest to die? Famine is in thy cheeks,
Need and oppression starveth in thy eyes,
Contempt and beggary hangs upon thy
back;
The world is not thy friend, nor the world's law,
The world affords no law to make thee rich;
Then be not poor, but break it and take this.
APOTHECARY: My poverty, but not my will, consents.

Shakespeare gives many clues in the lines of this scene to the outward condition of the apothecary: poor in health as well as poor in dress. What is given in the lines is helpful in a general way. It is the designer's task, however, to find some image that not only shows destitution but the furtiveness of the character's manner. The reason he is in dire straights is hinted at by Romeo but not explained fully: that reason is so many have sought the same service, the sale of poison, that the authorities in Mantua have passed the death penalty on its sale. What these others wanted was a means of doing in enemies, not themselves, as was Romeo's purpose. It is evident that the apothecary is still in business; nor would it escape the modern-day audience that certain modern-day associations are present, most notably the comparison between him and drug dealers of the present time.

The designer now has to make some decisions: how to merge the physical descriptions of the character with the nature of his trade. The use of a metaphorical image aids in this process; in this case it allows us to think of the character in terms that play on our revulsions and fears. Let us adopt for our metaphorical image that of a rat skulking about the dark alleys of a city slum. Using this image we begin to imagine not only a range of colors and textures for the costume—heavy shaggy textures in mottled grays and dirty browns, grizzled matted hair, long skeletal fingers with broken nails, perhaps dark sunken eyes with "*overwhelming brows*" but for the actor's movement as well. Metaphor used in this manner connects clues in the text directly to our own experience; thinking in this manner is the real basis of all theatrical thinking. It should also be noted, moreover, that the most important purpose for using metaphor in the design process is not to make the audience overtly aware of the imagery employed but, rather, to give a focal point to our own creative thoughts while giving a sense of direction to our work. Using metaphorical imagery is one of the few practical ways to integrate into the overall context of the production characters who appear for a few brief moments and then vanish. Metaphorical images should, therefore, resonate in the subconscious parts of the viewer's mind, not thrust themselves into the forefront of attention. No one in the audience should ever say when the apothecary appears: "Ah, a dirty rat!" What they should *feel*, however, is an unease and apprehension as the brief desperate scene takes place and to feel some of Romeo's own pity and loathing for both himself and for the situation in which he finds himself.

If there is one major trend discernible in the progress of costume design during the past hundred years, it is this: the costume designer has become less and less just a dressmaker who supplies vaguely appropriate costumes and more and more a creative artist whose techniques, knowledge, and artistry have progressed far beyond just knowing how to sew a straight seam, cut a pattern, or dye a piece of cloth.

The Scenographer's Relationship to the Director

In *Creativity in the Theater*, Philip Weissman writes, "no performance of a written work of art can be more than a single interpretation. The greatness of a director depends on his capacities to identify with the creator and to create in performance an optimal and original communication that enhances the author's creation without distorting it. A director identifies with the contents of the created work and interests himself in communicating its contents. He is more identified with the dramatist or composer than with the audience." In an article by Harold Clurman called "In a Different Language," a director says this of his profession:

That action speaks louder than words is the first principle of the stage; the director is the "author" of the stage action. Gestures and movement, which are the visible manifestations of action, have a different language from that which the playwright uses, although the playwright hopes that his words will suggest the kind of action that ought to be employed. The director must be a master of theatrical action, as the dramatist is master of the written concept of his play.

It is rarely the director's intention to alter the playwright's meaning. But it is a mistake amounting to ignorance to believe that the playwright's meaning is necessarily conveyed by merely mouthing the playwright's dialogue and following his stated instructions. In a sense the playwright's text disappears the moment it reaches the stage, because on the stage it becomes part of an action, every element of which is as pertinent to its meaning as the text itself.

The philosophy of interpretation that underlies these statements applies not only to the director but to the scenographer as well. It also, in part, helps to clarify the similarity of purpose and artistic bond between them. Although their materials and techniques differ greatly, the aims of both are especially similar. In a successful collaboration, both personalities might very well be evident, but just as some aspects of observations are directed by thought and some by purely visual response, so it is with the director's and scenographer's contributions. One might say that the scenographer's role is to act as another pair of eyes to the director-mind. This relationship is not unlike that of different parts of a single human body; they are separated but not unrelated. What these different parts do are part of a single function: interpretation of the playwright's words. In a successful production, it is often impossible to separate these two influencing forces into individual contributions. That all too often the work of the director and the scenographer exist side by side with little or no relationship of one to the other is testimony to the fact that this desired collaboration does not happen automatically or effortlessly. In fact, the odds always seem to be heavily weighed against it.

Perhaps we should take a brief look at the development of this relationship between the modern director and scenographer. From the middle decades of the nineteenth century until the early years of this, the philosophical approach held to be the most advanced solution to making theater an important art was this: *one person had to be in charge*. Even today the most common perception of how theater works is that any successful production must come from a single person with a single viewpoint. Subordinate talents are, of course, needed to implement this singular viewpoint, but the power to make conceptual decisions must not be shared. For almost one hundred fifty years we have been largely under the influence of such theatrical visionaries: Richard Wagner (who first articulated the concept of theater as an integrated work of art), the Duke of Saxe-Meiningen (who insisted on accurately researched settings and costume), Gordon Craig (the father of modern scenography), and Adolphe Appia (who first saw the dramatic possibilities of electric light). All held a similar view of what theater should be: an institution that would not attain its rightful place in the world until it produced artists whose vision was uncompromising and whose word was law. In practice, none of these men ever completely attained this vision, but they were instrumental in the creation of a mythical creature-the omniscient super director – that still is a stock character in many films and plays that have theater directors as characters. The route by which commands and ideas would be channeled down from the all-powerful director to an audience. Rudimentary as this diagram is, it does make clear that little give-and-take is expected or allowed.

It was not until the first decade of this century, however, that a man who fitted the desired description arrived on the scene. Max Reinhardt was the first of stage directors who came close to fulfilling the hopes of his nineteenth-century predecessors. Although there are many fanciful tales concerning Reinhardt and his style as a director, those who knew him best reported he was an eminently reasonable person who was exceptional in the way he was able to solicit the best advice of others, that his success was in large part due to the creative interaction of those he chose to work for him. Probably the only true superdirectors are those who work behind motion-picture cameras – the cinema director-and some few opera directors such as Franco Zeffirelli and the late Jean-Pierre Ponnel.

Reasonableness, quiet assessment of differing points of view, compromise all elements of any sound directorial approach – make for good theater. Both director and scenographer must be, in the truest sense of the word, *reasonable* people. This more nearly approximates the true path of concepts as they make their way from inception to a viewing audience. And the very first thing we see in this diagram is that any concept must undergo a series of steps, *all of which in some way alter the original intent*. As Tyrone Guthrie intimated earlier, compromise is the rule of the theater, not the exception. Far from being a limiting or negative process, new and original thoughts and concepts are brought about by such a progress. Furthermore, the continual testing of ideas by the process indicated better assures that needed changes to a production will be identified and accomplished. One should not forget, however, that concepts too quickly adopted often suffer two major misfortunes: (1) they never become completely integrated into the major design of the production, or (2) they cause the production to take a wrong direction, a situation that can subvert the intention of all concerned.

What we see is only a general outline as to how the director/ scenographer relationship might work. It is an abstract plan and, like all abstract plans, is not based on the actual way any one director/ scenographer team works.

It would be helpful to us, therefore, to listen to an actual director's thoughts on this subject.

Design Conferences

Each director relates to his stage designer and his costume designer in a unique and personal way.

In talking to the designers, it is important to begin discussion with a description of the general beauty. Leave discussion of mechanical details until a later time. In order to make the best use of the designer's creative imagination, it is valuable to begin by telling him what excites you about the play and why you find it beautiful.

In our early discussions, we agree on a metaphor. And [ask] designers [to] present ideas for the metaphors, such as photographs and paintings. It is essential that the director and designers agree;

there must be [an] agreement on the metaphor, because the metaphor will be a limiting factor (for) all of us in the preparation of the production.

It is crucial that the director be specific in sharing his impressions. Be very open with the designers, tell them your secret thoughts about the play, tell them extraneous thoughts, thematic thoughts, impressions, dreams, resemblances, jokes. Tell them what the play reminds you of. Tell them in poetic terms, in dream terms, in casual terms, in peculiar terms. We take this impressionistic approach because the designers are listening for clues. We cannot be sure in advance what will awaken their imaginations, so we talk freely about our impressions. We talk generally and vividly about the peculiarities of the writing. We talk about the rhythm, the speed of the play, the movement, the color. We talk about every impression, and we ask the designers for their impressions of the play. And among this great salad of impressions, the director and the designers gradually find an image emerging that increases their mutual enthusiasm. It is important to let them go home with their thoughts, allowing time for gestation and synthesis.

I always ask the designers to work in pencil and to come to me with rough sketches, because once a designer has done a completed rendering, replete with detail and color, it is almost impossible to get him to change anything. It is better that his ideas be expressed in many sketches so that we can work together on changes and modifications.

Some directors are easy to please and use everything that is given to them by the designers. I tend to ask endless questions. "Will this coat have inside pockets? How many steps will it take to get upstairs? Will the risers be five inches, seven and one-half inches, or nine inches? Will the banisters bear weight? Will the door slam? With a wooden sound or a metal click? Will the sofa be cushy? Will the panes of glass reflect light? Will the walls wobble?. I tend to plague the designer about these details, partly to assure myself, and partly to be prepared to tell the actor all about them. I want there to be as few surprises as possible when the technical rehearsal date arrives.

What underlies much of the advice Ball gives to the student of directing is that the director must make the scenographer part of his own function. This philosophy is an apt one: the expert use of experts is perhaps the director's most important function in the staging of a production. This all but precludes the dictatorial approach discussed earlier. The only place one is likely to find the autocratic approach to production in evidence is where experts are in short supply; smaller college and university theater departments or community theaters are more apt to spawn the all-powerful director than would be found in professional companies.

It would be well that we now look more closely into both the explicit and implicit assumptions. It is important that while such a plan as presented there is abstract and to some ideal, it still represents working philosophies more useful to the student scenographer than does the diagram outlining the dictatorial approach.

As Ball intimates in his remarks, he wants those scenographers working with him to understand his concerns and visions. Some directors, like Ball, are able to think in terms similar to the scenographer's (some, in fact, were scenographers before they became full-time directors; Franco Zeffirelli, quoted below, is such a director) and are able to speak the language of scenography, to make clear their ideas to the scenographers with whom they work. These directors, strangely enough, are often less dictatorial than those to whom scenography is a closed book written in a foreign language. Very few scenographers have not had the experience of working with a director who simply could not visualize in one scale—the working plans, models, sketches what would eventually be rendered in another. And how often has been heard the complaint, "I didn't know that that was what it would really look like," or the defense, "I don't know what I want until I see it on the stage."

There are directors, though, and the number is increasing steadily, since theater schools have begun training directors and scenographers to work together, that are able to express their directorial concepts in images and words the scenographer can understand and make use of in his own search for a scenic concept. Most scenographers do not, I think, feel this is an intrusion into their private areas of creativity. As a matter of fact, it is not uncommon for a scenographer to become so involved in the problems of the director that he actually begins to direct himself. Take for instance the example of Franco Zeffirelli mentioned above; a successful scenographer who has become an even more successful director. Although, as we saw earlier, Zeffirelli has during the past decade received criticism for his increasingly elaborate productions, we can still benefit from his comments made during an earlier period of his career. Let us then, as with William Ball, listen to his thoughts concerning the visual aspects of direction. As you read, particularly note that he is unable to keep his "scenographer's eye" from determining much of the action in the scenes he describes.

You don't need many ideas (in directing a play), you need one. On that you work and the idea carries you if it's right. Each of his interpretations he reports is based on a controlling image, a core. In *Cavalieria [Rusticanna]* I have always seen the core as a wide white street going uphill in a Sicilian village, that and the sky. At night the wind blows, and a tiny figure with a black shawl comes down running, closing under her shawl her pain and sorrow. It is the destiny of some Sicilian women. I built the set that way. The stage hands at Covent Garden can tell how fussy I was about the platform. The curtain goes up on the prelude. After that it's easy. You are on your path and you follow the consequence. What happens at dawn in Sicily? All the old women come to church. And so on. For *Lucia [Di Lammermoor]*, mine was the image of a woman shouting in a tremendous room, a castle hall, with her wedding veil covered with blood, crying and chasing her cries. How would a woman arrive at that point? How? I couldn't bear a kind of mechanical bird performance in the mad scene. It's a great tragic scene.

Zeffirelli is by no means—although in recent years he has become more so—only a pictorial director. He has in many designs demonstrated a strong commitment to the playwright's text as well as the scenic environment. Still, we see here a director reinforcing the concept that the correct scenic image is of great importance to a successful production. Zeffirelli does, in fact, use visual artists other than himself in his cinema productions. Much of Zeffirelli's motion-picture work clearly shows that both the director and the scenographer can, as separate creators, interest themselves in the other's function.

Sometimes, however, although the scenographer and director may work in close harmony and understanding, the resulting collaboration is something less than artistically successful. Why should this be; how does this situation come about? It is easy to understand failure when they do not cooperate with one another. What possible explanation could there be for failure when these two do work together? Peter Brook, in his book *The Empty Space* touches on this matter and offers some thoughts from the director's point of view.

In performance, the relationship is actor/subject/ audience. In rehearsal it is actor/subject/director. The earliest relationship is director/subject/designer. Scenery and costumes can sometimes evolve in rehearsal at the same time as the rest of the performance, but often practical considerations of building and dressmaking force the designer to have his work cut and dried before the first rehearsal. I have often done my own designs. This can be a distinct advantage, but for a very special reason. When the director is working this way, his theoretical understanding of the play and its extension in terms of shapes and colours both evolve at the same tempo. A scene may escape the director for several weeks, one shape in the set may seem incomplete then as he works on the set he may suddenly find the place of the scene that eludes him; as he works on the structure of the difficult scene he may suddenly glimpse its meaning in terms of stage action or a succession of colours. In work with a designer, a sympathy of tempo is what matters most. I have worked with joy with many marvellous designers—but have at times been caught in strange traps, as when the designer reaches a compelling solution too fast—so that I found myself having to accept or refuse shapes before I had sensed what shapes seemed to be immanent in the text. When I accepted the wrong shape, because I could find no logical reason for opposing the designer's conviction, I locked myself into a trap out of which the production could never evolve, and produced very bad work as a result. *I have often found that the set is the geometry of the eventual play, so that a wrong set makes many scenes impossible to play, and even destroys many possibilities for the actors*. The best designer evolves step by step with the director, going back, changing, scrapping, as a conception of the whole gradually takes form. A director who does his own designs naturally never believes that the completion of the designs can be an end in itself. He knows that he is just at the beginning of a long cycle of growth, because his own work lies before him. Many designers, however, tend to feel that with the delivery of the sets and costume sketches a major portion of their own creative work is genuinely complete. For them, a completed design is complete. Art lovers can never understand why all stage designing isn't done by "great" painters and sculptors. What is necessary, however, is an incomplete design: a design that has clarity without rigidity; one that could be called "open" as against "shut." This is the essence of theatrical thinking; a true theatre designer will think of his designs as being all the time in motion, in action, in relation to what the actor brings to a scene as it unfolds. In other words, unlike the easel painter, in two dimensions, or the sculptor in three, the designer thinks in terms of the fourth dimension, the passage of time-not the stage picture, but the stage moving picture. A film editor shapes his material after the event: the stage designer is often like the editor of an Alice-Throughthe-Looking-Glass film, cutting dynamic material in shapes, before this material has yet come into being. The later he makes his decisions, the better.

Of course it is impossible to set down an ideal work plan that the scenographer and director could always follow to ensure a successful collaboration; too many factors exist, and these factors change from production to production. Certain principles, however, can be evolved (as both William Ball and Peter Brook imply in the statements we have read) that help keep open channels of communication. Now let us proceed to a more detailed outline of some basic functions the director and scenographer directly share. As we have noted, the work of the director and the work of the scenographer moves on roughly parallel tracks. Both tracks, however, comprize eight levels of shared functions. These are:

1. Reads texts. Both read the text many times from various perspectives in order to determine the general outline of the narrative and way the language of the text serves the narrative.
2. Analyzes texts. Both make preliminary assessments as to how the intention of the text relates to the performer's physical requirements – properties, levels, spatial distances-and both attempt to determine how these relate to the performers' patterns of movement. Both also make preliminary determination of the play's eventual emotional background as described or implied in the text: perceived mood, color and tonality, times of day or year, weather conditions, qualities of sound.
3. Interprets texts. Both make individual judgments as to what direction to pursue but then must coordinate individual assessments into an agreed-upon plan of action: i.e., style of production, form of stage space, period to be adopted, level of

reality to be attempted, attendance to performer's explicit physical needs, range and nature of images and metaphors to be incorporated into production.

4. Research initiated. Both gather images that embody metaphors or shows visual interpretations of text's implications. Both search for documents, outside written sources and commentaries that support or explain selected images and text's requirements. Both assemble physical examples of tonalities, textures, images of objects required or to be interpolated into the production.
5. Research assimilated and assessed. Both make a unified presentation of all information gathered. At this point, however, the work of the director and the work of the scenographer begins to separate into specialized functions. While the visual records of the gathered ideas, thoughts, images, and metaphors selected will remain similar, the technical means of implementing them will begin to diverge. It is also during this period that a reevaluation of all initial decisions and materials gathered thus far should be undertaken.
6. Concrete planning. Both begin to record (but in their own languages) the decisions and agreements reached. For the director this means making visual patterns of action (i.e., blocking notes and diagrams) along with precise notes of production needs. For the scenographer this means getting or making not only firm commitments to the stage for style of production, period details, physical requirements of setting, objects, costume (if the production is totally designed by one person), spatial relationships but also decisions as to the means of scenic change, agreement on quality of light for each scene (if production is not lighted by scenographer, which is the increasingly more common situation).
7. Instruction to others. At this point both undertake supervisory functions. The director works primarily with performers. The scenographer works primarily with scenic craftsmen: carpenters, scenic painters, metal workers, property makers. It is important to note that there must remain a constant communication between the director and the scenographer in order to keep abreast of the many physical changes that

accompanies all productions. Every professional theater worker knows that the best reason to make detailed plans is to ensure the time necessary to change them.

8. Observation and refinement. Both the director and scenographer must continually reevaluate both their own work and the work of those they supervise. For the director, this means refining patterns of movement or reblocking patterns not viable, ensuring that themes and motivations are integrated with the performer's intentions and with the physical elements of the production. For the scenographer, communication with the director has a twofold obligation: (1) to assure that the physical elements of the production match the decisions made in point 6 of this outline and (2) to ensure that the various shops and craftsmen executing the physical production are aware of any changes made during the director's work with the performers.

This is the basic pattern of work followed in the translation of a dramatic text into a production for the stage. There will always be, of course, minor variations to the pattern; no two directors and no two scenographers work exactly alike. The pattern is also affected by the kind of producing organization involved. Nevertheless, the essential outline can be expected to remain roughly constant for all modes of production regardless of production type or size, or producing organization.

A few philosophical words are in order as we close this subject. In a scenographer's period of training, one frequently encounters directors who seem to possess total control over every aspect of any given production. In the professional theater, however, director and scenographer are more apt to consider each other as coworkers who are roughly equal in the interpretation of production's text. Each, ideally, has the primary intention of serving the best interests of the text. The master-subordinate relationship between director and scenographer is a rarity in today's theater. And while the director quite often is the first of these two to be retained, and, consequently, has started his conceptual work earlier than the scenographer, many directors make a conscious effort to "leave the door open" to the thoughts and concepts of the person who has been commissioned to design the production. This is because the intelligent director fully realizes that it is in his best interests to keep open and free channels of communication with other sensitive like-minded artists; a good director knows that an ill-considered design can irreparably mar an otherwise brilliantly conceived production. The best work on Broadway, in London, and, indeed, throughout the world gives testimony to the care with which directors forge alliances with "known quantities": Jo Mielziner and Elia Kazan, Harold Prince and Boris Aronson, Peter Hall and John Bury, to name but a few examples. The discussions that take place when these artists meet are only productive to the extent that both enter with open minds. In *Creating Theater*, by Lee Alan Morrow and Frank Pike, Emily Mann says that *"a director can find a play through the designers. I like to get them into the process early. Even as a writer I've often found a play first through a designer."* While all working scenographers over the years will have their patience tested many times in many places, the professional theater is still a much more reasonable place than popular conception of it often allows.

Scenographers cannot perform their jobs successfully unless they find ways to cooperate with the directors with whom they work while still preserving their own artistic integrity. It often difficult but it can be done.

The Language of Space

In *The Concept of Action in Painting*, Harold Rosenberg says: "Action is a means of probing, of going from stage to stage of discovery. If someone asks me a question, my answer will come from the surface of my mind. But if I start to write the answer, or to paint it, or to act it out, the answer changes. What is being done provides a clue to another thought."

The creation of static images is commonly thought to be the scenographer's primary function in theater; that is only partially correct. Scenographers do make visual images: sketches, set renderings, working plans, and numbers of other kinds of drawings. Contributing to the creation of active images on the stage is a better description of the scenographer's function. But, it is not possible to assess this contribution without an understanding of the kind of space he gives the performer to occupy. And the kind of space supplied depends upon how the playwright or composer regards its nature and what demands as to its use they have embedded in their written texts and musical scores.

Although concepts of space have existed throughout man's recorded history, it has only been during this century that any great attention has been given to the concept that there might be more precise meanings inherent in spatial relationships in the theater than heretofore imagined. (This kind of thinking, however, has been an integral part of Japanese art and culture for hundreds of years.) There is a much wider acceptance now, and especially during the last half of this century, that spatial relationships in the theater involve a more precise kind of language, a more reasoned approach than we formerly thought. The study of stage design has become largely the study of changing spatial relationships.

When we discuss space in the theater, we often assume a certain approach to the subject without sufficiently pinpointing the specific nature of that approach. We agree that there is a language of spatial relationships (and that they just *might* affect scenography), but we often do not seek further as to how this language relates to other elements of scenographic training: scenic sketching, the study of art history, or the understanding of stage mechanics. These subjects tend to remain isolated areas of study. Nevertheless even the least informed of present-day students seem to be aware of the implications of a language of space than were their counterparts a hundred years ago. But there appears to be a wide gap still between the recognition that such a language exists and the ability to make a knowledgeable use of it in a specifically predictable way. Few training in the theater today would not have some comprehension of what Peter Brook means when he says, "I can take an empty space and call it a stage." Very few, however, could adequately explain the meanings underlying such a statement or the philosophy that informs such a thought. And while I would expect many students of theater to comprehend Shakespeare's aphorism, "All the world's a stage, and all the men and women merely players," I would not really expect many to be able to specifically relate or explain Shakespeare's words to Brook's concept. And yet, simple as both the words and the concept are, I have often found that there is little understanding that Shakespeare and Brook have in common this basic philosophy: that the stage, no matter its restrictions or imperfections, is a place set apart from everyday experience; that it is a kind of no-man's land but at the same time every-man's land — a place that is both limited in time and space and at the same time unlimited in time and space, a place where anything that can be conceived can be shown. A closer look into this special conception of space is the subject we now need to investigate.

First, we should define more carefully the kinds of space that can be perceived. But while these are to a large extent arbitrary designations all of which overlap it is to our eventual advantage to attempt an understanding of how our concept of these designations affects our thinking and work in the theater. It is possible to categorize the modern-day conceptions of space in several ways. For our purposes, we will look at three of these: real, cultural, and scenographic.

Real Space

This is the kind of space we all live in day to day. Actually, what we call space is not a thing at all but simply the most convenient way of discussing the distance between objects and objects or objects and ourselves. The intensely exciting development of the ability to free ourselves of this planet with space vehicles has given such an emotional charge to the term *space* that the word has taken on a meaning that obscures the fact we are still only talking about relational distances, not a thing in itself. One of the most intriguing aspects of man's intellectual development is that he has come to regard certain relationships — and space provides a good example as something tangible, when, in fact, it is simply the absence of the tangible that is our real focus. We have even begun to use the term *space* to describe certain stages of being that do not actually involve physical distance; for instance, it is not at all uncommon to hear one speak of "*exploring inner space.*" Suspect as the term *real space* has become, however (and, of course, we must be aware that even such a designation is a contradiction in terms), our use of it here is necessary to bridge to a better understanding of the kind of space that Brook implies in his book and Shakespeare infers in his plays.

Cultural Space

During the past few decades we have seen a great interest displayed in seeking out information on the diverse cultures that inhabit this earth. This interest has resulted in a growing body of works that span a number of fields: archaeology, anthropology, religion, art, and, not least among these, theater. We have, as a world civilization, made tremendous strides in attempting to understand one another, to give respectful understanding of how we differ from one culture to the next, and to how national behaviors vary as we move from country to country. It is gratifying to note, moreover, that Western culture has made tremendous strides in freeing itself from the notion that there is an absolute hierarchy of cultural development directly linked to levels of technology and that Western culture (being the most technologically advanced) is the unquestioned apex of that hierarchy. This reassessment of the values of differing cultural views has given rise to an increasing number of studies that deal specifically with the social implications of the differences that occur as one goes from culture to culture. And one of the most important—and for the most part, most hidden—aspects of these studies is the way in which different societies give specific meanings to spatial relationships within that society. These studies have given a tremendous advantage to us not only in the understanding of other cultures but in the better understanding of the often questionable assumptions of our own. In our own culture we have always been aware that there were certain basic ways in which one group differed from another; these were often so visually evident that understanding got no further than observation of the fact. Nor did we ever question that most basic of assumptions that *familiar is good, different is bad.* While it is not possible to say that there is a universal lessening of parochial judgment, the willingness of many cultures to attempt an understanding of other points of view has led to a tremendous crossfertilization in the arts. The theater in particular has greatly benefited by these exchanges. But then, the theater has always, in a very real sense, been a peacemaker; when Shakespeare affirms that "All the world's a stage," he is saying that we are indeed all different, but in our differences, much the same. He does not excuse or apologize for those differences, just draws our attention to their existence. Notwithstanding the fact that we must all come from somewhere, and are what we are precisely because we do come from a particular background, those who work in the theater should realize that just as their art spans time and space, they too should make the attempt to free themselves from the crippling effects of too limited a view of the world in which they live. Nor must they ever be so careless in the practice of their particular art to forget that as they deal with the dramatic literature of different cultures and different times, there will always be something missing from their work if they investigate only styles of architecture, periods of furniture, dress or utilitarian object and neglect to search out those aspects of cultures foreign to them that tell not only what was used and how but in what special (and spatial) circumstances.

Just how is this information to'be gained? Where do we go to find instruction on this important aspect of a theater artist's education? A good start can be made by reading *The Hidden Dimension*, by Edward T. Hall, a work dealing specifically with the various ways different cultures approach spatial relationships. In this important study, Hall draws our attention to the difference between the traditional Japanese conception of space from the way it is perceived and used in European culture. He tells us: "The early designers of the Japanese garden apparently understood something of the interrelationship between the kinesthetic experience of space and the visual experience. Lacking wide-open spaces, and living close together as they do, the Japanese learned to make the most of small spaces. In the use of interior space, the Japanese keep the edges of their rooms clear because everything takes place in the middle. Europeans tend to fill up the edges by placing furniture near or against walls. As a consequence, Western rooms often look less cluttered to the Japanese than they do to us."

(In Japan, Hall tells us later, the Japanese have even given a name for that which we perceive to be nonexistent: the *Ma*, which like our word space, is not actually the name of a thing but the designation of the particular space that exists between objects. In Japanese philosophy and in Japanese art—much of which is an extension of that philosophy—this distinction demands a respectful understanding and is therefore given as much dutiful attention as are the objects that establish the boundaries of the *Ma*. In the paintings of Cezanne—one of the founding fathers of twentieth-century painting and both a student as well as admirer of Japanese art there is this same attention paid to negative space and its inclusion as an important aspect of composition.)

How an individual culture uses space, we can begin to see, tells much about what the values of the culture are. It is not possible, for instance, to understand the London of Dickens's time-nor Dickens himself, for that matter — unless we also understand that it was not only an overpopulated city but an aggressively social city in spite of the often horrendously uncomfortable conditions experienced by its ever-increasing population. In the cinema version of Reginald Barth musical Oliver, based on Dickens *Oliver Twist*, this understanding of how the inhabitants of London behaved was the conceptual basis of the film's choreography. If one wishes a better understanding of Londoner's feelings concerning the utilization of space during the nineteenth century, Henry Mayhew's *Poor of London* is a source of information difficult to match. This four-volume work (now available in a Dover paperback edition) is an invaluable compilation of facts and commentary detailing the lives of numerous individuals, groups, and social levels that coexisted in London during the middle and later half of the nineteenth century. All scenographers should be aware of this important work, one of the principal documents to come to us from that age.

Scenographic Space

In an article, "Recent Trends in Scenery Design: Twenty Years of Scenography," Denis Bablet says this:

> *The French word "decor" is a conventional term that we continue to use because habits are deeply rooted, but it is an obsolete one. The designer's task is no longer to ornament or to embellish, to create a shrine for the production the setting is today an interpreter of the play, an actor. In many cases, of course, it must still specify or evoke the scenes of the action, but above all it acts out and reveals the action, stresses or explains its meanings.*

The first step towards making dramatic action possible is to create the dramatic space. A Mertz or a Neher, a Svoboda, a Sean Kenny or an Acquart conceive, in agreement with the director, an organization of the scenic space that is functional in relation to the play, to the staging, to the actor and to the public. They model a stage floor, they portion out acting areas, create different levels. They trace axes, prescribe lines of circulation, in a word, *they establish a scenic architecture of which each element becomes indispensable, brings out the relationship that unites the characters, accentuates the signification of the actor's slightest gesture.* They are creators of space. It is understandable that many designers prefer to style themselves "scenographers," the term so justly employed in Central Europe.

We have arrived at the point where the term *space* must be given a deeper more precise meaning, since the way we will begin to use the term differs markedly from the way it is used outside the theater. It is also at this point we must begin the attempt to understand Peter Brook's first sentence in *The Empty Space*: I can take any empty space and call it a bare stage.

Tyrone Guthrie was once asked in an interview what his most precise definition of the stage was. He answered: "It is whatever I say it is." He was then asked: What do you you think Shakespeare would say if asked the same question? Guthrie thought for only the shortest of moments and then replied: "He would probably say that it was whatever *he* said it was." The interviewer then asked: Who would be right? This time Guthrie did not hesitate: "We'd work something out—we always have."

While these remarks were made with goodnatured lightness, they give, as Guthrie was asked to do, a precise definition of what the stage meant to him: it was, as he said, a place that could be whatever he wanted it to be and—although he did not specifically say so—a place where he had found it necessary to compromise. One cannot help but notice that what Guthrie said and what Brook says is remarkably similar; in substance their philosophies are identical. The stage is, for everyone who works on it, just such a place as Brook and Guthrie have defined. It is infinitely accommodating and must be accommodated infinitely. At the heart of all theater practice lies this Janus-like duality, this mysterious place that is every place and no place. Still, "It goes with the territory," as Willy Loman might say.

In Thornton Wilder *Our Town*, we can see this duality clearly at work. The play begins as the Stage Manager walks onto a bare stage. It is his function to lead us through the past lives of various inhabitants of a small New England town. He does this by sometimes taking a role in the play, at other times standing outside time and commenting on what is passing and what has passed in the town's history. In his first appearance, however, his job is to locate for us just where he stands and where we are: "The name of the town is Grover's Corners, New Hampshire—just across the Massachusetts line: longitude 42 degrees 40 minutes; latitude 70 degrees 37 minutes." It is doubtful if any in the audience take this information at face value; who there would seriously wonder how far they had to travel to reach home after leaving the theater? What Wilder has done, through the character of the Stage Manager on that bare stage, is to establish the point that we in the audience are no longer seeing events in real space or in real time, but in a different element, a different kind of world that, most important of all, demands a different attitude toward space and time. He asks that we compromise—as Guthrie and Shakespeare and Brook also ask with that socalled real world outside the theater in order that he be able to show us another *real* world: a world of the imagination that can transport us to anywhere at anytime to see anything. One should also note (a kind of paradox, if you will) that although the playwright has taken the greatest care to establish the setting of his play with precise measurements needed to locate a geographical point in that outside world, what he is really saying is, "You are now playing in my ballpark and I make the rules." Like Guthrie and Shakespeare and Brook, the playwright is, on a bare featureless plane with nothing else to aid him, *setting the terms of the bargain he wishes to strike with his audience*. Wilder is not unique in demanding such an understanding: many present-day playwrights feel that is an inherent right of the modern theater to use time and space in the freest possible manner, provided the purpose and understanding of this usage are not lost in the innovation. Nor do I believe this demand—despite an increasing use of scenic technology to create elaborate replicas of real things and places—puts an undue burden on the understanding of an audience; if anything, there is a growing awareness that spectators surfeited on television and cinematic reality actually welcome playing a more active role in the use of their imaginations.

It is also important for scenographers in today's theater to learn that while a great part of their day-to-day work depends upon subdividing that bare plane with the utmost care and accuracy, they should not forget that much of the real work of scenography lies in finding ways to assure that each scene of a production has set its own boundaries through its internal requirements. Just how this is done will occupy our thoughts during the rest of the text. For the moment, however, let us demonstrate one aspect of the principles we are examining in this section of the book. Let us also take note how a spatial relationship, having been established, can alter its basic nature as the time-space framework of the scene changes.

In Arthur Miller *Death of a Salesman*, the play begins in real time and is to be understood as taking place in an actual locale capable of being found geographically. Although Miller does not give us the exact location of Willy Loman's house—as the Stage Manager does in *Our Town*—he does state that Willy visits various places in New York and Boston of his time. It is certainly reasonable to assume, therefore, that this is Willy's selling territory and that he lives somewhere between the two cities. Miller also gives us, in his written stage directions immediately preceding act 1, not only a description of the house in which the main action of the play takes place but also information concerning the immediate surroundings: the back yard, the buildings that close in on his small lot. These specific directions (few of which are the original writings of the playwright but are, rather, the revised directions and descriptions applied to the play during and after its Broadway production) tell us two things: first, that the play is basically a naturalistic one, at least to the point that it deals with recognizable people experiencing actual situations in what we would call a *real world*, and second, that we cannot simply assume that that is the entire story; that within that framework of reality, some strange things might indeed happen; that time and place may very well lose its accustomed shape, form, and reality. This is, in point of fact, what does happen as the play unfolds. Within the first few pages of the play's text we see a bending of the laws of time and material; and it is the precise task of the scenographer to make this change of worlds not only evident to an audience but understandable. Jo Mielziner, in the original Broadway production solved the problems set by the playwright in the following manner:

1. Willy's entrance from the unseen garage is some distance (not the nearest) from the back door to the kitchen of his house. To reach that back door, Willy must take the longest route to it. Willy enters through a small trellis at the far side of the yard and starts the trek to the kitchen door. He walks slowly with some effort: this trip is in some ways a symbolic acting out of the many trips with the same heavy sample bags he has made over the years. But we can see even in this short walk that the years have taken their toll and that Willy is a profoundly tired

man. The scenographer in league with the director has forced Willy to take the *longest possible path* in order to reach the necessary entrance to the house. (We should note here the scenographer and director have already established important conventions for this setting: that is, although the house has no actual walls to it, the actor cannot step onto the platform at any point without violating an established convention; he can only get into the house by going to the designated kitchen door.)

2. Once in the room—which in actuality is only some inches above the outside of the house Willy's actions are restricted by the smallness of the kitchen area. (The actor could, of course, at any time he chooses, step off that slight level; he will not do so—until specifically given permission—because playwright, scenographer, director, and actor have agreed, walls or not, that area is the kitchen and that, seen or not, there are real physical barriers that cannot be violated. Acceptance of this convention, moreover, is an absolute necessity to the dramatic structure of this play.)
3. After preliminary conversation with his wife, Willy opens the refrigerator and removes a bottle of milk. The stage direction reads: *He pours milk into a glass. He is totally immersed in himself, smiling faintly*. As he does this he begins to talk to himself; his mind begins to wander back to a happier time, a time when he and his sons were on better terms, a time when he was not as old and tired; a time when he was still considered an important salesmen, a man to be envied and emulated by younger salesmen. Here the stage direction reads: *Willy is gradually addressing physically—a point offstage, speaking through the wall of the kitchen, and his voice has been rising in volume to that of a normal conversation.*
4. A short while after Willy begins his interior conversation with the past, he rise and walks off the platform that has, up until this moment, had "physical" walls surrounding it. At this point, Willy, literally, *walks through the wall* into the backyard; but more important still, he walks *backward in time*. Later in the play, he will not only go back into time but will step into another geographic locale—a hotel room in Boston—not merely his own backyard.

The actions just described and the spatial requirements made of them are extremely simple in concept and execution. What is important to note, however, is that a complex interaction of time, space, and movement was made with a minimum of physical change in scenery; at no time was it necessary to lower a curtain, revolve a turntable, or shift a wagon to effect the change or make the scene understandable to the audience watching it. It is doubtful if an audience of a hundred years ago would have "read" the scene in the way that a modern audience does; modern-day audiences, whether or not they consciously realize it, have come to accept a whole set of stage conventions their predecessors would have found incomprehensible. It has been during that hundred-year period that the theater has once again found ways to actively engage an audience's imagination. It should also be noted that only through the close cooperation of the scenographer and director that such actions are rendered comprehensible to a viewer in the theater.

Tyrone Guthrie was absolutely right when he said that the stage is *what I say it is*. Shakespeare would be absolutely right if he, as Guthrie supposes, answered the same. What scenographers must constantly keep in mind is that it is their special task to aid both to determine just what they think that "it" is.

There is, however, one very important point that we should understand before we end our discussion of stage space. That is, that any truly workable understanding of the physical stage can only be arrived at through actual experience on the stage. When Peter Brook states, as we have already read, that he believes "that the set is the geometry of the eventual play, so that a wrong set makes many scenes impossible to play," he is, in actuality, bringing to our attention the vital hidden requirement of the scenographer's work: the kinesthetic understanding of specific playing areas for specific dramatic problems. Just what does that mean?

"Every little movement has a meaning all its own." Thus goes the lyric of a well-known song. The idea behind these words is not difficult to understand or comprehend; the thought is part of our consciousness, part of our everyday working social relationships with others, which is as applicable to the stranger as well as a friend. We do, in fact, "read" the movements of others and obtain messages from those movements—"body language" has become a popular description of such an understanding. Some of these messages are obvious and occur to us as conscious thought; others are intuited and are received subliminally as feelings. In all cases, however, we are aware that movement does, as the song points out, have meanings that are the result of purposeful patterns of action. And although not as easily seen or charted, these patterns, taken in a sequence of time, require a precise physical amount of space. These patterns do not usually, though, leave physical traces: the dancer moving in a large circle does not produce an actual circle on the floor. Nevertheless, in terms of time one can make the case that the circle does exist; first, in the mind of the choreographer who conceived of it and, second, in the understanding of the scenographer who must either provide the physical space needed or at least leave that space unencumbered with physical objects. This circle is an actual *shape* that although only perceived in time must be allowed for in space. This is what Brook means when he talks of "shapes immanent in the text." Actors, much like dancers, create such shapes as they move through the enactment of a text. Just as it is important that the choreographer be able to *see* these shapes in the composition of dance, it is equally important that the scenographer – in tandem with the director – see in a written text the possible paths actors might take. Evolution of a total spatial pattern is the key to a workable floor plan for a particular play. The "sympathy of tempo," which Brook also seeks in his work with a scenographer very much involves the agreement of both as to the physical parameters of such a plan.

Now, it is quite possible that the entire work of a scenographer for a particular production can be done within the confines of a studio or at some place other than the actual stage on which the production will occur. But it is extremely important that the nature of that space be understood *kinesthetically* as well as *conceptually*. This sounds abstract, but it is actually a simple proposition in practice. What is meant here is that the scenographer, who has physically walked out the space on the empty stage where the eventual scenographic design is to be, before any scenic element has been conceived of or built for a particular scene, is much more able to conceive and design a specific plan, a specific place for actions immanent in, and appropriate to, the text to occur. If, on the other hand, spatial problems and actions suggested in the text are restricted only to oral discussions away from the site where they will be performed, then the understanding of the shapes immanent in the text will be at best arbitrary and tentative. As an example, consider this situation: someone wishes to know the exact distance between one point on a map and another. Looking at a topographical map of the area (which is analogous to a floor plan) will show exactly how far a mile is; and it is fully possible to determine where a hill is or where a stream might occur along a certain path of movement. But the person who has *actually* walked that mile, has climbed that hill, or has crossed that stream will have an understanding of that path the most detailed study of the map could not provide. The point is that the information is received kinesthetically, not conceptually, and is all the more valuable for having been experienced physically, not abstractly.

This analogy may seem strained; most scenographers simply do not have time or opportunity to "walk out" the stage in order to arrive at a kinesthetically experienced solution to the spatial problems a production poses. Nevertheless to fully understand those "shapes immanent in the text," which Peter Brook thinks it important to do, then the practice is not an idle philosophical goal. And it it important to understand that this kind of activity is a real part of the training that every scenographer should seek out in early training and first experiences. As Jo Mielziner recalls from his own past: "I confess my unbounded delight in my early days at seeing my settings revealed by glamorous stage lighting after they were completed at dress-rehearsal time. I almost resented the prospect of actors standing between my picture and the admiring audience. When I eventually realized how indispensable an imaginative, experienced stage director is to a production, *I began to read a script as though I were going to direct it myself. This did not turn me into a director, but it did make me a better designer*" (italics mine). Mielziner, subsequent to those early productions he recalls, did on many occasions meet with directors on the stages where productions were planned, and in many instances these topics of discussion revolved around the kinds of space they wished to impose on a particular production. The main point we should note here is that when a scenographer turns from the desire to create pictures-as Mielziner's words imply — to the desire to promote action in space, we can begin to glimpse the true relationship of scenography to the theater.

The scenographer should never forget, therefore, that during a performance of any work-play, musical, opera, or ballet — "empty" space is never actually empty but only unoccupied for the moment, that the necessary amount of that empty space is directly related to periods of time when it will be occupied. In sculpture there is a specific term given to a form or group of forms seen in motion. The accepted name for forms seen in motion is *virtual volume*: a three-dimensional shape that only reveals itself in time and movement. If time-lapse photography recorded any object over a period of time, the object at rest would appear considerably different from that same object in motion. (How the wires of a rotary egg-beater, for instance, appear to the eye when they rapidly turn is a good example of virtual volume.) Action, therefore, determines the specific amount and form of the space required. While not readily evident in the theater, actors—even performing the slowest or most static of dramatic works—require amounts of space that may not be revealed by any other means except by consciously predicting and combining *all* the kinesthetic needs of the individual performers into a plan. Since this plan can only be seen in time, it often remains unseen to those untrained to appreciate its implications. This kind of thinking is one of the great overlooked considerations in the thinking processes of those new to theater; they very well can see an acorn and can as equally well understand the concept that oaks grow from it; what is not fully grasped is the time frame that shows how the one gets to be the other. And it is precisely this process of performer-action-time-space that often eludes the most careful study of the most dedicated student.

The scenographer, then, is always required to consider both the total amount of space needed for a particular production and the precise shape—determined by the virtual volume needed for each—into which his design will be divided. This is the real meaning of Adolphe Appia's statement that the scenographer designs with his legs, not with his eyes.

It is not difficult to discern the effect of the scenographer's visual influence in a scenic environment, Crime on Goat Island by Ugo Betti. What is not so obviously apparent is how one arrives at certain configurations of object in space. What gives the scenographer the insight to know not only what to include in these configurations but just what spatial relationships are immanent in a text? For almost every scenic environment is, so to speak, arrived at in reverse from life outside the theater; that is, the performers whose actions will be affected by the scenographer's work often come onto the scene *after* the parameters of the space are defined and the physical relationship of the objects within those parameters set. In many instances scenic environments are created before the director and actors arrive. Just how, then can the scenographer know that his decisions will mesh with the work of the director and performer? A partial answer—and probably the only thing that can be said—is that scenographer is simply an extension of the directing process; it is not totally preposterous to see in the fashioning of an environment a direct link to performing. Let us examine one lost point before we leave this subject of spatial relationships on the stage. And that is that the scenographer exercises two basic influences on the stage environment: the first and easiest to comprehend is the physical influence. Out of the physical influence arises a second influence that could be categorized as psychological. While psychological influences will not be discussed until a later chapter, the purely physical influences should be mentioned in this section. These can be separated into four distinct categories and are as follows:

1. Floor pattern and level change
2. Objects directly used in the action of the production (furniture, seating possibilities, set properties, personal properties)
3. Barriers that restrict and direct the flow of the performer's actions
4. Scenic elements and objects that have a visual influence on the audience but not a direct influence on the performer

These influences have all been discussed during this section of the text. They are shown here to illustrate how all are combined into the actual scenic environment. There is an all-important fifth influence that does not fall within the purview of this text: light and the effects of light on physical form. It is in the use of light, moreover, that one sees the merging of physical and psychological influences. This subject, however, will be left to other writers and other books.

The stage, then, is not just a place where anything can happen but a place where something specific always does: the stage although free of any real time restriction is always in the active present tense. But every action on that stage is, or should be, a specific action to a specific purpose. Every little movement, as the song says, does have a meaning of its own. The role of the scenographer, in equal collaboration with the director and performer, is to fashion out of time and space the only place where the playwright's world can exist. And while we must always be aware that what we do as scenographers and directors must be rendered into exact physical dimension and form that may seem to stand apart from the "meaning" of the text, we cannot afford to dismiss or discount that "interior geometry of the play." Just what is a stage, one may ask? *Three boards and a passion,* is the aphoristic answer—which is to say, anything you say it is. The scenographer must never forget that size, shape, and arrangement of those boards must be given as much care as those things we later decide to put upon them. For every project we undertake, a strict attention must be given to sculptor Naum Gabo's astute words, "Space is a material by itself, a structural part of any whole." Scenography, in the final analysis, concerns itself with important questions such as how far Willy Loman must walk before he steps from his backyard into the past.

"The Building or the Theatre"

The Theatre has become a thing outside of life. Too far outside. It's a mediocre, minority, closed-group activity. It has nothing to do with people having bread or finding things that are exciting. In economically developing countries, people are finding, for the first time, that they can have things other than necessities. They can go places, do things, that weren't available to them before. If the theatre is to be an art form of our time, it must take these new excitements of ordinary people and develop them into a new voice. A new voice: a new theatre.

People are deserting the old form, the old theatre, because it's rubbish. There's nothing to it. We have to forget about the eighteenth-century drawing room behavior and all that nonsense. Let's relegate Chekhov, Ibsen, and Shakespeare to their proper place: a museum theater that would show how things were written and done in the past; how dancers, singers, and actors can interpret a life, a situation, a problem of another time. In art, people take a seventeenth-, eighteenth-, or nineteenth-century painter and consider his work a comment on things as and when he saw them—not a comment on today. What we call Modern Theatre is Theatre of Yesterday. We go on using it because we've developed no alternative. It's as though there were no more movies and we kept showing Charlie Chaplin and the Marx Brothers, saying: this is good cinema and this is the only cinema. Our civilization is becoming more and more a civilization of action. People don't want to sit down, like coy Victorians, to watch a semi-risque story and giggle. They want to take part; they want to do something; they want to shout, to answer back, to rebel and to acclaim. I think these people would want to take part in a new theatre, a theatre that would be theirs and theirs to enjoy.

They'd want to take part in a theatre that reflects what's really happening in this world. At the moment, we have culture salesmen, amateurs who peddle culture to the masses, proclaiming life is an extension of art, art is all. They say to the factory workers: this is what you've missed. But those characters in the factory are bored. What the hell do they know about Picasso? What do they care about folk-lorists or old musical instruments?

I'm not advocating a socialistic, commentmessage-ridden theatre. I want a theatre of excitement. A theatre where you don't have to wear furs, eat chocolate, and read programs. A theatre where you can go and have a ball, where you can drink, where you can do what you bloody well like: dance and jump around and sing.

This theatre, like a baseball hat, would hit you over the head with ideas. It would offer new breakaways, show new break-throughs, suggest how there can be more to life. It would show us how to be more individual—not better, not good, but more individual; it would tell us how to release the emotions half-hidden within ourselves. It would be a place for man: for each and every one of us.

I realize this sounds anarchistic, but in order to prepare the ground for a new theatre, we have to break down all the old barricades, the old ways of doing things. We have to get rid of and destroy, once and for all, the victorian Birdcage. We have to destroy the idea that theatre is designers, is theatre managers, is committees, is directors, is buildings.

Theatre is simply a playwright and a group of actors who want to tell a story before an audience. It doesn't require a building. A building can be a great liability. People who want to build a theatre think first of all of the structure. They don't think of the heart of the matter, the powerhouse behind it: the group of people who will be the theatre. At meetings of theatre people, everybody discusses the building and the stage as if theatre originates with these inanimate elements. They debate three-cornered versus four-cornered, five-cornered, in-the-round, in-the-square, or upside down. If we could find a good, well-designed stage, they feel, we'd have the answer. They are just evading the real issue: what is theatre, what does it talk about, what's doing in our world today? Tackling this does not require a building; any place would do, any street corner, any parking lot. If the people were inventive enough, they would send somebody down the street for a couple of beer barrels and a plank, and have him stand on it.

New theatres, in almost all cases, are not being built by the people. City halls are building them, and the structures they turn out have nothing to do with true theatre. They are badges of culture: symbols of how well we live and how well we conserve and publicize our culture. They are part of the prevailing cultural supermarket-and have no value to anyone but status seekers, people who put badges on their walls.

Speaking of myself as a designer, I don't think I set out to change the theatre or to make it into something different. I wanted to find out exactly what could be done with it, as it was and as it is, and how far it could be stretched. But the nature of a designer's role limits his ability to influence the theatre. He is an outside man; he is not and cannot be, too involved.

We designers spend most of our time arranging wallpaper, chairs, and settees, odd bits of things here and there, that are supposed to make some kind of comment on the story. But to me, design in the theatre is basically a waste of time. A designer can't change anything about the theatre as it is now, unless he stops being a designer and writes a story. Short of that, there is nothing more he can do in the existing theatre; he's just a prop man.

But the designer could do something for a new theatre. He could find a very good square, a good space where the theatre could begin again, where he would say to the actors and the playwright: here is a good place to tell your story in—not a building inside which you can tell it, but a place. It would be marvelous if this place could be found, but I suspect it will have to be different from what we have now.

The new theatre will begin almost as the old began; someone will go to a small town with a group of actors and give a performance.

In the prairies, in the mountains, it doesn't matter. There, like a dance, or a song, or a ballad that evolves into a story, theatre will emerge. And it will attain real significance when it succeeds in attracting the people in the streets and the children.

Our best hope for a new theatre may lie in the children themselves, for children have an idea of excitement beyond themselves. If instead of erecting stages in gymnasiums, the schools were to give platforms, chairs and materials to the children and let them do whatever they want, we might hear the beginnings of a voice called theatre. The children, as they grow up, might suddenly discover that there is one particular way in which they speak best of all, a way important to us. Tomorrow's audience, tomorrow's playhouse, tomorrow's playwrights, could be born in the schools. Just find a thousand acres, plunk the children in the middle with wood, nails, canvas—whatever they want—and say: now, you speak. It might be worth trying.

My feeling on theatre design, on problem of visual concept, is this: to hell with national theatres, to hell with provincial theatres, and to hell with Lincoln Center. Let's just have airplanes, trains and buses, Let's have squares and fields, But let's not build reinforced concrete theatres until we begin to find out which direction, which way our theatre is going to go.

Theatre should be like a floating crap game. It should be able to change its arrangement, to change its environment, to change its whole influence in relation to the things around it. Reinforced concrete foundations are a yoke. They won't let you move; they won't let you change. We are building theatres at this moment, designed for the next 80 or 90 years—however long they stand up—that are impossible to change. We are forced to exist inside them; we have to behave inside the architecture. This can't be theatre. We need structures we can knock holes in; we need to be able to move walls out entirely. The trouble with our theatre today is that if you push out the walls, the roof will fall in.

If this is a beginning period, a beginning time, then we need a beginning shape, and the only thing that we can have at this time is some kind of space tent or something, so that we can move in whatever direction our new theatre wants to go.

We need frames that can be changed; we need places where people can find their own physical ease for watching, sitting, lying, standing whatever it is. We need a new kind of space into which a director and a group of actors and a playwright can come and say: well, we'll put a platform here, and orchestra there, some of the audience here so they'll look like the Roman soldiers we're short of. The entire space could be designed, for each particular performance, for each particular story. The entire space should be always fluid, always flexible. A space that you couldn't even call a theatre, because it wouldn't exist until those boys came in and started to do something. Only then would it become a theatre.

All a painter asks for is a clean white canvas. We need a clean white canvas place, in which we can begin to tell a new kind of story. There should be no architectural statements made before we begin, no statement at all. We can do anything with whatever media we want to use; lighting projection, sound, everything in the world. But first we need this new kind of space.

In the new theatre the designer would be part of a cooperative team altering the place to suit the play. In some cases the designer might say to the director and the actors: you don't need anything from me, you don't need anything for this play; just play it with two chairs—the ones you're siting on right now.

And there are people who go in this direction, people like Littlewood, Wells, Guthrie, and Svoboda. There are lots of people who have ideas; individuals who really want to speak out, who want to reorganize, who want to adjust and say: let's go in a new direction. But control of the theatre is in the hands of the wrong people, the direction is in the hands of old critics.

John Whiting, while he was writing *The Devils*, asked me to help him place the scenes. The only thing I could say to John at that stage was-don't write *any* place. If you can, think in terms of a cinema idea, a television idea, because it should be possible to do anything, to create any place. It doesn't always have to be "enter down left and cross to fireplace"; these sorts of things don't have to happen in the theatre. And so a lot of the stage directions in *The Devils* simply come out: two men are walking, two men are talking. My advice to writers is to start where you want to; go ahead and write—the man jumps out the window onto the back of a white horse and the white horse, chased by ten more horses, runs away through the audience. There should be a freedom about writing for the stage. Why set handcuffs on the theatre?

3

Creative Research in the Theater

Introduction

We designate as artists are tacitly exempted from the first activity in the mistaken belief that investigation is an occupation more suited to police detectives, social workers, ambitious journalists, or literary scholars. On the other hand, interpretation is considered a matter of personal feeling and artistic insight, both of which lie beyond scrutiny. In the theater, however, whether we direct plays or design scenic environments, these two areas often overlap. They are, in fact, different aspects of the same activity. That this interrelationship is often slighted in the educational stages of a scenographer's development or, at best, given slight attention, is the primary reason the present book was written. It would be well for us to begin with a close look at these two words *investigate* and *interpret*. Here are brief definitions of the words themselves as found in most dictionaries:Investigate: To observe or study closely: inquire into systematically: to EXAMINE OR SCRUTINIZE. Interpret:

1. To explain or tell the meaning of: EXPOUND, ELUCIDATE, TRANSLATE
2. To understand and appreciate in the light of individual belief, judgment, interest, or circumstance: CONSTRUE

3. To apprehend and represent by means of art: show by illustrative representation: bring (a score or script) to active realization by performance (Italics mine)

It is not difficult to see that the activities that accompany these definitions are certainly not synonymous; *to investigate* has a more rational, logical purpose behind its meaning than does the phrase *to interpret*. But do not be misled into the mistaken conclusion that these activities do not overlap in significant ways; nor should it take much understanding to realize that both run on the same fuel: *the question* or, to use the term we will adopt in this book, the *informed question*. Moreover, the structure of any investigation or interpretation is determined by the nature of the questions posed. As Heinrich Engel, the noted German architect, observes: "The idea of any study is best understood and consequently best pursued when expressed through a series of questions. *For the question is not only the origin of all intellectual endeavor of man but also, if precisely formulated, indicates the sphere that encircles the answer*".

In its most elemental form, the dramatic text is simply a long list of questions—an investigation, if you will—clothed in the guise of dramatic dialogue. Those who come to the theater want answers to what they see on the stage. Their concern may range from "What is the meaning of life?" to "What is going to happen in the next five seconds?" Curiosity may kill cats but it keeps an audience's attention alive. Often, unlike the investigations of a Sherlock Holmes, these answers may not come as verbal explanations. The "answer" on the stage may very well come in the form of a revealing image. Actually the theater's most satisfying answers tend to be those that show us a resolution rather than *telling* us anything in words. But dramatic texts do not come with accompanying pictures; words are all we have to guide us. How, then, do the words become those affecting images? What steps must we must take in order to bring those images into being? That is the focus of our book. In order to understand how the word on the page becomes an image in the theater, we need to comprehend something that frequently escapes conscious attention: the first reading of the play.

There is an important first principle concerning the reading of any new or unfamiliar play that most theater artists through experience come to understand; a principle many practice faithfully to keep that all-important inner eye clear of the hidden dangers of habit. That principle is: *The first reading of any new or unfamiliar play should be done for enjoyment only; no other purpose need be considered.*

Simple as this proposition seems, the underlying advice becomes increasingly difficult to follow as experience accrues. Since the greater part of any theater research technique consists of stripping away the emotional color of a play's text in order to get at its underlying structure (i.e., untangling the web of questions that chart the play's development), it might seem time wasted not to begin the intense analysis of the text as soon as possible. But in this very eagerness to understand the hidden structure and the concealed meanings, the playwright has willfully or unconsciously placed there, such a reader may abort many important subconscious processes, processes that might never be recovered in subsequent readings. Expert readers have long known of this danger. Samuel Johnson drew attention to the fact that "what is read with delight is commonly retained, *because pleasure always secures attention*; but the books which are consulted by occasional necessity, and perused with impatience, seldom leave any traces on the mind".

This is good advice; still, it is often difficult to follow in the busy world most of us live. Nevertheless, impatience is the common enemy of any good research regardless of the field in which it is done.

Is it possible for the experienced director or scenographer to read a play with a mind cleansed of all past encounters with the stage? Probably not. A new play, unless it closely resembles or mimics some earlier work, often presents fewer problems in this regard than a familiar one. And while any new work may remind the experienced director or scenographer of previously read works, its unfamiliarity often helps to keep minds open. And yet is it possible that many experienced directors or scenographers can approach the rereading of *Hamlet* as if for the first time? For many of us who live with an intimate knowledge of this play, and have done so not only for years but for decades, the answer *is not entirely and never entirely*; the more experience encounters, the more experience colors what is known. For most theater artists even the new rapidly becomes tainted with experience gained from the old. Naturally, expertise in any activity must rely heavily on that residual stain of past experience and accomplishment: that is the basis of a seasoned director's or scenographer's effectiveness. Still, the very thing that renders us effective and reliable carries within it the possibility that our work may become, as

> *Hamlet says of his life, increasingly "flat, stale and unprofitable." The problem is not insurmountable; it is manageable if considered early in the scenographer's development. There are methods of overcoming the hidden dangers of bias as well as overcoming the blind reliance on past "tricks of the trade." This brings us to a second principle to consider. This is:* As you read—either a new play or a familiar one—put your imagination in the same world as the playwright's.

The playwright's text almost always takes place in a real world, fantastic as those worlds sometimes are. Almost all texts describe people, places, and things as if they might be encountered in the world outside the theater's doors. *Stage right, stage left,* and *the curtain falls,* all are applied to a play *after* the play is conceived and recorded. These and similar directions are part of the working world of the theater; they are mechanical necessities that have little to do with that seminal world of the playwright's imagination. The best playwrights, Shakespeare, for example, have little difficulty in bridging these two worlds; often the seams between the two are undetectable; in many instances Shakespeare himself commented on the curious relationship between that world of imagination and the world of the practical stage. But he was never in doubt that the first must come before the second: that the play of the imagination precedes the play in the theater. And it is this that we who must read plays for our instruction and as part of our profession must constantly keep in mind as we undertake our investigations and interpretations into those imaginary first worlds of the playwright. It is only to the extent that we keep our minds free of the prejudicial information of past experience that we will remain free to absorb-both consciously and unconsciously—the original elements of a new work or come to understand the still to be discovered secrets of those most familiar to us. The eventual shape of a production will, of course, rely on the nature of the logical questions to which we subject the playwright's text. But it is in those first attempts to *feel out* the play's emotional undercurrent and subtext, paying as little regard to the technical workings of the theater as possible, that we will make our most important discoveries. The key to all good research, whether as a director or as a scenographer, lies in our ability to make that all-important first reading as an *absorbing experience* as possible.

Active Eye: The Role of Research

In *Walden*, Henry David Thoreau made this complaint (which I am certain he was more than willing to endure its continuance): "Who placed us with eyes between a microscopic and telescopic world? I have the habit of attention to such excess that my senses get no rest, but suffer from a constant strain."

Every visual artist bears this same burden. Moreover, it is a burden that he must seek to make greater as his art matures. The eye is traditionally considered as something that is acted upon; passive until something strikes its view. The visual artist must, however, have a somewhat different philosophy as to how his eye works and, more important, how to make it work better for him. Of course, we must constantly be ready to receive and process the random image; the encounter with the unexpected is one of the great joys of art. But we must always have as the most basic tenet of our artistic philosophy and practice that the artist's eye is *active*; that, to use an extremely old phrase, we must "cast an eye" over the entire world we encounter if we are to keep the ravenous appetite of our artistic imagination fed.

There can be little doubt that man's most comprehensive sense is vision; while his other senses add to and qualify much of what is perceived through the eye, the ability to gather information and make evaluations through this sense alone has been tantamount to his survival as a species. The eye is also of primary importance to the construction and understanding of any communication system or form of culture. While vision has been important in many systems that transmit direct information, serious study of those messages that cannot be directly perceived (or perceived fully at a glance) is a fairly recent concern. The most prevalent mistake we have made as members of separate cultures is to accept without question the erroneous assumption that all human beings see alike; even the speculation that different cultures might see differently has been until very recently almost completely ignored. Although the mechanics of optical reception are similar in all human beings, little attention has been given to how groups with individual characteristics see. Now, however, we are becoming more and more aware not only that different cultures see differently, but that members of single culture cannot be said to see alike. This also brings us to another important point: the difference between seeing things directly and reading visual situations in the light of past visual experience; that is, seeing what we expect to see, not necessarily what is there. When we say we *know* something, it means that we have become aware of some piece of information or the connection between two or more pieces. Encounters with new information occur constantly, often without conscious effort on our part. Formal education is nothing more than purposefully putting oneself in the direct path of facts or theories while at the same time making a conscious effort to comprehend the content or effects of those facts or theories. This much is easy to understand. What is not so apparent is the way actually, ways—we absorb the content of what we seek to know; for *knowing* something involves more than simple confrontation and memorization of facts and theories. Additionally, different forms of information must be acquired in different ways. Gaining information (with the attendant goal of knowing the content) has four general paths. These are:

1. Things seen. In *The Science of Mind*, Kenneth Klivington says this: "All sensory systems serve a similar purpose, to bring information from the outside world into the brain. The general patterns of their organization are also similar, but there are some important differences. In each case a sense organ receives a signal: sound in the ear, light in the eye, and so on. It translates this signal into the language of the nervous system and sends the resulting message coursing toward the brain. *One of the most studied senses is vision*. Scientists have carefully unraveled the connections of brain cells in the visual system and have studied how they respond to light, so we have many clues about how the brain takes visual images apart. *What is particularly elusive, however, is how the brain puts the pieces back together, turning two-dimensional patterns of light on the retinas into our perception of the visual world*" (italics mine).
2. Things read. We have just discussed the difference between raw seeing and that piecing together of elements into shapes and objects. There we observed that things seen by the eye and processed through the brain cause the mind to create unified patterns out of separate elements: that is, lines form shapes, shapes form objects, objects form patterns, patterns form facts, facts form theories, and finally theories give rise to

meaning. On a rudimentary level, the meaning of anything results from searching patterns for likenesses and differences, then ranking those likenesses into complex orders and patterns.

3. Things perceived. Independent patterns when considered together can cause the mind to seek connections that do not actually exist. When, however, a number of elements that have no logical connection are linked together into a pattern, meaning can also emerge, since the mind—as we have noted—both actively and subconsciously seeks to impose a pattern even where none exists. The most logical of patterns has synaptic gaps over which the mind must leap in order to grasp a meaning. In the most complicated of patterns (and plays, novels, poems, paintings, music, are subject to this condition), there are unavoidable holes and gaps that the mind must cross if understanding of the pattern is to be accomplished. Intuition is an important element of perception in the knowing process; intuition is the assumed *reason* in the French aphorism, *The heart has its reasons that reason knows nothing of.* It is primarily through the act of active intuition that the actor finds meaning in his lines and that the scenographer finds reasons for his setting.
4. *Things kinesthetically experienced.* In his advice to the players in act 2, scene 2, Hamlet lays especial emphasis on relationship of physical movement to written text. He says, "Suit the action to the word, the word to the action . . ." Even four hundred years ago those who made theater a profession knew well the vital link between subjective thought and objective action. Stimuli encountered *directly through actions of the body in time and space* are not only crucial to learning processes but are often the key to understanding a fact or a theory. It should also be noted that only through kinesthetic action do all aspects of knowing come into play. The kinesthetic action brings into synthesis patterns seen, patterns read, and patterns perceived. All performers are aware of this way of learning. Theater designers are less attuned to the role that physical action plays in the production process. Understanding that kinesthetic action does have a direct impact has been commented upon by past designers. Remember Adolphe Appia's words—noted

in an earlier section of this book-that "a designer designs with his legs." Add to that this advice of Robert Edmond Jones that "we have to know the instant we see and touch a fabric what it will look like on the stage both in movement and in repose. *We have to develop the brains that are in our fingers*" (italics mine). Both attest to the role kinesthetic action plays in theater art.

Our mind has not only combined the individual line elements into shapes but has also combined the shapes into the image of a box perceptibly threedimensional. The mind has stopped seeing individual units such as lines and has begun to form those abstract separate elements into associative forms; in this case, a box or a cube. In a very real way we have stopped *seeing* elements and have started *reading form*. Despite the fact that the box or cube is only a combination of the same line elements, our eye has unconsciously assembled these forms into a meaningful whole. We no longer see the lines, only the box. (This, by the way, is the basis for the aesthetic aphorism that *a work of art is more than the sum of its parts*. We literally *loose sight* of the individual elements at the same time as we gain a vision of the whole.

The ability to work backward from wholes to elements is crucial to the work of any visual artist. This ability is not a natural one since our brain insists on working the other way: it always puts disparate elements into patterns as the initial step to comprehension. The mind cannot abide ambiguity, and it uses its instrument of perception the brain to incessantly scan all within its visual field to constantly assemble disparate parts into meaningful wholes. An important feature of all visual processes is that even when meaning is absent, the mind supplies the deficiency. It imposes patterns on what is perceived until a meaning—no matter how tenuous—emerges.

So insistent is the mind to put into order what it receives from visual stimuli that often it accepts as fact an image it knows cannot exist. For example, the "object" appears to have three tines leading to a base. But if one looks closely at the base, only *two* tines begin there. This object could not exist in reality. As a drawn image, however, a clever arrangement of lines makes the impossible appear possible. The ambiguity of this figure is processed by the mind by alternating between the acceptance of the three tines when focused on them and acceptance of the two tines when focused on the base.

These figures demonstrate that mind will find consistency and order even when it knows that what it perceives is a logical impossibility.

In addition to the mind's capability to make sense of ambiguity, there is another major way it processes visual information. This process is called *completion* and is sometimes called *closure*. Completion is the ability of the mind to bring disparate elements into a pattern or a whole. It is similar to what we observed in the object above in that the purpose of the mind here is to finish out what it perceives to to missing. It shows what appears to be a white triangle superimposed onto three black circles. There is no triangle, there are no black circles. There are only three small irregular forms strategically placed that produce the illusion of a white triangle. Again, we see evidence of the mind *reading* information beyond the limits of what the eye actually perceives. The ability of the mind to find continuity when it does not exist, to create whole images from incomplete parts, is a crucial part of every visual artist's understanding and education. It is also an essential tool in the practice of scenography. Scenographic designs in today's theater rely on the minds of audiences not only to complete whole images from isolated details but often to *read into* those fragmentary images meanings that support the action of the production or the sense of the text. Few spectators seeing such an arrangement on the stage would have little difficulty accepting performers behaving as if they were living in an actual structure. A cardinal condition of theatergoing is—has always been-a willingness to substitute symbolic representation for the common perception of reality.

The act of seeing, it is evident, is not as simple an activity as one might first believe. Even in the perception of the most uncontroversial of visual events—as we see in the illustrations above-there are a distinct, although related phases. Visual experience is progressively built by these steps that are continuously and, for the most part, unconsciously performed by every sighted individual. Although much we perceive is unconsciously processed, visual artists can never take their seeing abilities for granted or believe their visual training is ever complete. To a degree not required from most other individuals, the scenographer must search for those elements of an image *that evoke meanings and information that lie beyond recognition of surface features*. The scenographer, unlike the casual observer, must be an especially active looker, not simply a passive receiver of visual stimuli. The formative stage of any visual artist's training is not unlike that of the biologist who carefully dissects into constituent parts a specimen in order to understand more clearly the relationship of those parts to the living whole. While it is never possible to understand that whole merely through inspection of parts, our understanding is, nonetheless enhanced if we become familiar with the elements that make up the whole. Let us now expand on the ideas encountered above as we begin to relate these and others to the purposes of scenography. The basic steps involved in all visualization are as follows:

1. Visual sensation. Any visual stimulus has an immediate effect on the brain, but all sense stimuli are interrelated to the other senses. (When we see a cut on another person, for instance, quite often we experience a definite perceptible sensation in our own bodies. Looking down from great heights can also produce reactions in parts of the body that cannot be said to be purely visual responses.) The stronger the initial visual sensation, the more quickly are we forced to a second response:
2. Thinking. Upon seeing something, the mind begins immediately to fit the visual sensations it perceives into rational contexts. This process attempts to relate new visual sensations to past patterns of images and experience. (We speak of "making sense" to describe this process. We also use the phrase "at first glance." Both of these indicate the natural inclination to fit any visual experience into an understandable pattern, which does happen for the most part instantaneously; this process is so quick, in fact, that very strange sensations are often glossed over in the process. The visual artist must train himself to slow down this assimilation process; otherwise he will often miss that very creative process that is summed in that other hackneyed phrase, "like seeing it for the first time." This is often the visual artist's most important task: *seeing the familiar as if it were for the first time.*) The thinking process almost invariably leads to a third response:
3. Feeling. The residual effect of both the sensation and the immediate conscious assessment of what has been visually experienced leads us to a stage wherein we have "made sense" of the visual response. Having "made sense" of our reaction implies that we now have some emotional response and, as

well, added to that visual response. (Familiarity with an image or set of images can, however, be so familiar and so frequent that this emotional response becomes atrophied to the point of being nonoperational-witness the effect of violence to which we are subjected in the cinema and on television. While many would debate its ultimate effect on our actions, few would deny that violence perceived in these media produces little emotional reaction beyond casual recognition.) While all of these first three responses are taking place, a fourth-and perhaps a simultaneous—process is happening:

4. Intuition. This is the unconscious assessment of the image in terms of past experience and quite possibly an unconscious understanding of how this image might relate to future experience or action. Here we do not speak of "making sense" but, rather, of *sensing* something not immediately available to the conscious mind. It is quite possible that no awareness is present at all in the conscious levels of the mind, that the various sublevels of the mind are recording the visual event or relating it to other images stored there. This storage process cannot take place, however, without the objective image being present (although images already stored can, of course, summon up others not actually physical). This is, quite possibly, the best reason for the artist to expose herself constantly to images with no apparent need for their immediate use. Dylan Thomas, an unusually sensitive poet to things visual, often spoke of his formative years when he went about "with my eyes hanging out." It is this attitude that all visual artists come to espouse in time; it is, however, an attitude of which the evolving artist must become intensely aware before she can appreciate the need to train her eyes to work independently of directed intention.

Seeing and intuition are inseparable parts of one another. Nor is intuition the exclusive prerogative of some while denied to others. No doubt some persons are more predisposed to intuitive reasoning than others; but this does not rule out the possibility that it can be nurtured and strengthened in those who feel a positive need to do so. The investigative mind cannot, however, confine itself to that often very narrow band of rational and logical thought that often declines to acknowledge any solution to a problem outside its own boundaries. No artist, certainly not the scenographer, can afford to discount the powers of intuition or the pursuit of its attainment. Henri Cartier Bresson, a great artist whose primary medium is photography, says this concerning the role of intuition in his own work.

There is subject in all that takes place in the world, as well as in our personal universe. We cannot negate subject. It is everywhere. So we must be lucid toward what is going on in the world, and honest about what we feel. Subject does not consist of a collection of facts, for facts in themselves offer little interest. Through facts, however, we can reach an understanding of the laws that govern them, and be better able to select the essential ones which communicate reality. Composition must be one of our constant preoccupations, but at the moment of shooting it can stem only from our intuition, for we are out to capture the fugitive moment, and all the interrelationships involved are on the move. In applying the Golden Rule, the only pair of compasses at the photographer's disposal is his own pair of eyes.

I believe that, through the act of living, the discovery of oneself is made concurrently with the discovery of the world around us which can mold us, but which can also be affected by us. A balance must be established between these two worlds—the one inside us and the one outside us. As the result of a constant reciprocal process, both these worlds come to form a single one. And it is this world that we must communicate. For me, content cannot be separated from form. By form, I mean a rigorous organization of the interplay of surfaces, lines, and values. It is in this organization alone that our conceptions and emotions become concrete and communicable.

These words, by a photographer, apply equally to those who work in other visual worlds. But, as Henri Cartier Bresson also advises us, "It is essential to cut from the raw material of life—to cut and cut, but to cut with discrimination." The scenographer, as with all visual artists, must learn to make the power of intuition a working tool by which that raw material is gathered and processed.

Perhaps every creative person, artist and scientist alike, can take hope from the words written in a decision handed down by the U.S. Court of Customs and Patent Appeals a few years back. Part of that finding reads as follows: "Invention isn't always the offspring of genius; more often, it's the result of plain hard work; sometimes it arises from accident or carelessness; occasionally it's the happy thought of an ordinary mind; and sometimes invention is simply the product of sheer stupidity."

All students of scenographic art must give long and careful attention to the ways they visually perceive the world as well as to consider how they shape the vision of those who see their work. Let us leave this subject with these words of the nineteenth-century painter who shaped much of the vision of the twentieth-century artist Paul Cezanne: *Time and reflection change the sight little by little until we come to understand.*

Scenographic Vision

We often hear the expression, "To the trained eye"; it denotes that the person possessing such vision is able to perceive information that is not at first apparent or readily accessible to the casual untrained observer. A doctor can often predict, for instance, certain types of internal diseases or disorders simply by observing the color or discoloration of the skin alone; the farmer can, by look and feel of soil, appraise its value for growing certain crops, as well as predict an expected crop yield; dozens of professions rely on the ability of an individual to give precise evaluations from quick surface investigations of objects, materials, or mixtures: a calculated "guess" that will, at a later time, be borne out in proof. This vision, this "trained eye," this insight, while it may exist without antecedents or understandable reason in some—a Mozart or a Beethoven or a Leonardo da Vinci—is not an inborn trait for most individuals; it is a faculty which must be rigorously pursued and then carefully nurtured. The scenographer must, like every other trained professional, learn to use the natural sensory equipment he has in ways and at higher levels of perception than even the most sensitive or intuitive member of an audience could imagine; the work of the scenographer is, to a very great extent, a visual medium through which the vision of others must pass; an audience sees through the eyes of the scenographer, since he both rationally and intuitively selects what they view. Moreover, he controls not only what they see but also the context in which they see it. The objective vision of the scenographer very much determines the subjective reality an audience perceives.

The innermost nature of the theater depends upon the use of imagery. But, just as all imagery is not of the same kind, all the purposes to which imagery can be put in the theater are not similar. Basically, the purpose of imagery is to make the nonvisual elements of the production more effective. Philosophically, imagery is based on the assumption that in the theater things or acts directly seen have a greater effect than things or acts described or reported. Perhaps the ancient Greek theater's practice of reporting acts of extreme violence or catastrophe would lend support to this contention; while one could show the effects of violence—Medea's dead children, Oedipus's blinded eyes, the head of Pentheus after he had been torn apart by his mother and her followers—it was felt that showing the actual act would be too strong a vision for the audience to support. Since that period, of course, such restrictions in the theater have been disregarded, although the question concerning the showing of violence is still being hotly debated, especially as it relates to television. In any case, there can be no doubt that what is seen is many times more affective than what is described. The scenographer is, of course, an artist who constantly deals with images. But, just how often do we consider precisely the type of images we use daily or the import of the various levels of imagery we often employ unthinkingly? For not to consider these questions is, in part, to relinquish an important part of the control we as scenographers are given.

It is taken for granted that the scenographer works to be effective; that is, the training and inclination of the scenographer are toward the production of predictable and intended results. Yet a scenographer may be very effective and still not be an artist of the theater. A setting or scenic environment may be basically appropriate, workable for performers and may, indeed, even create an atmospheric mood. All these elements might be present in a design, and still something will be lacking when the total work is presented to an audience.

What we speak of here is not the skill to be *effective*, which, it should be expected, is the prime purpose of disciplined training, but the ability to be *affective*. While these words may sound similar, in fact they are often used interchangeably, they are far from being the same. It is, moreover, in the power to be affective that the scenographer contributes his own special art to the theater. It could even be said that scenography is largely the ability *effectively* to promote predictably *affective* images on demand. It is, more important still, in the construction of affective images that the undercurrents of a production are given form and direction. While the rational faculties of the scenographer must be under his strict control in order to create these supporting images, they will, to a very large extent, lie beyond completely rational explanations and definitions. An affective image is one, in the final analysis, whose full import must be experienced in terms beyond verbal exposition, its perceived meaning lying outside the most careful attempt to "explain" that import. And yet careful analysis is the most basic of the scenographer's tasks: analysis of a production's meaning in terms of text, imagery, physical needs, and audience perception. It is paradoxical (if not downright contradictory) to say, on the one hand, that a scenographer must know every step in the production of an environment as it relates to both the conceptual meanings of a stage work and its physical construction and, on the other hand, to affirm that this work can involve images that cannot be logically or rationally explained. Yet when we cross that illusive line from craft to art, our certainties as to intention and results often become less tangible. It is, however, when we cross that line that we must also begin to speak of levels of the mind that, although not completely clear in outline, do operate in positive and productive ways. It is when we venture into these areas where the truly creative processes begin to operate that we must begin to trust other systems that, for want of a better phrase, are out of our control. And it is in the acceptance that such systems do, indeed, exist and work for us in a positive manner that we make our most important step toward becoming that artist we aspire to be.

Most simply put, the scenographic process is an interlinked network of skills, historical understanding, sensual perceptions, love of dramatic action, deep appreciation of the power of all manners of language, and a willingness to probe all levels of the mind of oneself and of others. It also means a firm commitment to a life of selfexamination rather than one of self-expression.

To be *effective* is within the powers of almost anyone who is willing to invest the time for the accumulation of required skills; to be *affective* is to acquire skills beyond those purely mechanical, the most important of those skills being the ability to *see*. Perhaps, therefore, the greatest error the beginning scenographer can make is to assume without question that once those mechanical skills of the craft are mastered—which, indeed, must be done, or no further progress is possible in any direction—the natural and unique imagination we are all endowed with will supply any other minor requirement: that one can automatically draw upon an inexhaustible spontaneous natural store of imagery out of past experience that will supply the form and detail necessary for the effective design of an appropriate scenic environment. Nothing is further from the truth. But why is this so?

For our present purposes, the answer lies in the nature of man's vision. Let us repeat it once again: the most important skill for any student of the visual arts is to develop the ability to see. While this sounds too elementary for comment, too simple a requirement, in practice it is not as simple as it seems. And the reason it is not a simple matter is that theatrical vision requires not one but two distinct types of seeing. One vision addresses itself to the world of the objective; the other vision must deal with the world of the illusive subjective—a world that often is hidden from purely objective (if such a thing exists) vision and investigation. It is not uncommon for mature scenographers to speak of an "inner eye." This is not simply a poetic or mystical expression. What they are referring to is a real and necessary part of their working technique; an attempt to describe the kind of vision and understanding all visual artists must develop. Seeing is the subject of the following section, but it is to that subjective "inner eye" that the most of our attention must be directed. And while it is impossible to assure that every student of scenography will in time come to possess or make use of such a vision, we must discuss this area of artistic training at least to the point that we can assure to all that such a vision is a practical necessity for working in the theater.

Robert Edmond Jones once said that "stage designers are born, not made." A great part of what he means by that statement has to do less with natural selection or cultural background than with the particular ways certain natural predispositions are channeled into the theater. But the callings of destiny aside, just how does the vision of the scenographer differ from the vision everyone else possesses? Or is there a difference? Are not 20/20 or corrected vision and a certain level of manual dexterity the only real requirements for the pursuit of any visual art? Increasingly, I feel, the answers to these questions must be *no*.

We cannot ignore the growing evidence that each human being is, indeed, a truly unique entity; that, similar as we sometimes appear to be to others who either look like us, dress like us, sound like us, or have the same basic cultural background, we all possess individual minds that may altogether contradict the most identical of surface similarities. Even identical twins can have distinctly separate and basically different ways of perceiving the world. We do not, as the timeworn phrase might lead us to think, all congenitally "see eye to eye." And this can be especially true in the manner in which we encounter the visual world about us. Gordon Rattray Taylor draws our attention to some observations that directly affect our old notions of human vision; more importantly, he raises a distinct challenge to the idea that all sighted people see the same objective world.

Some authorities have asserted that no thought is possible without imagery, but that is almost certainly false. It was Professor Bartlett, at Cambridge, who in the course of studying memory, came to the conclusion that people fell into two distinct groups: visualisers and verbalisers. The late Dr. Grey Walter brought a little more scientific accuracy to the subject when he estimated, on the basis of the brain waves he studied, that fifteen per cent of the population think exclusively in visual terms, fifteen per cent exclusively in verbal terms, while the rest employ a mixture.

Visualisers find it hard to form abstract concepts and find it difficult to communicate with verbalisers verbalisers tend to operate in a domain of concepts which have, all too often, only the vaguest relevance to the real world. I suspect that many lawyers, legislators, bureaucrats and administrators have the same defect.

Few of us like to admit that we do not see immediately and perfectly. The truth of the matter, however, is that even the most perfectly sighted person sees selectively and, at best, imperfectly. This can be demonstrated very simply by the following quick test. Question: Just what did you *see*? If you said, "I see a line drawing of a man wearing a two-button jacket, a plaid vest, a figured tie, glasses, and smoking a cigarette," you would be right—but only halfright. The image also contains other items of information that have been purposely hidden in this relatively simple drawing. To be precise, it contains not only three hidden things but the clue to the number hidden. Now go back and look at the lower right side of the image; there you will see the name of the artist and a number beside it; the number is the clue. The clue to what, you ask? The clue to the number of times Hirschfeld has included the name of his daughter in the drawing; it appears three times. And where are those names? That is the game he has been playing with his fans for many years. The name of his daughter is *Nina*. Now, if you go back, it will take very little time to decipher the puzzle. It is easy to solve the mystery once you know that there is something to be found in the lines of the drawing; once alerted to the possibility of "hidden things" in the drawing, our vision is *actively directed* toward seeking out just what those things are. This *actively directed vision* is a necessary requirement for the practice of any phase of theatrical art, not just that of scenography. It should take very little time or effort to find that Hirschfeld has incorporated into the bends of the elbows and at the base of the ear of the figure the name *"Nina"*; being part of the design and sharing the same qualities as the other lines, the name becomes, however, very much like Poe's purloined letter—all but invisible to the *undirected vision*. Having once *seen* these names *as names*—not abstract lines representing cloth in a sleeve—we can never look at this drawing again without seeing them. In short, our vision has become *instructed*. And yet, those who do not know the "secret" of the drawing rarely see those names without being similarly instructed. This has nothing to do with native intelligence or perfect vision; it does very forcibly point out that intelligence and perfect vision must sometimes be directed toward a goal.

This simple test should bring home the observation that few of us do see immediately and with perfect understanding that which is seen; reception of an image and perception of that same image are not always in phase. It is especially sobering to realize that the vision of the scenographer must be trained to "see" when helpful clues, such as the ones Hirschfeld supplies, are few or more deeply hidden in the images we must use for theatrical work. Rest assured, however, there will always be similar "mysteries" inherent in the visual materials that scenographers use in their work.

Let us pursue this problem further; let us admit to ourselves that *seeing* of any kind can be *directed* and *deepened* by influences that have nothing to do with visual images. A picture is, it has been sagely observed, worth ten thousand words and perhaps no number of words can ever adequately take the place of the image or make it as apparent to the mind as the image itself does. And yet, as another wise person once pointed out, *it took words to make that observation apparent.* There is a principle every scenographer (indeed, every theatrical artist) must be aware of that words can directly affect images; that the most profound statements the theater affords are a direct result of this interaction.

When Hamlet, in act 3, scene 4, is admonished by the ghost of his father to be less harsh in his indictment of his mother, he finds to his surprise that what is perfectly apparent to him in a visual sense is neither apparent nor visible to her:

HAMLET: Do you see nothing there? QUEEN: Nothing at all, *yet all that is I see.* (Italics mine)

The scenographer's vision is much like the sight of Hamlet; it sees both with a special intensity and with a special purpose. His mother's vision, on the other hand, has serious blind spots in it precisely because it is an unquestioning act. She sees only what she expects to see, making no attempt to see further. This is the prime mistake no artist can afford to make: *seeing that does not question what is seen is uninformed, and vision uninformed is vision impaired.* In the simplest terms, not only must all artists possess a keen outer eye that perceives shape, form, color, texture, and spatial relationships, they also must have an equally sensitive inner eye. The artist's vision is at once objective in the analytical sense as well as subjective in the most symbolic sense. The kind of seeing we speak of here is not, however, a matter of idiosyncratic vision a strictly personal view such as the one practiced by the German expressionists immediately following the First World War—but a vision capable of interpreting forces and meanings contained in an object or image that escapes the superficial or cursory investigation of the untrained eye. Like Hamlet, one must be prepared to receive and perceive information that will always remain invisible or incomprehensible to others such as Hamlet's mother. It is a common mistake to think that if one can see at all, one can see it all. The Queen does not see the ghost, therefore it does not exist—at least for her; but everyone in the audience knows that he is there, that it is a necessity that he be there. Theatrical vision, then, is the sight Hamlet possesses. But, having said this, just how does one go about getting this unique vision?

Artists cannot develop their abilities to any significant degree without two very important characteristics present in their nature: (1) they must have a natural curiosity about the objective world in general, and (2) they must have an intense need to know the facts concerning particular situations beyond the common perceptions of reality. They must have, in short, a complete vision, reflective in nature but fed by objective stimuli. Scenic seeing is, essentially, the development of the eye so that it "thinks" as well as sees; to be able to "see" in more than one time dimension and, most important of all, to be able to distill from the obvious surfaces of the material world that which is dramatically poetic. For as Herman Melville has taken care to point out, "poetry is not a thing of ink and rhyme, but of thought and act, and, in the later way, is by any one to be found anywhere, when in useful action sought." The fact that the messages the scenographer sends through the medium of design are often not meant to be perceived by conscious perception does not in any way weaken the point that he must be perfectly aware of what those messages are and strive to incorporate them into material form.

Our first question concerning the development of scenic vision as opposed to just "seeing" might very well be this: Does not everyone with 20/20 vision, regardless of culture or background, see the same thing when looking at the same thing? The answer, all questions of natural intelligence left aside, is unequivocally and absolutely no they do not. The next question, invariably, would be, If not, why not?

This is a question that all beginning visual artists have, and usually, they do not seriously entertain the idea that they do not see all there is to be seen. It is a difficult pill to swallow for beginning artists to be told by their instructors or by more advanced compatriots that being able to "see" is a time-consuming and difficult undertaking. Usually the explanation of why this might be so ceases with the statement. But in fact, there is no one reason why the young artist does not "see" all that his more experienced counterpart does; there are many. Of all the reasons, time and exposure to the objective world are the largest, most important factors; not only does experience of the world teach us to see more, but the constant questioning of the very act of seeing is a necessary part of the artist's visual development.

Let us begin this search for understanding by looking at a famous sixteenth-century painting: *The Ambassadors* by Hans Holbein, painted in 1533. Examine the picture for the information it contains;

it is not difficult to inventory the visual contents of the painting: two men, both in costume of the day (although one is dressed in academic garb, not in court dress, as is the other figure). They stand at either side of a two-tiered open case that contains representative instruments of all the arts and sciences of the time. We see, in short, a factual record of two famous men, and we can infer, by the painter's juxtaposition of them to the objects included, that they are not only figures of breeding and position but inquisitive men of intelligence and accomplishment. Their grave but open faces, their ease and poise, their familiar relationships to the accouterments of learning, combine to give the viewer a message; a message not difficult to understand even some four hundred years later. And yet in this most meticulous rendering of objective reality, the artist has also included a strange object that defies rational explanation. Holbein, who in all of his other works scrupulously copied the outward appearance of reality, has, in this painting, introduced an irrational element that, in one sense, cannot be part of the total picture and, in another sense, cannot be separated from it. This "thing," which starts from the lower left of the painting and sharply cuts across the floor, is nothing less than a human skull; but it is painted in such a distorted manner that its true visual form cannot be grasped until the onlooker assumes another physical viewpoint that distorts the rest of the picture. Both views cannot be seen at the same time; both, in other words, cannot be understood at the same time; both do not belong to the same painting and yet they can in no way be separated. Why did he do this? Several ideas present themselves—but we cannot ever know for sure if our explanation for this strange work is the correct one (assuming in the first place that there is, in fact, a "correct" one). Any explanation cannot be entirely verbalized, entirely satisfactory; this painting will, quite probably, remain something of a provocative mystery.

This painting has been included here not for its value as a work of art nor because it presents a tantalizing visual mystery. Both are true. It is here in this text because it serves as a visual touchstone as to how the scenographer employs his own special vision. In *The Ambassadors*, Holbein gives a mystery to be sure; but he also has done much of the "work" for us. All we have to do is to assume the two different positions and the two different images will emerge: the real and the phantasmagorical. But that is really not the point to which we should bring our attention; having approached the picture from those two viewpoints, having seen the images in both, we are left not with an "answer" but with a question: *What was Holbein getting at – what was he trying to say?* And, even more important than being a tantalizing question, the fact that he forces us to move physically in order to make any sense of this work is a valuable lesson for the scenographer to learn. The image engages our attention but does so in a particularly dynamic way; we must do more than passively "see," we must actively work to bring the image into focus. Physically changing our viewpoint is required to understand this work at its most basic level: mentally changing our point of view is every bit as important and must be pursued in a similarly active way. It is an unsettling thought that we cannot or should not trust our ingrained and comfortable modes of perception, that we do not, as Hamlet's mother, see all that is. But it is with just such an acceptance of this situation that real progress in the art of scenography begins. The images we confront in our research do not, as with the Holbein painting, come equipped with such readily accessible clues; nor are there numbers, as with Hirschfeld's drawings, to tell us precisely the entire stock of hidden things. We must, as an integral part of our artistic work, seek these hidden factors out by less direct means, more difficult searches. As with the Holbein painting and the Hirschfeld caricature, there are ways of finding help and we should be aware that such aid does exist. Let us examine another image: a photograph taken in Toledo, Spain. Before reading any further, take a long look at the building in this photograph.

Now, ask yourself these questions: What did I *see*? What does this image project to my immediate vision? Is there anything *hidden* in the picture, any quality or fact I am not seeing or understanding? These, it must be granted, are difficult thoughts to entertain, since the question must almost certainly arise: *But just what am I looking for in the first place*?

Go back and look at the picture again. This time, however, ask yourself these questions: *If I were designing an environment that required elements from this locale – Mozart's* Don Giovanni, *for instance – what could I use from this image? What elements are appropriate; what would I choose to ignore? Does this picture tell me anything I need to know about Spain itself?*

These speculations do not give hard information; they do, however, begin an extremely important process: they cause us to change our focus from what is simply observed in the image to what exists in this particular image that can be used for a specific purpose. This line of thought is, by its very nature active rather than passive; our senses are alerted to the possibility that *something* or *some things* are included in this image that are appropriate to our specific purposes the setting for *Don Giovanni*. But what?

Robert Edmond Jones very likely had just such questions when he began his initial speculations concerning the design of *The Birthday of the Infanta*, a work performed at the Manhattan Opera House. He had, of course, several years earlier visited Spain and had seen firsthand much of the visual material he would need to incorporate in the design. But did he simply copy details from the sketch book we know he carried throughout that country; did he simply check out research materials from the New York Public Library? It is quite certain he did look at and study many images from numerous sources; it is also just as certain that he did not stop his investigation of the design possibilities when he had found a "right" picture to copy from. We do not have either his written thoughts or his reported speculations on this project. What we do have, however, is a review of the design Jones created as that design appeared in performance. This review, moreover, reveals a great deal about how Jones studied the information contained in that material.

Here is how Stark Young, who reviewed the first performance of *The Birthday of the Infanta*, reacted to what he saw on stage: "No where in Spain have I seen buildings like these. But I have seen in Spain that character of sterility, of color and mass. I have seen that barbaric and cruel barrenness of sheer walls emerge, though any amount of rococo and baroque or plasteresque ornamentation had been superficially laid on to soften the aspect of it. The character of Mr. Jones' setting, then, perfectly expresses the Spanish instinct, into which the actuality of the buildings has been translated by the artist. But that is not the important point just here. So far they have indeed become art, it is true, but not necessarily the art of the theatre. The important thing to be said here is that this is not architecture in Spain or anywhere else, but a translation of architecture into theatre terms."

Certainly the picture you now see is different from the one you saw before. "Barbaric and cruel barrenness," "superficially laid on," "the Spanish instinct": Have not these qualities become apparent to you in a manner that was not evident when you first examined the photograph? Is it now relatively easy to perceive that while the blind copying of details could give a certain "Spanishness" to the design, it was necessary for Jones to *understand the import* of what he did select? If he had only copied a building from Spain, it is doubtful that his underlying thoughts and feelings would have been projected to Young. Robert Edmond Jones was an artist who could and did make an active effort to distill from the mass of what he saw the precise forms, colors, and textures needed for a precise purpose. He possessed and used his inner eye.

It is very possible that you will never again be able to see either an image of a Spanish building or the actual architecture of Spain without the words of Stark Young in some way guiding your vision. It is also possible that your understanding of the architecture of other countries will become more discriminating precisely because you now have a kind of architecture with which to compare it. It is not difficult to comprehend the principle put forth here: that there is always more to any visual experience than at first appears; that it is very possible that while a picture is worth ten thousand words, words can add to the worth of that image. But, once having articulated this principle, it must be said that it remains only an abstract thought that must be reexamined and reproved every time it is brought into play. And that is why "scenic seeing" is the core of the scenographer's art; he can never take for granted that he has reached some absolute level of expertness where this vision is an automatic response to anything that comes into view. As Frederick S. Wight points out in *The Object as Self-Image,* "A man-made object has a way of revealing itself to be something else than it at first appears, and then that revelation proves to be a cover story, and the whole process of undraping the truth is a disturbing one, subject to unaccountable blockages." This is true for the scenographer's research whether he is examining a photograph or a drawing or looking at something in its actual context, as Jones did when he toured Spain. We must constantly force our minds to change their points of view much in the same way Holbein forces us to change physically our viewing points; otherwise we will always be on the outside looking only at the surface of things.

Before leaving this discussion let us take another "test" to explore how that inner vision that scenographers use works. To facilitate this, let us construct a short outline of questions that allows us to catalog our impressions and thoughts. This picture seen in isolation elicits few questions or allows few observations to rise to the surface of attention. When the two images are compared, however, the situation alters; although the two have little connection or relationship other than their present juxtaposition, certain comparisons and analogies unconsciously begin to form in the mind. Curiosity is aroused; imagination springs into action; chains of associations begin. What are these associations; how does the examination of one image affect what is perceived in the other? How does one, then, track the mind as it explores the random thoughts that arise from such associations?

These questions and others like them form the basis of our investigative technique. Such questions which one can easily see have few "logical" answers are addressed by simple investigative procedures that include the following:

1. Listing all visual correspondences: that is, *What visual qualities of one image are similar to visual qualities in the other? What visual relationships of form, line, texture, are alike?*

   After this phase of the exercise proceed to the following:

2. Listing emotional crossovers: that is, *What qualities of the sculpture alter your feelings about the skeleton of the dinosaur? What attributes of the skeleton do you perceive in the sculpture?*

Now begin to think how these thoughts and visual observations might be used in a design for a production. Consider how would you combine the two images into stage structure? Begin to make small sketches showing how you might use the visual qualities of both images in a single image. You might begin, at the same time, to consider what specific plays or musical works could use such imagery.

While it is a sound principle to seek out the help of those highly knowledgeable or expert in their fields—as we did when we read the remarks of Stark Young concerning the architecture of Spain—it does not relieve the individual viewer from using his own vision to question the vision of others. *An inquiring vision is also a skeptical vision*; even the wisest and most astute scholars can misinterpret what they see or what they *think* they see sometimes making mistakes in visual interpretation. One example is sufficient to show how this can happen.

The sixteenth-century portrait of Thomas More painted by Hans Holbein. In his book *Thomas More*, Richard Marius uses this picture as a springboard for an interpretation of the predominant character traits he believed More possessed and that he, Marius, thought Holbein captured in this painting. Here is a partial account of what he says: "The stupendous Holbein portrait done about 1527 shows us in part a conventional pose, a man who aims to look the part he plays in the world wearing the golden chain of Tudor knighthood—dignified, sober, wise. But no other Holbein portrait shows a figure so brooding, *with so much on his mind, with so many things to do that he must hold a little book with both hands as if to keep himself from jumping up and going back to work*".

Closely examine this portrait for yourself. Do you agree with Marius's interpretation? What he reports seems reasonable enough; if you read the rest of passage quoted as well as the rest of the book, what he relates about the picture makes good sense. One would have to agree that what he puts forth here seems to be both true and convincing.

There is, however, only one real problem with this interpretation: that is, that *the author is in error reporting what he sees*. For More is *not holding a book but, rather, a folded piece of paper*; moreover, this piece of paper is held by one hand alone, not by two. These, one must admit, are two rather insignificant points; they do little or nothing to detract from the import of this fine biography, quite probably the best written during the past fifty years on this important historical character. Still this does not alter the fact that mistakes in seeing were made. These are enough for the careful researcher to question any other observations Marius makes that deal with specific interpretations made from examination of visual research materials.

We have taken time to show how words cannot only explain images but can actually alter radically the perception of those images. A short codicil, then, should be added to our basic principle: *When you seek out the dwellings of other opinions, make sure you do not check your own eyes at the door.*

While "tests" of this kind we have been taking may seem to have no real purpose, the speculations and discoveries we make doing such exercises bring into focus two important principles of creative visual research: (1) *That scenographers must assemble many images in order to set the forces of the imagination into play;* (2) *that a strong element of skepticism accompany any research of any kind.*

The noted scientist Linus Pauling gives us good advice to accompany our research chores when he advises that "*in order to have a good idea you have to have lots of ideas*". I would add to that thought in advising that the element of play—as discussed earlier in this text—is also a necessity in good research technique. All visual artists, scenographers not least among them, in time come to realize that *all good research is a serious form of play,* that the element of puzzle solving is an important component in the process of designing for the theater.

Imagination, it is clearly evident, is not a fixed quantity. It is not something you "have or don't have," are born with or born without. Nor is it a randomly acquired human trait like freckles or red hair or blue eyes. It is, rather, the active combination of an ability to see, in the manner just discussed, individual attitudes (both conscious and unconscious) and—most important of all—the active employment of mechanical skills to serve the imaginative processes of the mind.

In order to feed the voracious appetite of the imagination, the scenographer must maintain an active awareness of the artwork of the past. To some extent this need can be supplied by course work in art history; but this approach can at best only supply a limited knowledge and understanding. Only if the interest is constant and the pursuit lifelong can an understanding of the past be gained or professionally used. In large part, knowing exactly what to take from that extensive body of work is the business of scenography. The extent to which direct use is made of precise forms or specific works is, however, a matter of judgment, and that illusive quality we can only inadequately call "taste"; but using a criteria of complete originality for the evaluation of the worth of an artwork has been, and remains today, contrary to the most basic practices of all past artists regardless of their individual art. Only in the twentieth century have we given innovation and originality such a high place in our judgment as to what is "good" or "bad" art; these are standards, we should also note, that are being substantially called into question as the only viable means by which to assign value to an artwork.

In a lighthearted moment, William Faulkner once observed, "*Immature artists copy great artists steal.*" While this is a humorous remark (but, nevertheless, a view that Faulkner is not alone in holding) that obviously overstates the case, it does point to an important truth concerning a continuing interrelationship between contemporary artists and their past counterparts. And while few would suggest we always blindly copy the work of the past, we should seek its guidance when appropriate. Faulkner's remark can also mean that the past's accomplishments are not "off limits" to us; the student of this art must come to realize (as the mature scenographer is constantly aware) that what we term past is also a name for a living heritage meant to be used as well as studied. Nor should reverence for that which is gone immobilize us from making the best use of that which has survived. A good example of the principles that arise from the assimilation of the thoughts just presented can be demonstrated by examination of the production of *Antigone* designed by Douglas W. Schmidt for the Vivian Beaumont Theatre in Lincoln Center. Schmidt used an original source for his design with a minimum of change: a section of a frieze from the Great Altar at Pergamon, a Greek work that dates from approximately 180 to 160 B.C., now part of the Staatliche Museen, Berlin. But, while he has retained the basic forms and design of the original fragment, he has found it necessary to incorporate a detail from another section of the same work in order to give completeness to his own work. This was made necessary, in all probability, by the different context in which the basic design ideas appear; that is, from museum fragment to theatrical setting could not be a simple one-step job of copying. The addition of the shield detail was, it is obvious, a conscious act on the part of the scenographer, which demonstrates that unthinking duplication of another's work was not the only act performed. The exact reason why Schmidt incorporated that detail quite possibly was an intuitive one, but nevertheless, it indicates that the scenographic mind was at work. Use of historical materials in this manner is a legitimate part of the scenographer's function; moreover it is a creative use of visual research materials. The greatest playwright in our language Shakespeare was not above borrowing ideas and plots (and occasionally a line of text from another playwright) from any source of information to which he had access.

The direct use of these original materials is not so much the question as is how they are used. While we cannot formulate strict rules as to how these materials should be used, it should expected that the exact manner will change from scenographeor to scenographer; one should expect to see similar "steals" incorporated into the same works in differing ways. For instance, while the Vivian Beaumont Theatre production used actual three-dimensional building materials (the panels were sculpted from Styrofoam slabs), another production of this same play used a projected image of statue from the same country and period, but from the British Museum in London. Similar sources do not determine similar results; there is always ample opportunity for "originality" even in the most obvious cases of "stealing" as these two examples have shown.

Theatrical Thinking

All work in the theater starts as an idea, a concept without physical form. The image we see on stage is no exception. However, it would be a mistake to believe that the transition from an idea or a feeling to a finished design is a single step; many steps, in fact, intervene, and the process is complex and multifaceted.

Probably the most often asked question of any director or scenographer is, Where do your ideas come from? The real answer is quite simple: everywhere. But explaining the answer is somewhat more difficult, and the entire process can never be fully revealed (and some aspects of the answer remain shadowy even to the scenographer himself). Nevertheless, while it is true that scenographers obtain what they need from literally everywhere, it difficult to dispel the myth that the individual artist relies primarily on an intangible property of the mind we like to call *imagination*. What is difficult to explain to anyone is that while imagination is required in the practice of any art, its real role in the creative process is to *select, judge, reject, and synthesize* the materials found in the research of external facts and images. As the eighteenth-century painter Sir Joshua Reynolds wisely reminds us: "*The greatest natural genius cannot subsist on its own stock; he who resolves never to ransack any mind but his own will soon be reduced from mere barrenness to the poorest of all imitations. It is vain to invent without materials on which the mind may work and from which invention must originate. Nothing can come of nothing."*

All artists including those who work in the theater are included in this important dictum. *Even the greatest minds,* is no idle phrase; for some our own century's most important theater figures have relied heavily on the work of not only those who lived in the past but their contemporaries as well. Bertolt Brecht, certainly one of the greatest innovators of the twentieth century, often used the work of others in ways that might surprise those who believed that his plays sprang full-blown from the esoteric levels of his own individual imagination. One example—though not unique in the career of Brecht-should reveal the somewhat blatantly direct manner in which the creative mind works. Brecht meant the scene to be a comic one and instructed his scenographer accordingly. But what very few in the audience watching the play knew was that the visual source for this scene was a sequence in the Marx Brothers motion picture, A Night at the Opera. This is where Brecht got the inspiration that was crucial to the designing of the setting for the scene. Doubtlessly von Appen also found it necessary to do other research; research that provided him images. This kind of historical research is also necessary to support the time period during which Brecht set his play. But the fact remains that the real impetus for the scenographer's design came from a Hollywood farce. Brecht was one of the first in the modern theater to demonstrate to us that ideas may come from *any* period and from *any* source as long as they are used to support the playwright's dramatic concepts. Since Brecht and his scenographers first formulated the theatrical philosophy of *conscious anachronism,* this mode of thought has become one of the most widespread practices in the staging of plays and the design of scenery and costume. There are very few scenographers working today who have not designed productions using this approach.

It is interesting to observe how closely Brecht, in his actual staging of the wedding scene in The Caucasian Chalk Circle, took the positioning and grouping of the performers suggested by the scenographer in his scenic sketch. This does indicate that while the initial idea of the scene was Brecht's, he allowed others to aid in the development of that basic idea in production; in fact, Brecht himself often wrote that he counted heavily on his scenographers to flesh out his sometimes sketchy suggestions. Let us examine another external source that was in great part responsible for a design on the stage. We see a frankly theatrical, almost abstract stage arrangement; but this design is an almost direct copy of an image found outside the theater in the actual world. And this is the very photograph the scenographer used in his research for the play: a long narrow path in an English park with its final destination lost in the distant winter fog. This image was not decided upon immediately but only *after* the director and the scenographer began a search for an image that was first suggested by another literary work that graphically summed up many of the thoughts and feelings

Storey wrote into his play—a sonnet by Shakespeare.

That time of year thou mayst in me behold
When yellow leaves, or none, or few, do hang
Upon those boughs which shake against the cold,
Bare [ruin'd] choirs, where late the sweet birds sang.
In me thou seest the twilight of such day
As after sunset fadeth in the west,
Which by and by black night doth take away,
Death's second self, that seals up all in rest.
In me thou seest the glowing of such fire
That on the ashes of his youth doth lie,
As the death-bed whereon it must expire,
Consum'd with that which it was nourish'd by.
This thou perceiv'st, which makes thy love more strong
To love that well, which thou must leave ere long.

Here the scenographer took his entire inspiration from a single image in a medical textbook printed during the period that Rabelais actually lived. This image was then reproduced on the stage as a grossly enlarged structure that was variously used as a banquet table, a platform, and for numerous other purposes as the play progressed.

Rarely, however, does the scenographer literally reproduce any image in its entirety on the stage. More likely, elements of the original source will be used selectively.

It is easy to see that a scenographic idea often has strange history and that an idea or an image for a scenographic design rarely comes from one source alone or from one branch of arts exclusively. It would be more accurate to say that what finally appears in the theater is an amalgam of *all* human activities, all arts and crafts, and is gleaned from all possible research sources. The main point to be observed here and we will in later sections of this book explore more deeply this question of the sources of imagination—is that in the initial stages of seeking out a beginning point for the creation of a scenographic design, there is really no limit to the images or ideas available to the scenographer for his use; nor should the scenographer ever arbitrarily restrict his search to those from his own mind or to those of the playwright. It must also be remembered that it is the imagination's chief function to synthesize images from the outside world into physical realities on the stage that best serve the total production, not to demonstrate the scenographer's artistic prowess.

When, after some image is found or a visual idea occurs to the scenographer, a number of options lie open to him as he begins to put these ideas into physical form. Many scenographers assemble sketches and images onto collagelike boards before proceeding with actual three-dimensional experimentation. On the other hand, the scenographer may begin his work directly with actual three-dimensional materials found objects, boards and papers, wire screening and meshes, cord—without any prior graphic work. But, as the student scenographer will probably discover very early in his study, the development of most ideas into scenographic form means that a great deal of both kinds of work-graphic and three-dimensional must take place; that rarely does one kind of work ever take entire precedence over the other, and that often the one kind of work invariably leads to the other and then back again much in the way one plays leapfrog. By that I mean that rarely is any artwork a straight-line activity with clearly defined steps, one following the other in a strict order of cause and effect. Scenography, like all other artwork, tends to proceed in stages, each made up of differing (not always predictable) forms of experimentation. A sketch might precede an experiment on the model stage, or it might just be a graphic record of what is assembled there. But it is also possible that that sketch might, in turn, cause the scenographer to alter on the model something suggested by the sketch. And this process may take place dozens of times before a viable solution to a design problem for a particular scene finally occurs. The scenographer will doubtlessly find that as he works on project after project, it becomes increasingly difficult to separate his work into neat self-contained steps. The professional scenographer must be expert in all forms of artwork and must continually develop that outer eye that can capitalize on the rich visual world surrounding us all.

I would not like to leave the impression that all scenographic design is simply a matter of finding a striking image to copy or the cannibalization of the creative work of others; obviously that is not so. The imagination is also capable of visualizing original concepts although almost always based on some aspects of the objective world from which a design will develop. Before the actual work on a production begins, before the scenographer starts his own experimentation or the director begins to rehearse his performers, most productions are thoroughly discussed so that certain agreed-upon intellectual and visual directions will be correctly charted. Often the scenographer and the director working together—using the written images of the playwright or the librettist—will create their own imagery; imagery they believe will best serve that of the text or libretto. Read, for instance, these words of the noted British scenographer John Bury concerning the Royal Shakespeare Company's Wars of the Roses, a group of Shakespeare's related historical plays that were performed as a unit:

> The Wars of the Roses was designed in steel—the steel of the plate amour—the steel of the shield and the steel of the broadsword. In this hard and dangerous world of our production, the central image the steel of war—has spread and forged anew the whole of our medieval landscape. On the flagged floors of sheet steel tables are daggers, staircases are axe-heads, and doors the traps on scaffolds. Nothing yields: stone walls have lost their seduction and now loom dangerously steelclad—to enclose and to imprison. The countryside offers no escape the danger is still there in the iron foliage of the cruel trees and, surrounding all, the great steel cage of war.
>
> The costumes corrode with the years. The onceproud red rose of Lancaster becomes as a rusty scale on the soldiers' coats; the milk-white rose of York is no more than a pale blush on the tarnished steel of the Yorkist insurrection. Colour drains and drains from the stage until, among the drying patches of scarlet blood, the black night of England settles on the leather costumes of Richard's thugs.

Certainly, the mature scenographic imagination is at work here even though what is discussed is nothing more than a list of materials, objects, and literal descriptions of the effects of war and the passage of time.

Nature of Research

No matter how creative the individual director, no matter how clever the scenographer, no aspect of theater art can be pursued without frequent recourse to research in some form. In the producing theater the importance of this multifaceted, many-leveled activity should not be minimized; it is as important that both the director and the scenographer be adept in finding appropriate source materials that will aid them. They must know as well just what and how much to take from those sources. Yet there is a vast difference between mere research – that is, finding something that relates to the text's requirements in a vague way and creative research, which seeks to find *exactly the right thing* for that particular production of that particular play. As the great French critic Andre Malraux stated, "Genius is not what it encounters but what it annexes."

The simplest form of research is satisfied with superficial representation of period style or detail alone. Many hundreds of costume films made during the past seventy years attest to the unthinking manner that research can be done. In many of them works what we see is a world that superficially *looks* like a particular place at a particular time but does not persuade us that the picture is a true depiction of the spirit of the time or representative of the cultural climate. it seeks to portray; ostensibly *accurate* in detail but unconvincing as a whole. Creative research concerns itself more with the *evocation of a past time* than it does with the literal replication of it. Research is only useful to the extent it assists the director or the scenographer to clarify the underlying themes of a production or to elucidate for a modern-day audience a play's oftentimes obscure text. Simply to reproduce a picture of a past age is not the purpose of the theater. Museums do that much better than the theater can. Creative research makes it possible, however, for interpreters to show a present-day audience considered syntheses of living cultures distilled from collective pasts. The theater allows us – to borrow an apt phrase from the poet W. H. Auden – *To break bread with the dead.*

Yet how does one know what to select, and how does he know what he selects is *right*, is useful to the purpose just stated? For out of a world of possibilities, there must finally be a limited number of selective judgments made, definite choices that preclude all other possibilities; definite choices that will push the text in one direction or another, slant the meaning of the words in the text. What test of use or criterion of selection should we adopt in our search for these *right* things? Any form of interpretation, of course, has its attendant dangers. John Kenneth Gailbraith reports that as George Bernard Shaw grew older, "he became less and less interested in theory, more and more interested in information." Gailbraith goes on to say, "I now pick up magazines and leaf through them looking for articles that are rich with facts; I don't care what they are. Evocative and deeply percipient theory I avoid. It leaves me cold unless I am the author of it myself. My advice to all young writers would be to stick to research and reporting with only a minimum of interpretation."

Should the director or scenographer heed this advice? Is there anything in the experienced attitudes of a Shaw or a Gailbraith that would apply to the kind of research we do in the theater? This is a question all researchers must consider if not resolve. Let us attempt, therefore, to be clear as to just what are the *goals* of the kind of research that goes beyond simple annexation of superficial detail. As a basic outline of intent these aims could be listed:

- To explore
- To find
- To distill
- To understand
- To choose
- To assemble
- To show

These goals outline the work all researchers do. Keep them in mind as we progress from subject to subject in the remainder of this text. Precision of intent should inform the work of both director and scenographer alike. A short example as to what is meant by this phrase *precision of intent* should suffice.

Several years ago a student selected *Hamlet* as a project to design; the scene where Polonius is stabbed through the curtain (called an *arras* in Shakespeare's time) in the Queen's bedchamber was under discussion. The basic task for the class was to consider what a director and scenographer would agree upon as the design of this curtain; what would be appropriate in terms of historical research, and what would be useful to the director's concept of that particular scene. The student was questioned about what factors would influence his decisions in the making of a design specification for the curtain. "Well," he said impatiently, "I haven't picked one out yet or designed it. Just a tapestry." He was asked if his selection of this tapestry—or his design—might in any way help reinforce the director's work, or if it would possibly tell something *about the Queen's character*; something that might allow the director to bring to the attention of the actors something about the purpose of the scene itself. After all, as a character in the play, she might have had some influence on the way her bedchamber was furnished. What sort of things does she select. What does it say about her tastes? Or is it not possible that somehow this tapestry might subtly underscore, even intensify the feelings of the audience who will witness the coldblooded murder of a harmless old man as he hides behind the hanging? The student thought about these possibilities. (He also admitted that he had not considered the selection of the rooms' furnishings in any detail, certainly not very carefully.) Finally he came to the conclusion—although it took some time and further research to arrive at a new understanding of the scene—that although the tapestry need not be greatly symbolic in any way, consideration of those questions could help him recognize the right tapestry among the several examples he found.

Purpose behind Theatrical Research

Everything man fashions needs or wants, even the institutions that mold his social life—speaks a silent language not easily comprehensible and has a story to tell that superficial investigation will not reveal. Simple research will isolate these things so that they may be named and categorized; creative research, on the other hand, not only does this but also deals with their interpretation and meaning—it hears and translates that silent language into practical information. The theater artist—no matter whether his job is to instruct the actor or design their costumes or create the worlds they live in-must learn to see *through* the surface of things, as opaque as that surface often is.

Remembering Robert Edmond Jones, Jo Mielziner draws our attention to just such an artist:

> *I recall the time when Jones was supervising the execution of the stage setting for the seventeenthcentury Spanish room in The Buccaneer. A week earlier he had completed his design, and on this particular day the crew of fine artists in Bergman's Studio was executing the set on the paint frame below Jones's studio. Bobby couldn't bear the idea that they would think of their work as simply the job of executing a large painting; so he scurried out with me to gather up bits and pieces of what he called "living things" which related to the setting: a lovely antique bench of the period with the patina of age and the beauty of line that he loved so much; a swatch of antique yellow satin, with some black lace and a huge artificial red flower; a yard or two of heavy gold lace; one lovely Spanish Renaissance tile. These things he placed on the floor beside the setting on which the painters were at work, because Jones wanted – for himself and for all who were working with him – to be conscious of the relations of this painting to its final achievement and appearance on the stage.*

Robert Edmond Jones could be described as a dreamer, but he was also a doer. Idealist he was, but certainly he cannot be dismissed as a mere visionary. A prophet, yes, but at the same time a most practical craftsman.

This, then, is the crux of our problem when we endeavor to do more than mere literal research. As Jones wrote "we may fairly speak of the art of stage designing as poetic, in that it seeks to give expression to the essential quality of a play rather than to its outward characteristics." Although these words come from a time that had a view of theater somewhat different from the one we profess today, the essential truth and good common sense of Jones's view still applies, is still valid. In the final analysis, creative research is a means to the poetic art of scenography that Jones felt was so important. What he sought then, although much has changed in theater since, is still basically what we seek now, what we as scenographers still attempt to do.

John Ruskin, the noted nineteenth-century art critic, once wrote: "Great nations write their autobiographies in three manuscripts, the book of their deeds, the book of their words and the book of their art. Not one of these books can be understood unless we read the two others, but of the three the only trustworthy one is the last". It is an accepted principle of most historians that all activities of an age reflect either directly or indirectly the spirit of the time. Music, philosophy, religion, and political theory, as well as architecture, sculpture, and painting, all exercise influences one on the other and interrelate to such an extent that the theatrical use of any one element cannot help but call a knowledge of the others into question. Not even so great an artist as Michelangelo, despite his personal genius and singularity, can be fully understood without consideration of his close working relationship to the church and the doctrines of the day. Nor could the church itself be fully understood without examining its relationship to the secular, political milieu of late Renaissance Italy. To comprehend the visual image of a period along with the myriad facets of that image—and this is the scenographer's ultimate aim—he must also understand the forces that had molded the people who in turn determined the character of the age in which they lived. It is a common fault of young scenographers to limit their research into a period too narrowly; the veteran artist seeks his images and concepts from behind the surfaces, from the obscure, out-of-the-way nooks and crannies of the past. Simple research, that which stops at surface examination, can be carried out by the most uninterested of workers; creative research, that which goes into the deeper layers of what is being examined and seeks to understand more than a cursory glance can reveal, is a highly personal activity and the necessary business of an artist; discovery of a fact may be important, but understanding and interpreting the forces that created that fact is essential if the resultant findings are to have any real worth to the scenographer. It was precisely in this area the difference between these two ways of approaching research that the scenographers of most nineteenth-century productions fell short. They were more than conscientious and meticulous in reproduction of historical detail, but contemporary drawings and early photographs reveal that what they produced would have been more serviceable for Madame Tussaud's Wax Museum than for a living theater. Accuracy of detail alone is not sufficient to ensure that the contemporaneity of the past can be evoked.

In speaking of the craft of poetry, Dylan Thomas once pointed out that "the best craftsmanship always leaves holes and gaps in the works of the poem so that something that is *not* in the poem can creep, crawl, crash, or thunder in." Creative research is not altogether unlike this; often a scenographer feels he is looking for something (having read and studied a playscript or libretto), the nature of which he is not quite sure. Often the most knowledgeable and experienced scenographer cannot with absolute certainty always know just what this unknown quantity is until it is found. And it is quite possible that he overlooks what he needs by looking too hard. As Jean Dubuffet, the French painter has noted:

> *I am obsessed by the idea that there is something both false and unprofitable in looking at things too closely and too long. It is not normal for a human being to stare at objects for the sole purpose of inspecting them and making an inventory of their constituent parts. Such a position in our relation to them seems to me to destroy completely (if not to empty them of all content) the mechanisms of communications that exist between man and the objects around him, the way he perceives them and the way they affect him. Man sees things without trying to see them. While he is looking at one thing he sees another as though obliquely.*

I must say my feeling is always has been-very strong that the key to things must not be as we imagine it, but that the world must be ruled by strange systems of which we have not the slightest inkling. This is why I rush toward strange things. I am quite convinced that truth is strange; it is at the far end of strangeness that one has a chance to find the key to things.

What Dubuffet is saying (and he is certainly not the first or only artist to realize these hidden forces that influence any art form) is that awareness is never a completely logical or "conscious" process, that there are, indeed, other ways of being aware, ways that directly influence what an artist produces but that are neither under conscious control nor, for that matter, always predictable. This is an important point to understand when we begin any research for any purpose: that specific task-oriented projects must take into account an entire spectrum of "awareness." As Gordon Rattray Taylor points out in the *The Natural History of the Mind*: "Of all the problems which arise in connection with the notion of 'mind' the most difficult is the fact of consciousness itself. Consciousness is often defined as awareness—awareness of self and of the environment—but this does no more than substitute one word for another, since we are equally unable to explain the subjective aspects of awareness *consciousness is not a single entity but varies in kind as well as degree*".

What this means is that we must learn to cooperate with our own minds (and to give way at times to inner promptings that seem to defy our "logical" sense of rightness); to create within our own selves the climate for the fullest utilizations of all levels of our consciousness, not merely that top layer that we have heretofore called *awareness*. In short, we must learn (and more important, put to use) the meaning of Dubuffet's words: "it is at the far end of strangeness that one has a chance to find the key to things."

But what do these words mean to the scenographer? Is this type of research valid, this philosophy of vision acceptable or usable to him; is it even employable in the practical world of theatrical production? Yes, it may very well affect the manner is which the scenographer approaches his research chores. And yet this does not mean to infer that research is wholly an intuitional activity, or that the scenographer merely goes to the library or his files methodically examining everything in sight until some psychic bell rings; there are methods and principles of research that will both expedite much of the guesswork and still leave room for the "strange systems" alluded to by Dubuffet to do their work. As Ben Shahn, another famous painter, has pointed out in his book *The Shape of Content*: "The subconscious may greatly shape one's art; undoubtedly it does so. But the subconscious cannot create art. The very act of making a painting is an intending one; thus to intend and at the same time relinquish intentions is a hopeless contradiction, albeit one that is exhibited on every hand."

What Shahn says about painters applies equally well to scenographers; one must trust his intuition to a great extent but never use intuition as an excuse for not digging into a problem of research. It does little good to tell the novice scenographer that in twenty years the task of locating useful material hidden away in libraries and museums may still be difficult but not as difficult as it is today; for the professional scenographer never outgrows the need to perform research in the practice of his art. It is obvious that experience will ease the difficulty in finding appropriate source materials; but the process becomes neither entirely automatic nor ever anything less than a chore. For the student the problems in learning to perform scenographic research are real and substantial. And while there has been a veritable explosion of printed materials that should make the job of finding information easier, this profileration has in many ways made the job of research more difficult than ever. So, if it is not possible for us to say *where* to find information, we can, at least, point out a few guidelines that may be helpful in learning *how* to approach this all-important subject. Let us begin by examining how the *element of chance* affects the process of research.

Role of Chance in the Creative Process

Creative research is as much an attitude as it is a specific goal-oriented pursuit. These attitudes often are products of accidental experience, not conscious thought; linear research technique is not always the most productive. At times, when we are least looking for a specific answer to a particular question we accidentally *happen* upon information that may instantly illuminate our understanding, even causing us to abandon long-held preconceptions. Accidental encounters may even provide information relating to questions of research we have yet to discover. We cannot discount the mysterious side of research procedure.

In my own experience such encounters frequently occur. For example, during my student days, while spending an afternoon in London's Victoria and Albert Museum, I chanced across information that substantially altered my previous understanding of the past. Having no purpose in mind with the exception of avoiding a late winter storm, I found myself idly wandering among cases of costume accessories and period jewelry. One case contained objects that appeared to be unusually long hatpins. Too large and too ornate for hatpins, I was puzzled about their use. Although of French origin, they were owned by upper-class and aristocratic English women during the first half of the eighteenth century. The names of these objects were unfamiliar. Asking a nearby attendant for further information he replied, "Lice stickers the only way to get to them out when the hair was done up a few months." This isolated fact revealed in the pragmatic way it was—sharply focused the curious double standards of another age. Questions that had unconsciously accumulated in my mind concerning this time instantly became clear. Soon I was to design a production set in the period these pins were made and used. At that moment my mind was far from the project. My attention was not on the characters I would in a few months have to house and clothe. The words of the museum attendant shocked me. I already knew that all European countries, especially France and England, placed great emphasis on outward refinement of dress during most of the eighteenth century. I also understood that class and status demanded that its members maintain styles that identified as well as separated them from lower classes. Yet until now my concerns with the period reached no deeper understanding than that which the casual eye perceives from words and images in books dealing with the period. With all my art and social history studies I did not differentiate between museum exhibits and living worlds of the past. While sure of the exact dates and period features in Fielding Tom Jones or Sheridan *School for Scandal*, I was less sure how people of the time lived day to day. I had read Pepy's diaries that revealed the age immediately preceding this one and was also familiar with Samuel Johnson's writings and Boswell's anecdotes. While I had much information at my fingertips, I now realized I did not really *know the people themselves;* that although I was intellectually familiar with the *name* and *look* of what they wore, knew precisely what they sat on, had considered the places they frequented both "in the season" and out, I did not have a living image of everyday life. With all the information at hand I still possessed little understanding as to how those living then felt or thought. I did not know, I realized, *how they lived from day to day.* Yet here—in a glass case only inches from my own hand-was an object that another hand two hundred fifty years ago used for specific purposes, purposes that gave me such an empathetic feeling that I found myself involuntarily scratching my head. Never before do I remember an instance where the past so forcibly engaged my imagination. As I examined the object before me, I began to perceive the concerns of eighteenth-century daily life not only the constant need to dispatch vermin from hair but also the deeply felt need "to be in fashion." I began to understand that one must not only seek out specific dates and pictures of past ages but must find ways of knowing the people themselves in ways museums and collections of objects can in no way show. Knowing from earlier study that cleanliness beneath expensive dress and excessive makeup was not a dominant concern of the time, I sensed that my twentieth-century revulsion to the unsavory aspects of the period acted as a barrier, an opaque screen, preventing me from accepting that these people actually lived in a world not that different from today. Leaving the museum I had no firm design concepts in mind. I felt better prepared, however, to believe that the early eighteenth century had existed; that I might with diligent study and help from other revelations—come to understand it better.

Months later, I began work on the The Beggar's Opera, John Gay eighteenth-century ballad-opera (a work that Bertold Brecht would adapt in the twentieth century and rename, The Three-Penny Opera). My research began attempting to recall those feelings experienced in the Victoria and Albert Museum. It also included examination of materials I gathered from other museum visits while in London from Sir John Soane's house—which is not so much a museum as it is a private house open to the public. There I had encountered another important "key" by which to enter this period: the paintings of Hogarth. Of especial value to my current project were a series of paintings—which Hogarth also issued as prints of drawings—called *The Rake's Progress*. Not only did these works show many visual details in the appropriate time period that concerned my project, they even dealt with the same class of people who people The Beggar's Opera. Little effort was needed to see links between the world Hogarth painted and the world Gay wrote about. Another idea occurred to me at this time. "Now," I thought, "since they-Hogarth and Gay—lived in the same period, did they know one another?" A little research revealed they did. This led to a further thought: since they knew each other, they must have known other writers and artists. *Who were those others*? With this simple question, a chain of associations began. My research now took on aspects of investigative reporting.

As a result of these speculations, two kinds of material began to accumulate: (1) Visual materials—such as Hogarth paintings and prints, images of items, furnishing, clothing, crafts—from everyday life and (2) written materials garnered from those living at the time who had recorded their everyday experiences. Beginning with Hogarth's images and Gay's words as "letters of introduction," I began to "call" on their friends and acquaintances. The circle was wide and varied; among the group, however, several stood out. One in particular addressed many of the visual and written descriptions I had assembled. Jonathan Swift--the Irish writer who lived in London for most of his life—recorded particularly vivid (at times savage) descriptions of the life one might find in London during the first half of the eighteenth century. From his writings alone it was possible to obtain a coherent picture of the period; and it was he more than any other who gave me entry to the time of The Beggar's Opera. One instance although many exist as to how the process of combining word and image to gain a picture of a past age should suffice. This print records a moment in the daily life of a group of itinerant actors. The focal point of the picture is a woman who could serve as visual information for several of the characters in The Beggar's Opera: Polly Peacham or Lucy Lockit among them. The title for the print derives its name from this person: The Strolling Actress. If one carefully examines the picture, many distinct items are evident. The drawing is so animated and specific that it is possible to speculate on individual personalities and relationships of those shown. Now, since the drawing is accurate—the eye of the artist being highly selective in the detail included—what more can any scenographer wishing factual information hope to find? In not this visual record sufficient to show us *how the people of the time lived,* since we can see clearly *how they appeared*? This is the juncture of research where Swift is able to enhance perceptions of what is visually evident, a demonstration as to how *words and thoughts* change attitudes as to what is seen.

This often savage, ultimately devastating portrait details the daily life of a person that not only Swift and Gay probably knew well, but that Hogarth quite possibly often drew or painted. But can one glean the particulars of this life from the evidence of Hogarth's drawing alone? The clues are there, but the image is a sanitary one compared to the images Swift draws in the mind of the reader. While it is painful to imagine what Swift records, if one reads The Beggar's Opera carefully the description rings true. We even are warned early in The Beggar's Opera of the kinds of people we are soon to meet: in the prologue a beggar directly addresses the audience telling them not only what the play is about but who they will see. Among the types all from the lower and criminal classes of London—are thieves, highwaymen, pickpockets, fences, murderers, prostitutes, pimps, many bearing the colorful names that surfaced during Shakespeare's time and earlier: jades, trulls, trollops, queans. But, as the beggar says: "All is human." After reading Swift's poem, we are not likely again to see Hogarth's paintings or prints in quite the same way.

A twofold principle of creative research can be formulated from the kinds of experiences encountered above: (1) that creative research is a continuous process frequently subject to the vagaries of circumstance and chance, and (2) that imagination is not a fixed quantity of chosen individuals but an ongoing bargain artists make between eyes and mind.

How, then, can one be trained to know precisely the ways to gather an often diffuse body of fact, image, and opinion? This, in brief, forms the basis of the question students of scenography most often ask: *Where do I find the answers to questions I may not know how to ask?* While this may seem to be a nonsensical question on the surface, it presents a real problem in research: finding factual materials that satisfy intuitional needs. One of the more bizarre aspects of such creative research is that often a scenographer will discover the answers to these needs purely by accident *by chance.*

This statement is not as illogical as it might first appear. Principles can be fashioned that take into consideration the random nature of researching needed materials. Moreover, there are many who have sought to know just how these principles can be made operational. Among the clearest expositions of this fascinating problem is a study by James H. Austin. In his book, *Chase, Chance, and Creativity*, Austin provides a good understanding of the ways chance can be put to work for anyone engaged in searching out answers to problems that appear to have no straightforward solutions.

What is chance? Dictionaries define it as something fortuitous that happens unpredictably without discernible human intention. Chance is unintentional and capricious, but we needn't conclude that chance is immune from human intervention. Indeed, chance plays several distinct roles when humans react creatively with one another and with their environment.

Chance I is the pure blind luck that comes with no effort on our part. If, for example, you are sitting at a bridge table of four, it's "in the cards" for you to receive a hand of all 13 spades, but it will come up only once in every 6.3 trillion deals. You will ultimately draw this lucky hand—with no intervention on your part—but it does involve a longer wait than most of us have time for.

Chance II evokes the kind of luck Charles Kettering had in mind when he said: "Keep on going and the chances are you will stumble on something, perhaps when you are least expecting it. I have never heard anyone stumbling on something sitting down."

In the sense referred to here, Chance II is not passive, but springs from an energetic generalized motor activity. A certain basal level of action "stirs up the pot," brings in random ideas that will collide and stick together in fresh combinations, lets chance operate. When someone, *anyone*, does swing into motion and keeps on going, he will increase the number of collisions between events. When a few events are linked together, they can then be exploited to have a fortuitous outcome, but many others, of course, cannot. Kettering—was right. Press on. Something will turn up.

As we move on to Chance III, we see blind luck, but in camouflage. Chance presents the clue, the opportunity exists, but it would be missed except by that one person uniquely equipped to observe it, visualize it conceptually, and fully grasp its significance. Chance III involves a special receptivity and discernment unique to the recipient. Louis Pasteur characterized it for all time when he said: "Chance favors only the prepared mind."

Chance can be on our side, if we but stir it up with our energies, stay receptive to its every random opportunity, and continually provoke it by individuality in our hobbies and our approach to life.

While these observations do not give exact formulas for accomplishing creative research-nor can anyone answer all questions concerning the role of chance in the artistic process—they give positive reinforcement to the principle of "keep going." As the comments of Austin infer, research is an activity to be approached in the spirit of adventure; we should neither be afraid of the paths where our research might lead us nor be hesitant to follow what may seem at first glance a frivolous direction. To paraphrase the old French aphorism: *creative research has its reasons that reason knows nothing of.*

While not possible for any interpreter to unearth every reason why a playwright wrote a certain line in a certain way or to seek out in every instance the exact cause why a character says certain words—in many cases, the playwright may not consciously know all these reasons himself—the search for useful information must continually go forward. That is what interpretation means. If we constantly keep in mind that there are always many more facts to be found in a text than will be found, then our anticipation of finding that information will make us—as Austin thinks—more active searchers. As a result we will increase the probability as well the certainty that more will be found. On the other hand, when we blindly accept the words or directions of a playwright strictly at face value with no further scrutiny, we decrease our ability to get to those levels of a text that reveal the playwright's deepest concerns or his hidden worlds. Chance, as we have seen, is not a fixed operation immune to human intervention. It can be prompted; an active belief that this is so will help us to capitalize on information that comes by the most indirect route.

Let me cite one more experience when my path accidentally crossed that of a playwright to show how this accidental encounter greatly aided my understanding of the environment necessary for the play.

At the beginning of A Streetcar Named Desire, Blanche du Bois comes to live in New Orleans with her sister, Stella. The house in which Stella and Stanley—Stella's husband live is a cramped, run-down structure at the edge of the Old French Quarter. A few days after Blanche arrives Stella plans an outing for Blanche and herself to a well-known restaurant. She is aware that Blanche not only is ill at ease in her new surroundings but actually feels threatened by the situation in which she finds herself. Believing that a night out will lessen the shock of Blanche's recent displacement, she tells Stanley of her plan:

STELLA: Oh, Stan! (*She jumps up and kisses him which he accepts with lordly composure.*) I'm taking Blanche to Galatoire's for supper and then to a show, because it's your poker night.

STANLEY: Well, isn't that just dandy! How about my supper, huh? I'm not going to no Galatoire's for supper!

Later that night the two women return; before entering the house, this exchange takes place.

STELLA: The game is still going on.

BLANCHE: How do I look?

STELLA: Lovely, Blanche.

BLANCHE: I feel so hot and frazzled. Wait till I powder before you open the door. Do I look done in?

STELLA: Why no. You are as fresh as a daisy.

BLANCHE: One that's been picked a few days.

Once again, Blanche must enter the claustrophobic house, a microcosm of that world that both oppresses and frightens her; a world so different from the environment in which she and Stella grew up. The crude and vulgar character of the house, as well as the area that surrounds it, is an inescapable reminder that Blanche has seen better days, more "genteel" surroundings. Stella, on the other hand, has not only adjusted to this world but finds it is entirely suitable to her real nature even though it is the antithesis of the past life that Blanche champions (all the more fiercely now that it has vanished). Shortly after they go in, Blanche meets Mitch for the first time. She immediately perceives that he is not of the same rough disposition as the other poker-playing friends of Stanley. She attempts to form a closer relationship with him, to draw him out, since she instinctively feels his shyness and sensitivity.

MITCH: You are Stella's sister, are you not?

BLANCHE: Yes, Stella is my precious little sister. I call her little in spite of the fact she's somewhat older than I. Just slightly. Less than a year. Will you do something for me?

MITCH: Sure. What?

BLANCHE: I bought this adorable little colored paper lantern at a Chinese shop on Bourbon Street. Put it over the light bulb! Will you, please?

MITCH: Be glad to.

BLANCHE: I can't stand a naked light bulb, any more than I can a rude remark or a vulgar action.

In the context of the play, every remark made in the scene seems natural; every word is unremarkable in its casualness: people talking to one another about nothing much in particular. Yet hidden in these aimlessly spoken lines lie deep insights into Blanche's nature and character. The playwright has, although the clues are carefully masked, supplied us with almost everything we need to know concerning the character of Blanche and how she views the world that she now finds herself. He has done one thing more that would, probably, escape the attention of anyone who did not personally know the city of New Orleans or had not had the *chance,* as I later did, to discover how intricately motivated those casual exchanges of dialogue. I had read this play many times; I believed I detected most of the possible meanings behind the text. It was not until I had moved to New Orleans, however, to work in the theater in the French Quarter that I realized how intricately Williams wove actual places into the actions and emotions of his characters in this play or how much a part the city itself plays in all his works, both dramatic and literary, or how important the city is to this play in particular. My realization as to just how specifically the atmosphere of this unique city is captured in the text of A Streetcar Named Desire happened in a flash of insight and occurred the first time that I--as Blanche did—went to Galatoire's restaurant to dine. I knew of this famous restaurant both from its reputation as well as from personal recommendation of many friends. Although they had also informed me that this was the place many native New Orleanians preferred to more famous names associated with the tourist trade, no one thought to give me indications of its physical description—or of its particular *atmosphere*. Nor was I at the time thinking of either the play A Streetcar Named Desire or of Blanche du Bois. However, upon entering the front door both immediately leapt to mind. My first words were, "My God, how did she stand it?"What I had encountered in that first moment was this: a large single room constituted the main part of the restaurant; the walls were painted a stark white, and around the room were large wide mirrors—the entire area brightly lit from hanging lights; there were numerous "naked bulbs." The emphasis here, it was quickly apparent, was on food served with efficiency-and ample light to see what you had ordered. Later, as I recalled that moment, I began consciously to fit my own spontaneous reaction to the information the playwright provides in the text. What follows is, in a more or less orderly and logical presentation, what I came to understand about the place *to which Williamsent Blanche* on her first outing in New Orleans and, most important of all, why he chose it out of all others. First, let us venture some speculations as to why Stella acts in the manner she does; that is, makes the choice of Galatoire's:

1. Stella—who is unlike Blanche in almost every way and, more important, is actually considerably younger than Blanche despite Blanche's "little white lie" that Stella is the older of the sisters -- takes Blanche to the restaurant she considers to be the best: Galatoire's. Her reasons have nothing to do with considerations of the restaurant's atmospheric qualities or decor but, rather, with the quality of the food served there.
2. Stella—neither excessively vain nor yet at the time of life when age is a real concern—does not consider that her sister is morbidly sensitive to the passing years and is, consequently,

extremely apprehensive at being seen in a bright revealing light. In actuality, as with most relatives, Stella hardly *sees* her sister at all; certainly she does not see her as a middle-aged woman. For Stella, the bright light holds no sinister aspect; nor does she appreciate the light's threat to the youthful illusion Blanche seeks to maintain. Stella does not realize that she is taking her sister to the *one well-known restaurant where Blanche would be most self-conscious and tormented*: Galatoire's. With its glaring light and mirrors that reflect one's image back at every turn, this restaurant would be the one to avoid at any cost; as it is, we can easily understand that the experience is a veritable nightmare for Blanche. And can she really say to Stella: *Let's leave – here everyone can see how old I really am!* No. She is caught. Is this selection of this particular restaurant calculated or only coincidence? Probably elements of both are present; certainly the element of chance came into the play as I walked in the same door as had Blanche. There is no doubt in my mind, however, that Williams had picked out of his own experience the one place (perhaps unconsciously) where Blanche would suffer the pangs of being viewed under the worst of conditions. But while this decision of the playwright could very well have been "accidental," it does, in point of fact, begin a chain of events of reactions, more specifically that are central to the progress of the play's actions and absolutely essential to the play's dramatic force.

3. Blanche—on her way back to her new "home"-buys a Chinese paper lantern. This act is certainly motivated by her earlier encounter (not mentioned, however, until her return from the restaurant) with the hanging light in the room where she is forced to live; but it is also possible that it is motivated by her recent experience at Galatoire's. Her real reason for getting the lantern, ostensibly an impulse purchase, is to modify the harshness of the "naked bulb" hanging in the room where she must spend an unforeseeable time to come. But it is also possible that the purchase was spurred by the desire to prevent insofar as possible a recurrence of the Galatoire's experience. We can easily deduce that Stella is blithely unconscious of the effect that strong white light has on aging skin (and is also something of a less-than-dedicated housekeeper, since she

has apparently never made the effort to provide a shade for the bulb), and that Blanche feels compelled to take immediate steps to keep any light in her vicinity under strict management in the future. (It has already been established that she will not come outdoors until after the sun has set.) While Blanche's lantern is seemingly a modest gesture toward making the room more attractive, it has a very practical self-protective motive at bottom: to screen out the age-revealing qualities of the "naked bulb," (And you can be all but certain that the color of the lantern she picked was pink: the same color that hides best those small lines that herald the approach of old age; it is also, coincidently, the color of the theatrical media that aging actresses demand as a standard provision in their stage performance contracts.) At every step of these apparently unimportant events we can see the playwright's hand pulling hidden strings. As Chekhov remarks: *If a pistol is introduced in the first act of a play, it must be fired before the play is finished.* So it is with Blanche's Chinese lantern; put up to mask the harsh light, it must be removed before the action of the play ends.

4. The chain of actions continues. The purchase of the lantern gives Blanche an opportunity to seek — with all the antebellum charm she can muster — the aid of Mitch to put it up. She only met him minutes before; still she does not miss the opportunity to involve him in the seemingly insignificant — but incalculably effective-modification of her living space. More than that, she uses the event to cast the first thread of the web in which she hopes eventually to catch Mitch. Not only is it an extremely masterful stroke on the part of Williams's craftsmanship, it is a virtual necessity to the fabric of the play that the *same person who puts the lantern on the light must also be the person who will eventually tear it off.* Mitch, in a very real way, is made part of Blanche's destruction (and to a lesser extent, his own) in the intricate pattern of cause and effect that innocently began with Stella's decision to take her sister out to have a good meal. Nor does this pattern reach its eventual end until late in the play when a stormy scene takes place between Blanche and Mitch, after which he rips the fragile lantern from the bulb and brutally holds her face up to the harsh white light. In a sense, he returns Blanche to the "real" world that does not understand or tolerate

her mysterious avoidance of the light. Such an outburst as recorded here cannot be achieved only at the last moment; it is the result of causes that have been building from the very first moments of the play, from that time, perhaps, when Stella took Blanche out for a good meal.

Much of what has just been said is, of course, interpretative; conjecture, speculation, and plain guesswork have been the foundation of statements that are, at the very least, personal points of view. Do such suppositions really aid in the work of the scenographer? I think they do. Moreover, I can affirm that my own work is made more meaningful (if not easier) by such research. Chance, in this case, did provide many valuable clues to a deeper understanding of certain hidden motives that related directly to specifically written actions. Let us, however, for the moment cast some doubt on this process; or rather, let us raise a possible objection to the value of such an admittedly time-consuming and *chancy* way of working.

The question then might arise: Since the restaurant where Blanche is taken for that stressful dinner is not an actual part of the action seen on stage, why consider this tangential information at all? What possible difference does it make to know where she spent an uncomfortable evening? The general answer to this question is that *anything* that gives a more thorough understanding of any character in a text is a positive aid in understanding that character's physical environment (whether or not that environment is ever to be shown in its entirety). But a more specific response to such a question is this: Knowing exactly the contexts of a character's "offstage" experience can contribute extremely profitable information about how the onstage environment should be considered; for it can be taken for granted that the playwright did consider just such encounters as well as the consequences of those encounters. Nor is it outside the scenographer's ability to discover these useful pieces of information. This line of investigation is, admittedly, oblique in nature; it is, however, relevant to the total research inquiry and should be undertaken seriously. For instance, it seems reasonable to me—and not a difficult feat of investigation to have performed that Blanche bought the delicate paper Chinese lantern required in the acting of the play not simply as a passing whim *but as a direct response to her exposure to the merciless white light she experiences in that particular restaurant the playwright causes her to go.* And I am very certain that it was Williams's exact purpose that this restaurant—rather than a more romantically lighted one where she could safely hide her age in the shadows of discreetly shaded lamps or candlelight—should be the one to which Stella, who is thinking only of the quality of the food and not of the atmosphere, would unthinkingly take her sister. The playwright does not, of course, ever have time or opportunity to include in the play's text every indication of the hidden geneses of actions and words; but it would be extremely shortsighted of any interpretative artist working on this text not to realize that such information exists and is often possible to unearth. If we, as scenographers, doggedly pursue the reasons leading to the actions of characters-such as the seemingly insignificant and impulsive buying of a cheap paper lantern—we are much more apt to "know" the atmosphere and physical parameters of their environments. In the case of Blanche, such considerations not only tell us the kind of situation in which she finds herself but also indicate the small ways in which she seeks to change her physical environment to suit her own desperate needs. The hanging of a cheap paper lantern over a "naked" (her words) light bulb may seem the most casual of actions, but this one act is integral to the development of this play; without it, the highly charged scene between Mitch and Blanche in the latter part of the play cannot take place. It is imperative that *he* rip off that lantern and expose her again to the merciless white light (in exactly the same manner as she was exposed in Galatoire's). In a very real sense Blanche begins the play with an offstage experience that shows her just how important it is to preserve the increasingly fragile illusion that she is still young. Her ability to maintain this illusion is eroding rapidly, which the playwright shows us by the integration of this seemingly insignificant object into the mainstream of the action.

The deep searches we must make into the structure of a text are not simply to verify the exactness of background locale or period accuracy but to seek out the very nature of the playwright's world, the innermost character of his concerns, intentions, and—not least—his obsessions. While the visual arts of the theater ostensibly rely on the information we find in period research and the simulation of form found in the observable world outside the theater, that information must be subjected to a scrutiny that lies beyond purely aesthetic judgment. We who interpret that information must also think in much the same way as the archaeologist, psychologist, and social historian. More important, our methods of approaching texts in the theater are not unlike those puzzles Sherlock Holmes or *Hercule Poirot* have repeatedly found so fascinating. We – like them – must look closely at the facts as they surface; our "little gray cells" must probe as deeply those mysteries of character and circumstance the playwright sets before us, knowing all the time that the facts we encounter in a text for the stage often mask complex and all but undiscoverable human motives and actions.

It is relatively easy to make exact replicas of past works; architecture, costume, furniture, crafts, all can be simulated in today's scenic shops with amazing verisimilitude and accuracy. It is, however, considerably more difficult to restore a living meaning to those works if something else, something more, does not accompany that expert copying of detail. But this something more is precisely the task of the scenographer; he alone is given the great responsibility of assuring that that former life will become part of the physical work of selection and simulation; he, more than any other artist of the theater, is given the charge to *link the playwright's world of words – no matter how distant in time or different in nature from that we call "real" – to the actual world of the stage.* To find exact information that illumines the look and feel of the New Orleans where *Streetcar* takes place is important; to understand the particular life of Blanche, Stella, Stanley, and Mitch as they live in it requires stepping beyond the bounds of archaeological tourism.

Nor would it be stretching the point to say that the New Orleans in which Williams sets his play is seen in two distinct kinds of physical light that essentially determine the particular nature of this particular play: (1) the warm romantic glow of candlelight and Chinese lanterns and (2) the harsh glaring light of an unpretentious restaurant or a naked bulb in a cheaply constructed dwelling in an unfashionable part of the city. These two qualities of light are as integral to the interpretation of this play as is the adversary relationship of Blanche and Stanley or the desperately hopeful relationship between Mitch and Blanche. Both must be played out in certain qualities of light that stem from the physical world Williams had witnessed in actual life and from the world of the play that he constructed for the characters of his imagination. We will see later how important qualities of light are in another Williams play The

Glass Menagerie. There light becomes an important part of the play's dramatic structure, so much so that not to carefully consider what role it plays is to seriously jeopardize the meaning of the play. The director's and the scenographer's task is to bring onto the stage environments where the battle resulting from the clashes of character and light are clearly evident to those watching. This understanding of the play in the terms just set forth does not make itself readily apparent to the eye of the casual seeker; it must actively and carefully be sought out from many sources, many of which are difficult to find. But that, of course, is the function of the scenographer: to be an active and informed eye, not simply a mechanically recording one. My own understanding of this play was fortuitously aided by several accidental encounters with the exact place where Williams sent Blanche and her sister to dine. I also lived and worked in the place where the playwright chose to set his play. Still, one cannot rule out other possible ways of obtaining the same information we have looked at here. I have not related this experience—or any other, for that matter—to demonstrate my unique vision or to boast of my singular good luck. I merely wish to affirm that such encounters do exist and happen to every artist who is active in his art. Such information, such encounters happen to all artists constantly; it is how they obtain the raw materials of their art. All artists must be *lucky* or they would soon cease to be artists. Perhaps what we call "lucky" is simply another name for the necessary activeness of creative research.

Before leaving this subject to attend the more practical chores of research let us pause for a brief word of warning. It is very possible for artists to be too intellectual in their research of a project. Part of the task in becoming a good theater researcher is to know the difference between useful information and the frivolous speculation. There is a real and vital distinction to be made between the seeking out of information useful in re-creating the playwright's world and the often fruitless overextended academic exercise. You can, in other words, *think too much.* (Although I cannot remember too many instances of this pitfall surfacing in my own classrooms.) Ivor Brown, in his entertainingly helpful book *How Shakespeare Spent the Day,* nearly pinpoints the kind of speculation that hinders an interpreter's insight and understanding instead of aiding it:

What curious discoveries are made by the probing and learned academic mind! For example, in The Question of Hamlet, *Professor Harry Levin of Yale, who has carefully read his way through the deterrent jungle of Hamlet literature and can tell us in brief what the scholars have told us at length down the centuries, decides at one point that " Hamlet is reenacting the classical Eiron, the Socratic ironist who practices wisdom by disclaiming it. More immediately, Shakespeare was dramatising the humanistic critique of the intellect as it had been generally propounded by Erasmus." Of the "to be or not to be" soliloquy Proffesor Levin writes: "Such is the doubter's model of dialectic which leads him back – through complementary semicircles – to his binary point of departure. This is the question,* esse aut non esse, *which metaphysicians from Plato to Sartre have pondered. The ontological question becomes an existential question and the argument lifts from metaphysics to ethics." One can imagine that Shakespeare, confronted with a commentary of that kind, would have torn in bewilderment what hairs may then have been left on that exalted head when he was reaching middle age.*

Two Primary Approaches to Research Technique

If one draws a line through the middle of nineteenth-century theater, it is possible to gain a reasonably accurate understanding how philosophies of production before and after circa 1850 changed. Before the middle of the nineteenth century those responsible for staging theatrical works showed little consideration for historical accuracy. Those who worked for the stage showed scant concern for any of the following:

- Historical facts: dates, periods, verifiable facts
- Cultural awareness: customs, mores, religions, beliefs
- Artistic accuracy: dress, crafts, pictorial symbolism
- Geographical awareness: borders, coastlines, climate, flora, fauna
- Archeological knowledge: dates, periods, styles, artifacts

These areas were not considered worthy of deep investigation. From the beginning of western theater (the Greek theater of the fifth century B. C.), verisimilitude was never a serious concern. During and after the middle of the nineteenth century, however, attitudes changed radically. A new principle of interpretation emerged that profoundly affected how playwrights conceived their characters and how actors approached the playing of them. Briefly this principle holds that characters on the stage should be presented as actual people living in a real world, a world that mirrors the one outside the theater. A philosophy was also adopted that not only should these characters be shown in their own time but in visual contexts compatible with historical fact as revealed by research. The present-day theater still operates within the basic principles of interpretation established during the middle of the nineteenth century. For instance, when plays such as Abe Lincoln from Illinois, Amadeus, or The Private Life of Henry VIII are produced on the stage, one can expect these productions to accurately reflect a careful research of the period in question. While naturalism as a style of production only briefly dominated the theater during the early part of this century, the philosophy of both playwrights and interpreters is still based on perceivable reality. A sense of actual place, a sense of chronological order, and a sense of believable events occurring for the first time permeates most works seen in the present-day theater.

Plays written before the nineteenth century — whose characters are not conceived of "real" persons, such as Molière's Miser or Shakespeare's Puck — when produced today must now be considered in ways that would have never occurred to producers of earlier periods. The question of "doing a production in period" — a term that would have been incomprehensible to those working in the Elizabethan theater-is now routinely asked. Producers today freely choose periods other than those during which the play was written or out of the period in which the playwright originally set his action. So far, I know of no production of Hamlet set in the twenty-third century A. D. but it is only a matter of time until one will appear. Such a production would be more defensible than imposing that century on a production of Amadeus or Long Day's Journey into Night.

The characters a playwright includes in his play may or may not have historical models. Even when characters do not have real-life counterparts, in many instances there are good reasons why they should remain in contexts the playwright intended. Although Lady Macbeth retains a persuasive reality in times and cultures other than that Shakespeare intended (as Kurosawa proves in Throne of Blood, a successful adaptation of Macbeth, set in medieval Japan), Blanche Dubois, on the other hand, is irrevocably tied to her own particular period and place. In most of Tennessee Williams's plays, the sense of time and locale is so integrated into the sum and substance of the work that it is all but impossible to consider these characters as universal symbols. Like flies in amber, their setting is inseparable from their meaning. As with the Elizabethan concept of the Great Chain of Being, where everything in nature had its own place and function, all unchanging and unchangeable, there are some characters who cannot at least should not be pried from their niche in time. When dealing with the past, or when considering the period and style of a production, common sense that all-too-often uninvoked state of mind must be our guide; Mozart in a Star Trek spacesuit or even Abraham Lincoln in a miniskirt is a factual possibility on the stage; no law of theater prohibits it. Still, one hesitates even to voice the idea. We will list a number of general principles of research in outline form. These principles are intended for the student with little experience in scenographic research. As the student scenographer grows proficient in the craft of theater design, approaches to research will alter significantly. Creating personal methods of research grows in tandem with other skills. No two scenographers work in the same manner for long, nor does the individual scenographer work the same way during the span of a career. Here principles of research will be divided into two basic units: external research and internal research. The first category will include those elements of information pertinent to, but not actually found in, the written script. The second category will deal with items of information explicitly stated in the text or gleaned from close investigation of it. This division, of course, will result in some overlapping of materials; in addition, the need for research will vary considerably from script to script. A large part of the scenographer's research—especially the visual aspects of it are comparatively easy to understand for the beginning scenographer. The understanding of what lies below the surface details of historical or unfamiliar artifacts, or comprehending the cultural forces that molded them, often eludes casual inspection. Often the order and pattern of the research process greatly change from production to production. Only experience can speed up the process or give assurance to the scenographer that correct choices have been made. Still, most scenographers who constantly work in the theater become intuitive researchers developing an understanding for the substrata of an historical period or of a geographical location. Thus they can imbue their productions with the spirit of a past age or a sense of locale without blindly copying exterior trappings of a distant time or an unfamiliar place. The following outline of research principles is necessarily incomplete; nevertheless, it may prove useful as a general guideline or as a checklist of possible leads to follow when seeking out that illusive spirit of a past age or unfamiliar location. Following this section a suggested method for creating an inventory of needs for specific productions will be given. For now, keep in mind this observation made by the painter Jean Helion: "The artist is born with a definite feeling that Unity exists throughout the incongruous, and that we do not see it only because links are hidden, or missing, or misunderstood."

External Research

1. Date of the Text

a. *Date of the text's composition.* No matter what the date of the play's action, it is always a sound idea to examine the time *when the play was actually written.* In some cases, as with some of Shakespeare's plays, this date may be unknown or disputed. Still, no matter when an author sets the action of his play, some of his own time will undoubtedly creep into the fabric of the text; it is well to pinpoint that time as exactly as possible.

b. *Date of the text's action.* This date, along with the above, gives the scenographer a specific period of time around which all his research will center. In many instances, an author, wanting to treat a contemporary problem, will choose a time with similarities to his own so that he may call attention to some topical point or thesis. Shakespeare in his defense of, and allegiance to, the monarchy of his own age used examples of corrupt governments and rulers from the past, both foreign and domestic, to demonstrate how fortunate his contemporary countrymen were to have the rule they had. (To prove a point, he is not above unfairly maligning men or groups who differed with him in opinion. Witness the unfair treatment he gives the characters Richard III and Joan of Arc.) A careful study of both dates, while these alone will not provide the only dates he will need, will give the scenographer an excellent starting clue for his further research.

2. Period of the Text

The *period* is a deceptive concept; such divisions in time do not exist except in retrospect and after sufficient time has passed. Only then are we able to see the large outline of what has passed. But to assign a name and inclusive dates to a period of time is dangerous in that it leads to thinking that the past automatically divides itself into convenient compartments of time. It is dangerous also in that the inhabitants of any particular period become stereotyped images rather than living people. Invariably, more is omitted from this stereotype than is included; at times important things are left out simply because they don't neatly "fit" the simplicity of form that stereotypes demand. Still, many books and articles are written, and visual materials compiled, on the assumption that a span of time can be separated from others and given an appropriate name and character. The conscientious researcher should not be misled, however, into believing that a single book on any one period, no matter how extensive the coverage of that source, is sufficient. To understand the romantic era, for instance, it is imperative to examine works about the eighteenth century and also those of earlier periods and cultures against which that period revolted. Certainly all periods have their roots in those that preceded them. The astute researcher is prepared to trace these roots carefully as far back as they extend; quite often finding the meaning of an object or a practice, incomprehensible in itself, easily understood when traced to an earlier time. The understanding of words and especially their meanings can only be fully understood by going back to root uses and meanings. Shakespeare may have used many terms we recognize today, but often the entire meaning of what he said has shifted to concepts and usages that can be diametrically opposed to present-day understanding.

3. Geographical Factors in Scenography

It is self-evident that the geographical location of a play will dictate much of the detail of its setting. Even when a play is produced in a style other than realistic, there is usually some attempt to manifest the geographical spirit of the actual place. This might show only in the basic colors of the production – golden yellow and brown for the desert, cold blues and greens for northern climates. (This is especially true in the cinema version of Othello with Laurence Olivier; texture and colors, with a minimum of historical detail, allowed the scenographer to give the viewer an accurate sense of place and time without making imitative pictures of Venice and Cyprus "as it really was.") Geographical location, moreover, has an altering influence on similar styles of decoration and fashion, even though the differences may go unnoticed to the casual eye. Recent large-scale studies and publications such as *The Age of Expansion*, edited by Hugh Trevor-Roper , deal with particularly limited spans of time, in this case 1559 to 1660, and are able to clearly show the difference in developments in the arts, sciences, politics, and religious activities of various countries during this period. It is possible to see in Trevor-Roper's study deviations both great and small as each individual country is examined, and this can be of immense value to both scenographer and director. While material can sometimes be found altogether—as in the case of the English historian's book—more often than not, the scenographer must compile such information from various sources. Temperaments and points of view that emerge from a climate and geographical location—or from a play's characters or author—are so enmeshed in the work that ignorance of these qualities and the underlying reasons for them could lead to serious dislocations of visual ideas. While the sense of environment is important to a play, it is not always easy to distill from visual material alone.

It is not often possible for a working artist to go directly to a place and study firsthand the country from which material is needed. Travel books are helpful, especially pictorial ones, and most scenographers maintain files and personal materials on various countries in their permanent collection of sources, a practice that should also be emulated by the director. Still, one can sometimes miss important points without firsthand knowledge. All theater artists, regardless of area, should be constantly on the lookout for writers who have been places and have written about their travels. Often, this reportage, along with pictorial materials, can be invaluable to the scenographer who has not had the opportunity to travel extensively. A good example in support of this recommendation is Henry Miller's entertaining and informative account of his first visit to Greece. When Miller describes Greece in *The Colossus of Maroussi*, it is a Greece he saw in more than one time dimension. While he looked carefully at the country as it existed then, he was also able to see what it had been—an ancient Greece with its history and myths evident in every vista. His book is a record of his feelings and perceptions as he experiences a world where time present and time past coexist. Although there is not a single illustration or one reference to the Greek theater, any scenographer reading Miller's book would have his visual imagination stimulated and influenced by the power of Miller's words. Similarly, Mary McCarthy's *Stones of Florence* although it does have visual materials — is filled with perceptive observations. Nor should any cultivated researcher remain unacquainted with the writings of Jan Morris whose many works span all continents and many ages. Travel accounts are no substitute for travel itself, but the perceptive writer can often inform and inspire us when we are unable to go ourselves.

4. The Artistic Climate of the Time

In any period of history, the various artistic endeavors will reflect, better than any other form of record we have, the form and texture of the time. During the austerely religious period that followed the fall of decadent Rome, one might expect the simple but powerful Gregorian chant, massive cathedrals, and the sculpture of saints and martyrs. By the same token, it is reasonable to expect to find the spiritual lightness of the eighteenth century mirrored in the music of Mozart, the paintings of Watteau and Fragonard, and the excessively mannered busts of Bernini. Perhaps the arts are the most faithful lens we have to see into the past. Many times history, recorded only in words, can barely hint at what the arts can make very plain. Still, some arts are more useful to the scenographer than others. Architecture and sculpture very often show how humans would like to be, what they aspire to rather than what they are. Painting, on the other hand, while it too has often been used to glorify both men and gods, tends to capture our more human attributes. Painters, even when they are thinking least about the present moment, cannot keep it out of their work. For this reason, the painter-draftsman, with his more quickly accomplished works, is probably of more value to the scenographer than any other group of artists, even though a scenographer cannot exclude thorough study of them as well.

5. The Religious Climate of the Time

The religious philosophy of some periods has been their guiding force, and all other activities have stemmed from it or have been affected by it. The ceiling of the Sistine Chapel, one of the great monuments of Western art, was a commission of the church. Even the placement of each individual panel was dictated and supervised, along with the particular subject matter for each, by church officials, not by Michelangelo. When religion has been a prime factor in the structure of a period, it usually is so strong that not to consider it as a molding force of the visual elements of the time, both spiritual and secular, is to miss the point entirely. A play such as Arthur Miller's Crucible (although he was also dealing with the state of America in the twentieth century) or John Whiting's Devils requires a thorough study of church doctrines during the seventeenth century as they relate to witchcraft and Satanism. The Whiting play is difficult to produce without an intense examination of Aldous Huxley's book *The Devils of Loudun* on which the play is based. Even when religion does not play a prominent part in the structure of a work, it is sometimes much easier to understand the characters of a play if their beliefs are given attention; a scenographer's job is not so much to reproduce the minutiae of the past as to capture the spirit of it.

6. The Political Climate of the Time

Since a great many plays concern or have political happenings current at the time of the play's composition, it is sometimes necessary to delve into the political history of the period to make any sense of the play itself. Danton's Death by Georg Büchner, written in the early part of the last century, and the Marat/Sade of Peter Weiss , in our own day, both deal with the French Revolution and the forces that motivated it. While both plays have different motivations and purposes (the Weiss play deals more with the present day than it does with the past), it is not possible to produce intelligently either play without a comprehensive understanding of the political events that brought about that revolution. Although this area of research may be more useable to the director and actor, the scenographer cannot completely ignore or remain ignorant of what those events were or how they came about.

7. The Author's Commentary on His Own Time

Most works of art are, either consciously or unconsciously, evaluations made by their creators on the institutions and concepts they come in contact with during their everyday life. The stage has often been used as a platform for the expounding—sometimes subtly, sometimes not—of ideas and philosophies. Sheridan, Shaw, and Brecht, to name but a few, have strong opinions concerning contemporary figures and their behavior. If the scenographer is not aware of the author's state of mind, he might very well misunderstand the author's intention and create settings that defeat rather than aid the playwright's purpose. Usually the author is explicit in exposing his ideas through the medium of the play; in School for Scandal—a play whose subject is the often gratuitous, always malicious, fabrication and perpetuation of scandalous stories—Sheridan attacks not only individual characters but often entire levels of society whose behavior he found offensive, unthinking, or simply not in agreement with him. And, on at least one occasion Shaw's thoughts concerning a play (Androcles and the Lion) exceed in length the play itself. Sometimes, however, the scenographer must turn to other writings by the same author or about the author to answer questions concerning the play.

8. Style of Production of the Play as Originally Produced

The theater of any period had some singular style of production that employed the accepted conventions of the day. Today, in many instances, in order to recapture some of the original force of a work, it is produced with what are now outmoded conventions. But, even when the play is presented with modifications of those original conventions, a thorough knowledge of those conventions is essential. Much research has been done on all the important plays of the past still being produced today, and much information has been unearthed concerning theaters in which the plays were performed details of setting, lighting practices (if any), and mode of costume. It is sometimes almost a necessity to understand fully, if not reproduce exactly, the basic format of the original production in order to secure the results the author desired. During the last part of the nineteenth century, Shakespeare was given such extravagantly designed productions that the plays scarcely survived the scenic devices superimposed on their dramatic structures. To facilitate scene changes in these plays, scenes were altered or transposed to such an extent (in many cases important ones simply cut) that little or no regard was paid to the integrity of the play's internal structure. Research since that time has shown (oddly enough) that the simple, often crude Elizabethan theater was, from what little we do know of it, an almost ideal form in which to produce the plays of the period and to a great extent actually determined the writing of them.

These, then, are some of the basic investigations a scenographer must make in seeking material about a production. Just when the external research must be done may change with different projects (as well as how much). In one production he may find one category important to explore, another useless; in another production, just the reverse might be true. Keep in mind, therefore, that any sort of research is rarely if ever—a straight-line activity; jumping from group to group and from fact to fact, sometimes working forward, sometimes backtracking, are all part of the technique. It shows a London street in the middle 1880s. This engraving contains a great amount of visual material observed firsthand and recorded meticulously. If we look closely at this drawing it is almost impossible not to be puzzled about some of the things it contains, curious about the smaller details of the buildings, the street, and the activities of the people in those buildings and on the street. Fortunately we see more from the high angle the artist has chosen than if the picture had been drawn at ground level; this high viewing angle allows us to determine not only how the place *looked* but how it was used as well. Such images that show the activity of human beings in everyday surroundings are often more valuable to the scenographer than pictures of isolated buildings, empty rooms. Details devoid of human context are less valuable to the theater artist than images showing human activity. It is important at any stage of research to keep in mind that the actor, not the scenographer, is the primary teller of the playwright's story. Every image in a production should play a subsidiary role to the human actor. Even on working drawings, many scenographers place a simple line drawing of the human figure to remind him and all who work on his drawings of the human scale.

A singularly beneficial thing that can happen to a scenographer when in the initial stages of research is to become sidetracked, that is, to find materials, ideas, and images unexpectedly. Good reasons exist for allowing even encouraging diversions from the straight and narrow path of research. When this happens, the researcher is exposed to the possibility of an idea-a "happy accident" that does not fall within the scope of logical research patterns (see previous discussion of this subject in "The Role of Chance in the Creative Process" above). By allowing chance to operate, new and inventive solutions may occur. Chance discovery should be encouraged in all art forms, not least in the theater. Another possible reward is that discoveries not presently employed may be useful at another time. Most professional scenographers will admit that in many instances what they needed to complete a design they found accidentally. It is not unreasonable to compare artwork to night vision: during the daylight hours we can see an object directly in front of us without difficulty, whereas in the dark, our eyes are so constructed that one is able to see the object in front of him *only by looking to the side of it.* As a matter of fact, as Jean Dubuffet noted, it is possible to look too hard for something and in that way miss it altogether.

Quite often, too, the necessary information the scenographer is seeking comes in an aggregate form, that is, hidden among things not important, much in the manner in which we looked at the engraving of the London street. Keep in mind, therefore, that the best historical research materials are often the richest in detail. This means that the scenographer's task is not only to find such a source (that is scarcely half the job), but to be able to interpret and understand emotionally as well as intellectually what he needs from it. Scenography is much like refining gold; there is always more dross than anything else and the process of refining is tedious.

Internal Research

1. Explicit Directions

These directions are usually the minimum amount of information to denote entrances and exits or necessary physical actions to clarify dialogue references. But stage directions are not all the same type, nor do all convey the same kind of information. In most past periods of theater, stage directions actually written as part of the scripts have been scanty or nonexistent. On the other hand, it is a practice of today's playwrights to give elaborate and lengthy directions to supplement the dialogue. Some producers of plays, both directors and scenographers, make it a practice to remove or ignore all written directions when they study the playscript; they do not wish to be too influenced by the author's instructions because they feel that he, the playwright, is not necessarily the final arbiter in actually bringing the work to the stage. (While most playwrights do not like this practice on the part of their coworkers, some have seen the wisdom of it and have said so in print.) Most directors and scenographers, in defense of this attitude, think that the better the playwright has done his work in the text, the less he will need to explain it in a stage direction. Here is a brief outline of the various types of stage directions a scenographer might encounter in a script. While it is not, perhaps, necessary to try blindly to follow their advice, it is imperative for the scenographer to know precisely what these directions attempt to say and then to make an evaluation as to how far they should be observed or disregarded.

A. Factual descriptions. Shakespeare wrote very few directions; most of the directions that are found in his work have been supplied by later editors of his plays. Most plays, in fact, until about the last one hundred sixty-odd years, have little more than act and scene divisions and oneor two-word locale references. Since that time, however, the pendulum has swung the other way. It is now a common practice to write lengthy stage directions. George Bernard Shaw's directions were, for instance, often long and carefully worded essays to give background material primarily concerning the characters of his plays. Often he would also discuss the setting where these characters lived, since he felt that that, too, revealed a great deal about what they were or had become because of this environmental influence. Most playwrights working today, while not writing as voluminously as Shaw, present their directions more or less in this manner.

B. Poetic descriptions. Some authors, not many though, attempt to give the reader hints concerning the mood of the play by evocative and poetic descriptions (although not in verse form) of locales and characters. Perhaps Tennessee Williams is one of the best examples of a writer who uses this device. Take the beginning of *The Glass Menagerie* for instance:

The Wingfield apartment is in the rear of the building, one of those vast hive-like conglomerations of cellular living-units that flower as warty growths in overcrowded urban centers of lower middle-class population and are symptomatic of the impulse of this largest and fundamentally enslaved section of American society to avoid fluidity and differentiation and to exist and function as one interfused mass of automatism. The apartment faces an alley and is entered by a fire escape, a structure whose name is a touch of accidental truth, for all of these huge buildings are always burning with the slow and implacable fires of human desperation.

While this is not poetry, its intention is poetic. Eugene O'Neill did much the same thing in his earlier plays, but in a colder prose form. Both try to give more than just a factual account of the places where the action of the play takes place and a keener insight into the people who inhabit these places. Jo Mielziner, in speaking of Williams's practice of writing directions in this manner, has said: "If I were teaching an advanced course in scene design, I think I might ask the students to read the production notes that Tennessee Williams writes for almost all his plays. After reading his notes in the early script for Summer and Smoke, I felt that it would be truly difficult to design a setting for this play that was poor in concept. It might be inadequate in execution, but the extraordinarily knowledgeable and sensitive eye of the dramatist created a picture that even a mediocre designer could not spoil."

C. Stage directions in acting editions of plays. Most young students in the theater are surprised to learn that many of the directions in a published version of a Broadway success were not written down by the author but by the production's stage manager. He usually does this on the instructions of the director, since it is the function of the stage manager to compile and record the official promptscript. This promptscript, later used as the basis for the published version of the play, usually gives detailed information about all entrances, exits, directions of movements, and quite often, key words that indicate interpretations and vocal timings. The author's original directions and admonitions often get cut, inverted, or swallowed up in the general process of rehearsal and tryouts in front of test audiences. These scripts also contain detailed lists of properties, sound and light cues, costume plots, and floor plans for a particular production. In most cases, although there is a tendency especially among amateurs to regard this information as somehow sacrosanct, it can be and should be completely disregarded or at least carefully scrutinized.

2. Deductive Evidence Gained from Direct and Indirect References by Characters in the Play

It is often possible to glean information about a play's setting by careful study of oblique remarks made by the characters in their dialogue. It seems to be characteristic of well-written plays that the deductive evidence is of greater value to the scenographer in his research than explicit directions or descriptions. One of the drawbacks of seeking information by deduction is that unless the contributing factors that lead to the deduction are fairly specific and easy to interpret, the resulting information may be subject to wide interpretation. (The design and use of the Elizabethan stage are some of the best examples of the confusion that can result from interpretative study of internal evidence.) Nevertheless, the deductive process is one most followed by almost all artists and is the area in which the scenographer can make his greatest contribution to the production.

Dramatic Inventory

Texts contain many kinds of information. Analyzing that information into a logical pattern is an important step in the research process, since information is useless if not organized. How best to accomplish this requirement concerns us here. The time-honored guidelines employed by journalists and reporters provide good models for categorizing information. Emulation of these procedures is useful in scenographic research. But what are those procedures; how are they implemented?

The basic method used by all news reporters incorporates these five questions: Who? What? When? Where? and Why? For scenographers, the first four of these categories are necessary to all forms of research. The last question—Why?-addresses motivation, an area of research usually left to directors. Scenographers cannot, however, avoid this question, since much of the information they gather is explained when this last question is considered. The basic information needed for all scenographic inventories includes the following:

Who: (1) *Succinct descriptions of both the physical qualities as well as the psychological makeup of each character in the text and (2) brief descriptions of the relationships that exist between and among characters.* In many works written in the twentieth century the playwright provides this information in stage directions before and during the text. For plays previous to this century, few prefatory descriptions of characters exist; such information—as well as relationship between and among characters—is disclosed through internal reference.

What: *The action of the play described by notes before or during action of the text.* While it is a sound practice to make such chronologies for oneself, help from outside sources should not be disregarded. A number of commercial printing houses specialize in publishing critical notes in inexpensive formats that are useful when studying the classic or representative modern plays widely adopted in academic play anthologies. The increasing availability of well-written dramatic criticism – such as that contained in Thomas Cousineau's reader's companion to *Waiting for Godot* or Michael Hinden study of *Long Day's Journey into Night*, both from Twayne Publishers of Boston represents a growing response to the need for useful information about recently produced dramatic works. These sources represent the exception; most notes available are too rudimentary to be comprehensively helpful. For most plays, however, useful commentary is difficult to find or nonexistent. When: *The inclusive time units of the play as presented by the playwright*. Time factors are important to consider in the overall scheme of the text's action. Frequently such studies are given inadequate attention. Often significant features of a text are revealed when precise knowledge of its time frames are determined. Where: *The physical location(s) of the play's action as presented (or assumed) by the playwright*. Most dramatic texts unlike those of the Greek theater-do not obey the unity of time, place, and action. Where a scene takes place is often important to the understanding of what is happening. Why: *The psychological substructure of the text's elements*. Motivation in dramatic works divides into several parts: (1) why do characters say what they say; or (2) why do characters do what they do; and (3) why does a playwright set the action of the text in a certain place an aspect of the subject discussed in Where; or (4) why does a playwright begin the action at a precise time or end the action at another precise time; this is also an aspect of the subject discussed in When.Although the information needed to complete an inventory varies from project to project, many of the following categories remain constant. While the relative value of the kinds of information also change from production to production, most inventories follow the outline given below. The scenographer usually begins this inventory, however, *after* the first reading of the text, not before.

Dramatic Inventory

I. Inventory of basic information

1. Date of play's action (inclusive dates)

2. Chronology of play's action
   - A. Times of day for each scene
   - B. Time lapses between scenes
   - C. Times of year (seasons and activities associated with seasons)
   - D. Climate of locale and weathers conditions of each scene.
3. Date of play's composition (Estimate if unknown.)
4. Period of play's action (salient features of social behavior: art, government, religion, rituals and superstitions)
5. Period of play's composition (similar or dissimilar to above)
6. Geographical description of each scene (Note differences between actual geographical features found by external research and geographical features created by the playwright.)
7. List of scenes in order (Name locale and briefly describe immediate adjacent areas.)
8. Purpose of each scene in the fewest possible words
9. List of characters in play (Give title, relationship, or function of each character in the play's action.)
10. List number of characters in each scene (not names of characters)

II. Production requirements (Do not orient any information to any actual stage facilities: describe all information as if it existed in the world outside the theater.)

1. Note brief description of place of action
   - A. Entrances, exits, windows, other architectural or geographical features of place (Give period or style of architectural features.)
   - B. List of furniture, set properties, absolutely necessary to action of scene
   - C. Levels, etc., absolutely necessary to action of scene
   - D. List of of properties absolutely necessary to action of scene (Give period or style of properties.)
   - E. Examples of above selected from magazines, books, etc., photocopied from library material

F. Shape of playing area drawn in simple diagram with appropriate notes (Determine this shape in same way as demonstrated in "Research into Action: *Romeo and Juliet*" in part 5.)

III. Tonalities perceived in play (Cite period, climate, geography, social history to support choices.)

1. Major tonalities with brief explanation for choice
2. Minor tonalities with brief explanation for choice

IV. List symbols perceived in text. Metaphors perceived inherent in the text. Many visual theater artists find it productive to put their thoughts into short statements that detail in words visually important features found in study of a text.

It is evident from study of the above that the dramatic inventory is reductionist in nature; that is, it gives information required for the production but does not show the interrelationship of the various elements. Although inventories provide a way to determine basic needs of a text, much thought is needed to find the internal relationships between its many parts. Understanding how these parts relate to the whole is the major step in understanding what the text means.

Chronological and Psychological Order of the Creative Research Process

The young scenographer might well ask, "When do I do the exterior research, when the interior?" The answer is, there is no good way to determine a definite priority. Student scenographers learn quickly that research is a timeconsuming, often tedious process. The myriad paths that lead to materials have many unproductive sidetracks. Steps in the process are rarely marked; directions as to how to obtain information are often vague, even contradictory at times. Perhaps the only useful advice concerning research processes is that one thing found almost invariably gives meaning to what follows.

Visual research lies not so much in the skill to assemble unrelated watch-part "facts" as it does in the ability to track *feelings* – for want of a better word through uncharted labyrinths of information. Frequently information found is visually exciting but is not appropriate to underlying concepts of the production. Other research materials, although deceptively simple, ultimately prove useful—even critical—to a production's meaning. Veteran scenographers often admit that they are unsure as to how the process works speculating only that time and careful thought is necessary to determine meaning or importance to the vague feelings they experience when looking for "the answer." It is often difficult for students of scenography to comprehend that an important part of an artist's working technique is to recognize the useful or correct detail when accidently encountered, to accept that solutions to research problems often rest on decisions for which artists have no *conscious* reason for feeling as they do. On the other hand, rational selection is a fundamental part of an artist's working procedure. Taken together, one is left with the realization that an openly inquisitive nature is as important an ability to foster as is skill in drawing and painting or knowledge of stagecraft technique. An active curiosity is in itself a highly important and integral part of the scenographer's artistic apparatus.

In most instances scenographers work from opposite points in the spectrum of factual possibilities. On the one hand concern for discovering "facts" gathering information from study of historical or documented materials—is critically important to scenographic design. Such information influences the design of a production no matter how abstractly or theatrically that information is used. On the other hand, the scenographer works to satisfy all interior demands both factual and symbolic of the production. Specific needs of the performers—both physical and psychological must also be met.

Before proceeding to the next section, let us attempt to understand what is happening in the scenographer's mind—both on the conscious and subconscious levels—during this period of gestation. The forces and influences that affect the scenographic design include:

The written script (A)—the needs of the production (the actor's, director's, and technician's needs): this is determined primarily as demonstrated in "Internal Research".

Factual material (B) concerning period, etc: this is determined from investigation as outlined in "External Research." Internal and external research approaches were discussed during an earlier section. These play a significant role in the scenographer's conscious work pattern. But as all working scenographers know—these are *not* the only materials that condition how they work or what they must eventually accomplish. They must also realize that there are:

Practical considerations (C)—limitations of budget, inadequacies of stage facilities, time deadlines, and—not least in every producing organization—oppositions from others concerned with the production: these are all present-oriented problems but tend to be limiting in nature. Although these three categories constitute the rational part of a scenographer's task, there is one last area to be considered. This area determines the artistic value of a scenographer's accomplishment:

Intuitional responses and decisions (D): this area is primarily past-oriented. It is composed of personal preferences, backlogs of assimilated information, previous solutions to design problems, and—not least of these influences—prejudices. Depending upon the bent of the individual artist, this area tips toward conservative solutions to design problems or to those more radical and revolutionary. Since the subconscious is the more difficult area of the mind to control, it is also the area most difficult for the scenographer to use directly. It is understandable, therefore, that a scenographic design can never be a simple straight-line accomplishment. One should expect, moreover, different areas of research to assume different directions with different projects; the research needed for a production of The Odd Couple, for instance, has little in common with the research needed for a production of *Macbeth.*

Creative research is, finally, too personal or subjective to be captured in a series of specific admonitions. Since the research process is only useful to the extent that it is individually internalized, one must expect that the evolution of a successful technique will take many years to accomplish. As James H. Austen astutely comments: "Experience tells me that research is a series of contingencies, of zigzags, joined by one fragile link after another. You would never realize this from reading the tidy, aseptic research accounts that fill our libraries. For balance, someone should present a different side of the picture-show some contemporary research in all its haphazard, unpredictable complexity." A useful explanation how the artist's mind works is contained in Anton Ehrensweig *The Hidden Order of Art.* This difficult book presents a persuasive view of how the unconscious mind of the artist processes information gained from past experience. It is recommended to all students concerned with understanding how conscious and unconscious processes of artists work.

Diagrammatic Map

The designer said that this *Macbeth* takes place on various levels in Hell. Now, I have always been under the impression that *Macbeth* took place in Scotland.

Dramatic texts are complex language structures: metaphors, similes, allusions, analogies, all guide interpreters when it is necessary to change these words into actions and images on the stage. The scenographer's job is to translate words of the text into the things they suggest. In his book, *The Twin Dimensions*, a text that deals with the nature and perception of time and space, Geza Szamosi, writes: "One of the few things on which cultural historians of Western civilization all seem to agree is that three important developments occurred, took root, and flourished in Western civilization only. In many ways they characterize our civilization: polyphonic music, perspective painting, and experimental science. *It is remarkable, though seldom noticed, that all three came into existence as people struggled with basically the same problem: how to use the senses to find reliable measures of time intervals, spatial distances, and their various relationships. How to impose, in other words, mathematical order on the perceivable world. It is also remarkable – and equally seldom noticed – that in this crucial enterprise, the arts preceded experimental science*".

The underlying thought here is that human beings are curious creatures by nature; they must always know exactly where they are and what their situation is. This basic need motivates the construction of diagrammatic maps, a productive way to assemble and display information gathered from internal and external research sources.

Research of any sort is time travel in the imagination. For any kind of travel actual or imaginary maps provide tools to find places we want to go. Real travel—that we do on planes, on trains, or in cars—requires maps that show routes to our destination. Although some maps for the real world are difficult to find, with effort we can obtain them. Maps to imaginary places, on the other hand, are more difficult to discover. In certain instances, however, they can be found: J. R. R. Tolkien's maps for his *Lord of the Rings* trilogy, maps he drew himself, give his readers ways to find their way around the imaginary world depicted in Tolkien's story. Maps for most fictional places—for the island of *The Tempest*, the Greece of *A Midsummer Night's Dream*, or the Elsinore of *Hamlet*—must be individually constructed.

How, then, do we begin a visual reconstruction of a playwright's imagined world? What atlas shows—for instance the crossroads of Beckett *Waiting for Godot* or the Illyrian seacoast of *Twelfth Night?* How do the "mountains of the moon" look in Arthur Miller *After the Fall?* Or-for that matter—what is the topography of Jane Greenwood *Macbeth?*

In virtually every dramatic work there is a geographical substructure that allows a reader or an audience to follow the wanderings of the play's characters. Often the information that relates the lay of the land is introduced early (the first scene of any Shakespeare play contains many clues as to where the action takes place as well as the nature of the actions that transpire there); frequently this necessary information is buried within the dialogue. There are many instances when what is disclosed is not factually accurate or does not make sense historically. For instance, in the second scene of Twelfth Night, Viola, is shipwrecked on the coast of Illyria, the ancient name of an actual region bordering the Adriatic Sea. External research gives us information of its history; quite possibly we may find how Shakespeare came to know of it, even why he used this setting for his story. (We are reasonably certain that he had a profound interest in the writings of those who made adventurous voyages to unexplored regions of the world, and more than once he set his plays in these exotic locations.) Such information is necessary to interpreters of the play. But Twelfth Night is a romantic comedy in which Shakespeare creates a world that only superficially borrows from the historical record. As the noted English director Jonathan Miller points out, Shakespeare's archeology is often wildly inaccurate, his history frequently slanted, and his chronologies often border on the unbelievable. We as visual interpreters. of the play must, however, find a means to survey the territory where the characters of Twelfth Night live as Shakespeare conceives of them. The diagrammatic map is a map drawn more from the parameters of the play's internal directions than from the pages of history. Many playwrights freely fabricate geographical locations. Ambiguous locales can and often are used for dramatic purpose; the plays of Beckett are prime examples of worlds that could only exist on the stage.

The chief difference between real world travelers and interpreters of dramatic texts is that those who decide to visit present-day London today easily obtain helpful maps, Visiting Falstaff's London, however, can only be done through imagination; maps for that London must be assembled from many visual and verbal sources. While external research gives us some visual clues to these imagined worlds, it is our responsibility to decide their borders and to define their features.

In the real world of travel, seldom do we start our journey without seeking out helpful maps. But if one desires to obtain maps of an imaginary place, two possibilities exist: (1) we can seek out ready-made maps—such as Tolkien's, or (2) we can ourselves draw the maps we need. I recommend the second of these possibilities. The advice is not as whimsical as might first appear. Moreover, good reasons exist why scenographers should seriously consider creating these maps to imaginary worlds as an adjunct activity to other research tasks.

What is the nature of the map proposed here? More important to the interpreter, what function does the diagrammatic map serve when analyzing dramatic texts? Most important of all, how do these maps aid the conceptual process preceding stage productions? How, for that matter, do the two concepts—map and diagram—relate? A dictionary definition of diagram says this: A graphic design that explains rather than represents: *A drawing that shows arrangement and relationships (as of parts to the whole, relative values, origins and development, chronological fluctuations, distribution).* About maps John Noble Wilford tells us: "The map you spread out on the table and ask to transport your mind to faraway places or point the way to the next town is one of the oldest and most basic forms of human communication. The idea of drawing a map to communicate a sense of *here* in relation to *there* evolved long ago and independently among many peoples in many parts of the world. *People were making rude maps long before they developed written Language*" (italics mine).

Maps and diagrams, then although similar in function are related ways of processing information into more accessible concepts and images. The diagrammatic map is an amalgamation of the ways of presenting information individually fashioned by the interpreter—in this case the scenographer—to make the playwright's verbal descriptions visibly manifest; it is a means by which a clear picture of the playwright's imagined world is gained.

The diagrammatic map permits us to locate scenes of action in time as well as in space; it clarifies the relationship of scene to scene; it further permits us to record in visual form the nature and sequence of the actions required. We also have opportunity to include on these maps verbal comments that relate information affecting peripheral aspects of the play.

Diagrammatic maps are especially helpful in working with intricately plotted multi-scene plays, since they clearly demonstrate how a world imagined for one play cannot serve for another. A diagrammatic map for *The Tempest* clearly has little in common with the worlds of the other two. Similar differences to those that exist in the maps just seen can be demonstrated for other playwrights as well.

The diagrammatic map is never a literal representation of actual terrain; it does not show how a particular place appears. It is, rather, a graphic representation of spatial relationships that arise directly from the context of the story's internal structure. The diagrammatic map's primary purpose is to tie spatial relationships to the playwright's web of events. It is possible, moreover, to inspect events *before* the beginning of the play's action and in so doing clarify situations that are not explained in the main body of the play. These maps are most useful when the information revealed suggests visual ideas that later become incorporated in the design of specific scenes. These drawings also suggest metaphorical relationships to the scenographer. For example, the central feature of the *Hamlet* diagrammatic map — the castle at Elsinore — suggests a construction known as the classical seven-ring labyrinth, an archaic form of architecture. The labyrinth — and its counterpart, the maze are nothing more than large physical puzzles that the individual must solve by physically entering them. (It takes little imagination to see that the concept of the labyrinth or the maze has particular resonance to the plot of *Hamlet* as well as to the actions of Hamlet; *Hamlet* is, if nothing else, a monstrous puzzle of which the castle itself is the physical counterpart. Nor should we forget that the Elizabethan meaning of the word *amazing* is literally *to find oneself in an actual full-scale maze*.).

As we work with these maps, relating what we find in our external research to what we interpret from the text itself, it becomes apparent how the links between spatial-geographic location of specific scenes builds support for the dramatic philosophic base of the production. Making diagrammatic maps is, admittedly, time-consuming. For the conscientious scenographer it is time well spent. As Anthony Storr reminds us in his study of the creative mind, *Solitude*:

The act of drawing sharpens the perceptions of the draughtsman; an idea passionately advanced by Ruskin, who believed that it was *only by trying to capture the external world in form and colour that the artist learns to apprehend it*. . . . If naming things is the first creative act, as Bazin alleges, perhaps drawing is the second. *Drawing is comparable with forming concepts. It enables the draughtsman to experiment with images separate from the object which originally engaged his interest, and thus gives him a sense of mastery over that object.*

Constructing diagrammatic maps is an important form of communication that allows interpreters of dramatic texts to—as the telephone directory Yellow Pages advertisement promises—"*let your fingers do the walking*."

Time Frames in Dramatic Works

Early in the fifth century C.E., Saint Augustine wrote: If you ask me what time is, I do not know. But if you do not ask me what time is—I know.

Some fifteen centuries later his dilemma is still ours. A playtext has an infinite number of possibilities for subject matter; under all, however, lies a common factor: *the passage of time and its effects on the characters the playwright chooses to follow*. Shakespeare several times writes prologues reminding his audience that although he might *tell them in words* the outline or meaning of a story, unless they invest time to view it "the two hours' traffic of our stage" understanding of the tale will remain incomplete. The nature of a text's internal time structures is often difficult to determine, frequently difficult to understand. Time in dramatic works occasionally defies an effort to cast it into logical sequences. Long before Einstein's theory of relativity, playwrights wrote works that distort commonsense notions of how time runs. How playwrights incorporate time in their work is a subject that demands conscious examination by all theater interpreters, since on the stage time assumes aspects contrary to reason. The interpreter is a *fashioner of time*.What does this term *fashioner of time*-mean? This subject we examine in the following pages. There we examine time (1) as it is determined by the playwright, and (2) as it is manipulated on the stage. An important skill for both director and scenographer to develop is to understand that time witnessed in the theater is different than time experienced in daily life. Three terms are essential to the understanding of our subject. These are *event, time line*, and, *time frame*:

1. An *event* is an abstract concept that includes under one heading a number of disparate things. World War I had innumerable aspects to it; when discussed, however, common relationships spring to mind; the same holds true for World War II or the Viet Nam War or the War of 1812. Although it does not have the complexity of a war, works for the theater are events. To study any event, large or small, we need conceptual tools with which to work. For our purpose, the two most important are the concepts of *time lines* and *time frames*.
2. A *time line* is a way to chart elements that form *events*. While an *event* is difficult to comprehend as a whole, a *time line* is relatively easy to discern. Works such as *The Timetables of History: A Horizontal Linkage of People and Events*, by Bernard Grun , makes the task of finding *time lines* easier for interpreters to seek out not only *time lines* but the ways they are used by playwrights. As historian Daniel J. Boorstin tells us: "At a glance, *The Timetables of History* can give us a feel for the fluidity and many-sidedness of past experience. Here we plainly see that the historian's neat categories parse experience in ways never found among living people. While, even in this volume, the authors have found it necessary to separate events into political, cultural, artistic, and scientific categories, *when we cast our eye across any page we see how overlapping, interfusing, inseparable, and arbitrary are such separations.* Often the most interesting—and most surprising—are the miscellaneous items which the authors list in the last right-hand column under 'Daily Life.' Precisely because these items are commonplace in their time, precisely because they were so

obviously in the foreground of the experience of non-historians, historians have been reluctant to give them the dignity of 'history'" (italics mine).

Although *The Timetables of History* was among the first books that show time lines, others have followed in its wake: *The Macmillan World History Factfinder*, and *The Harper Atlas of World History*, two works in a growing list give nonhistorians accessibility to the various strands—the *time lines*—that compose the web of history.

3. *Time frames* are the combination of *events* and *time lines*. In common experience, *events* begin at a certain point and end at some later time. It is often difficult to conceive of a situation where the arrow of time does not flow in one direction only or of places that have no location. But in the imagination these conditions are possible. In the Greek theater of the fifth century B.C. such was not the case; strict rules for time shown in dramatic works existed. These rules specifically demanded that all plays observe a unity of time, of place, and of action. This meant that once a play began, the action of the play had to be continuous; that the location where the play started had to remain the same until the play ended and that no gaps in time could exist. It was a further practice for playwrights to make the time of a play's action coincide with the starting time of the performance. Plays such as *Oedipus* and *Antigone* both set at dawn actually began shortly before sunrise. From the Elizabethan period onward, however, rarely has the playwright observed the unities demanded of the Greek playwrights. It was during the Elizabethan age, moreover, that playwrights began to incorporate into their plays a concept that time has *no fixed nature, that it can flow at varying speed in any direction, that it can be freely manipulated to serve the needs of plot and action*. Modifying *time frames* has become an important element in the playwright's "bag of tricks." (See *"The Language of Space,"* in part 2, and *"The Nature of the Scenographic Concept,"* in part 5, for examples of *time frames* used.)

Here is an example—the final speech from *Dr. Faustus* by Christopher Marlowe—how time was consciously manipulated by Elizabethan playwrights:

FAUST: Ah, Faustus, Now has thou but one bare hour to live And then thou must be damned perpetually! Stand still, you ever-moving spheres of heaven, That time may cease and midnight never come; Fair Nature's eye, rise, rise again, and make Perpetual day; or let this hour be but A year, a month, a week, a natural day, That Faustus may repent and same his soul! O lente lente currite noctis equi. The stars move still, time runs, the clock will strike, The devil will come, and Faustus must be damned. O, I'll leap up to my God! Who pulls me down? See, see, where Christ's blood streams in the firmament! One drop would save my soul – half a drop ah, my Christ! Rend not my heart for naming of my Christ; Yet will I call on him – O, spare me, Lucifer! Where is it now? 'Tis gone; and see where God Stretcheth out his arm and bends his ireful brows. Mountains and hills, come, come and fall on me And hide me from the heavy wrath of God, No, no-Then will I headlong run into the earth: Earth, gape! O no, it will not harbor me. You stars that reigned at my nativity, Whose influence hath allotted death and hell, Now draw up Faustus like a fogy mist Into the entrails of yon laboring clouds That when they mount forth into the air, My limbs may issue from their smoky mouths, So that my soul may but ascend to heaven. (The watch strikes.) Ah, half the hour is past; 'twill all be past anon. Oh, God, If thou wilt not have mercy on my soul, Yet for Christ's sake whose blood hath ransomed me Impose some end to my incessant pain: Let Faustus live in hell a thousand years, A hundred thousand, and at last be saved! O, no end is limited to damned souls! Why wert thou not a creature wanting soul? Or why is this immortal that thou has? Ah, Pythagoras' metempsychosis – were that true, This soul should fly from me, and I be changed Unto some brutish beast. All beasts are happy, For when they die Their souls are soon dissolved in elements, But mine must live still to be plagued in hell. Cursed be the parents that engendered me! No, Faustus, curse thyself, curse Lucifer That hath deprived thee of the joys of heaven. [The clock strikes twelve.] It strikes, it strikes! Now, body, turn to air Or Lucifer will bear thee quick to hell! (Thunder and lightning.) O soul, be changed to little water drops And fall into the ocean, ne'er to be found. My God, my God, look not so fierce on me! [Enter DEVILS.] Adders and serpents, let me breath awhile! Ugly hell, gape not – come not, Lucifer-I'll burn my books – ah, Mephistophilis!

This is a long speech, but it certainly would not require a whole hour – the time period it purports to follow – to give. There are, it is clear, no time lapses during the speech. The beginning is specifically indicated in the text. The passage of time, moreover is commented upon by Faustus himself. And yet although Marlowe chronicles the passage of the entire hour before Faustus dies, the scene only takes a quarter of an hour as measured by the clock; clock time in the theater becomes *symbolic time*. The rise and maturation of the Elizabethan theater marks the beginning of our present-day theatrical concepts of time. It was during this period that experimentation with time became part of a playwright's modus operandi, that bending the ordinary concepts of time to the purposes of narrative became an accepted practice. Gezá Szamosí tells us how time can be fashioned to suit particular purposes:

> *A new and uniquely human world of time and space started with the evolution of language. But this world is not perceivable.* It is purely symbolic. *When I describe where I was an hour or a year ago, when Homer wrote about* The Trojan War, *or when Einstein calculated the motion of the perihelion of the planet Mercury, it was all done by using symbols: words, number, and the like. When we measure the length of an object or estimate some time span, the results are expressed in units and numbers which are, again, human symbols.* Thus can we speak of symbolic time and space accessible to the human mind only. *Rhythms, melodies, stories,* plays in a theater, *poetic meters, holy days, and eternity, all signify symbolic times. There are all different from each other, and all are different from the, say, symbolic time a digital clock describes with digits when humans refer to "space and time," they usually mean* symbolic space and time in one of its many forms. A symbol is just a symbol and never the real thing. *(Italics mine)*

The passage of time in the theater is a flexible commodity. But how do the ideas listed above affect those who work in the "practical" world of theater? Do such considerations have any real application for a director's work or for a scenographer's design? Theater interpreters—scenographers among them soon discover that they do. Understanding the precise time frames of a play is an important step in understanding the way to produce it on the stage. Is it simply the great plays of the past that demand a different relationship to the perception of time in the theater? Tennessee Williams, particularly sensitive to the quality of time as it relates to theater, says this concerning time as used by modernday playwrights:

> *Carson McCullers concludes one of her lyric poems with the line: "Time, the endless idiot, runs screaming 'round the world." It is this continual rush of time, so violent that it appears to be screaming, that deprives our actual lives of so much dignity and meaning, and it is, perhaps more than anything else, the arrest of time which has taken*

> *place in a completed work of art that gives to certain plays their feeling of depth and significance. In the London notices of* Death of a Salesman *a certain notoriously skeptical critic made the remark that Willy Loman was the sort of man that almost any member of the audience would have kicked out of an office had he applied for a job or detained one for conversation about his troubles. Facing Willy Loman across an office desk, meeting his nervous glance and hearing his querulous voice, we would be very likely to glance at our wrist watch and our schedule of other appointments. But suppose there had been no wrist watch or office clock and suppose there had not been the schedule of pressing appointments suppose, in other words, that the meeting with Willy Loman had somehow occurred in a world outside of time. Then I think we would receive him with concern and kindness and even with respect. If the world of a play did not offer us this occasion to view its characters under that special condition of a world without time, then, indeed, the characters and occurrences of drama would become equally pointless.*

In Williams's own plays, time frames form the skeletal structure of plots. Each scene unit-vital links in the plot chain—has both a specifically fabricated time frame that renders the narrative understandable while at the same time propelling the story to its necessary conclusion. These time frames almost invariably pass without calling attention to their artificiality. Good playwrights—like Shakespeare and William—bend time to their purpose and get away with it. Bad playwrights more often than not call attention to this manipulation to an audience as simply unbelievable. In *Hamlet* Shakespeare piles coincidence upon coincidence to the point of absurdity; careful analyzation reveals that the plot is nothing more than a series of improbabilities where time has been made to serve the playwright's narration. The first chore of any interpreter of a play, therefore, is to analyze the entire text into easily comprehended outlines that show the time lines that the playwright has imposed on narration.

By analyzing plays in this manner we can discern not only factual time structures but also the shape of a playwright's intention. Blanche emerges in this play as a "fly in the ointment" of Stanley's slovenly comfortable life (one reviewer of the play also called her "a moth that, attracted to the strong flame of Stanley, is destroyed by it"); at any cost she must be removed from it. The time structure of any Tennessee Williams play needs careful attention; often it is the passage of time as well as what happens to people and relationships that underlies his concern. Of the many plays Williams wrote, this play along with *Summer and Smoke* and *The Glass Menagerie* are in particular *time* obsessed. Williams is not, of course, the only playwright who was *time obsessed*. Let us briefly examine two other plays in which the playwright uses time frames for dramatic purposes: *The Cherry Orchard* and *Long Day's Journey into Night*. *The Cherry Orchard*, is customarily considered typically naturalistic in that it purports to show how Russians lived during the last years of the nineteenth century and the first years of the twentieth. (This approach to Chekhov is primarily due to Constantin Stanislavski. We know that Chekhov himself dissented from Stanislaviski's insistence that the theater should reflect directly life as perceived outside the theater.) It is now clear to us that the plays of Chekhov while set in certain places at certain times are not literal pictures of Russia dramatic snapshots made to *remind* us of what some people looked like a century ago. When we examine the way in which Stanislavsky produced these plays, we find indelible marks of a strong director that demonstrate how lasting a particular interpreter's point of view can be. Subsequent perceptions of a play's text often are distorted by such directors. By approaching Chekhov's plays *only* through the eyes of Stanislavsky, however, we could easily miss important elements of the playwright's own intention as to how the text should be put on the stage. In the case of *The Cherry Orchard* we would certainly miss the true nature of the time frame that Chekhov gave the play. Ostensibly, the play is nothing more than four scenes placed in a rough chronological order all of which transpire during a brief summer stay at a Russian country house. In the text these times are listed thus:

Act 1 – Spring: nursery; early morning

Act 2 – Early summer: sunset to evening

Act 3 – Late summer: evening to late night

Act 4 – Fall: early morning

The selection of time periods appears casual; they follow a simple chronological order: the characters arrive in the spring, they live quiet uneventful lives for a few months, and then, in the fall, they leave their summer home to return to their city homes. Two things make this visit memorable, however: (1) this is the *last* time they will come to this particular place, and (2) the unproductive cherry orchard – the playwright's symbol for the privileged Russian gentry will be cut down to allow for twentieth-century progress. This is the outward pattern of the play. Chekhov's hidden plan, however, shows an entire period of time a span of many months-cast in the time frame *of a single day*. Moreover, he takes great care that each of the four acts is placed squarely within its proper quarter of the day. What he does in this play is impose on the larger seasonal cycle the diurnal pattern of a day. In adopting this hidden time frame, Chekhov gives us both a precise picture showing how these people spent the time during the period of residency and a symbolic set of images showing how an old way of life is passing. The time structure of this play provides ample opportunity for an audience—during the span of an evening's performance—to examine in minute detail the lives of a doomed class of people. Although audiences sitting in the theater are not consciously aware how their attention is manipulated, the sense of an age and a class of people passing into oblivion is communicated. Whether or not Chekhov's method is calculated or intuitive--it probably includes elements of both—is of little importance to an interpreter. Manipulation of time stretching or collapsing it—is integral to the playwright's purpose, an important part of the playwright's method. In *Long Day's Journey into Night*, by Eugene O'Neill, the reverse of what we see in Chekhov's play takes place.

We do not know if the title for this play came quickly to O'Neill, or if he selected it after long deliberation. What we do know is that it possesses a dual meaning for O'Neill. Unlike Chekhov's *Cherry Orchard*, the time period of this play is limited to one particular day in O'Neill's life; the action begins shortly after sunrise, progresses from afternoon into evening, ending at the threshold of a new day. The hidden time frame for this play is not one day but several months, roughly comparable, perhaps, to the season in Chekhov's play. Although we must give careful attention to the implications of the title, we should not accept the title at face value. Although the action of the play ostensibly transpires in a single day, the substance of the play is a distillation of as much as half a year in "real" time.

The title— Long Day's Journey into Night—is at once ironic and chillingly appropriate. O'Neill wrote this play many years after he lived the events it portrays. The episodes of many months—his mother's return to drug dependency, his father's parsimonious refusal to provide adequate medical aid for him or his mother, his brother's increasing inability to extend support or guidance, his own increasingly serious tubercular condition, events that in actuality took months to experience—precipitate into one torturously long day. The play begins in a bright early morning light, but as the play progresses from act to act, Edmund's world begins to darken both figuratively as well as literally. At the end of the play, his mother lapses back into a world of the past, his brother retreats from his own unsatisfactory world into an alcoholic stupor, while their penurious father's only real concern is to save money on the electric bill by turning off all but the smallest of lights in the room. All sit alone in the dark room, the same room that had been filled with light at the beginning of the play. To strengthen his time frame, O'Neill ties specific features of day and night to the conceptual background of the play: light as it progresses from morning into night—to the inexorable spiritual darkening of his own life. We do not know exactly what goes through the mind of Edmund in the final moments of the play; O'Neill gives him no words to tell us directly. We can surmise that this is the lowest point in his life, the moment when he realizes that no guidance—no light—will come from those closest to him; that if there is to be any light by which to find a way, it must come from within himself. Those who knew O'Neill in later years spoke of his eye's unusual brilliance. "It was as if," as one friend said, "he had within him a fire that he only allowed to show through his eyes."Understanding the ordinary nature of time is at best perplexing; when we encounter a playwright's personally constructed version of it, the confusion can be confounded. An important part of the scenographer's task is to understand (1) the nature of the time frame required and (2) how the a scenographic design can reflect that scheme on stage. Here are three general principles I find useful in discussion of a text with others while working on a common project:

1. On the stage *time* is both a *temporal framework* and a *dramatic blueprint* for the action of the play. Always discuss this framework with others.
2. A play begins at the *latest possible moment* and ends at the *earliest possible point.* Determine what these moments are and why they are chosen.
3. *Diurnal rhythms* and *seasonal patterns* are clearly linked to dramatic purpose: the key to a play lies in the *time frame* established. Make an exact calendar of the play's specific

chronology and annotate specific time frames that compose it.

Just as the passage of time is reflected in the change we see around us, the nature of time for a particular production must be reflected in the scenographic design. Time although invisible in most ways—can, when necessary, be seen on the stage. A significant part of a scenographer's job is to understand fully how the playwright regards time and to visually aid an audience's perception of it on the stage. The key to a play's meaning often lies in understanding precisely the various ways time is treated in it.

Historical Accuracy and Conscious Anachronism

In the late nineteenth century there was an intense desire in the theater to dress the stage and actor with settings and costumes as correct in period detail as was possible to determine from research. To our eye, the results of this activity, if we accept the visual materials that have come down to us as representative, have a certain quaint but essentially moribund charm. Part of this feeling can be explained by the time lapse between then and now; styles and customs of the past have always seemed slightly humorous. Yet much of the strangeness associated with these settings and costumes stems from a lack of understanding on the part of the scenographers of the period that accuracy of detail alone does not, cannot in fact, ensure that the intangible spirit of the original will automatically be recreated in the reproduction. All too often, when we study a costumed actor (and we have had photographs of actors for over a hundred years) what we see is a real person in a mode of dress he did not ordinarily affect, not a believable character wearing appropriate clothes; what he was *not* is more evident than what he was supposed to be. The same relationship (or lack of it) doubtlessly held true for the actor's involvement with his scenic environment. Even though the theater has developed in many directions since then, the desire to be *real* and accurate is stiff a dominant attitude in production today. It is unfortunate that we unquestioningly accept accuracy as a true test of theatrical accomplishment; this attitude is slowly changing, but it is apparently too deeply embedded in both producers and audience to disappear quickly or altogether.

Many student scenographers follow a fairly consistent pattern of development in regard to the problem of historical accuracy in design. There is at first an almost total disregard of any research at all. This cavalier approach is often replaced (after is is discovered that research need not be an unavoidable chore when inspiration fails) by an intense insistence on complete accuracy. There is a third period-which engenders an attitude that comes only with maturity and experience—that can only be described as one where the scenographer allows himself to be consciously anachronistic: to combine periods or use a detail from one period out of its time. The reasons for doing this cannot be completely or logically explained; it is a practice, however, that many scenographers follow. Peter Brook, the eminent English director who often either works very closely with a scenographer or designs his productions himself, has said this on the subject in his book, *The Empty Space*:

One of the pioneer figures in the movement towards a renewed Shakespeare was William Poel. An actress once told me that she had worked with Poel in a production of Much Ado about Nothing that was presented some fifty years ago for one night in some gloomy London Hall. She said that at the first rehearsal Poel arrived with a case full of scraps out of which he brought odd photographs, drawings, pictures tom out of magazines. "That's you," he said, giving her a picture of a debutante at the Royal Garden Party. To someone else it was a knight in armour, a Gainsborough portrait or else just a hat. In all simplicity, he was expressing the way he saw the play when he read it—directly, as a child does—not as a grownup monitoring himself with notions of history and period. My friend told me that the total pre-pop-art mixture had an extraordinary homogeneity. I am sure of it. Poel was a great innovator and he dearly saw that consistency had no relation to real Shakespearian style. I once did a production of Love's Labour's Lost where I dressed the character called Constable Dull as a Victorian policeman because his name at once conjured up the typical figure of the London bobby. For other reasons the rest of the characters were dressed in Watteau-eighteenth-century clothes but no one was conscious of an anachronism. A long time ago I saw a production of The Taming of the Shrew where all the actors dressed themselves exactly the way they saw the characters—I still remember a cowboy, and a fat character busting the buttons of a pageboy's uniform—and that it was far and away the most satisfying rendering of this play I have seen.

This third period can only be reached by going through the second (and few scenographers ever completely fall out of love with the past and the desire to render it faithfully on a stage). Let us assume, then, that the student scenographer is currently approaching, or is in the second phase of, this development, that he has learned research can be an engrossing activity as well as a necessary part of his work. He will, almost certainly, find that many plays that demand extensive research quite frequently contain puzzling questions seemingly with no logical solutions. For a moment, therefore, let us examine one such question that quite possibly might arise from a study of the play Hamlet.

Suppose that a director and scenographer agreed to produce Hamlet as much in period as possible; that is, as close as possible to the time when the story was intended to occur. If the play were Julius Caesar, the problem would not be too difficult; the facts and dates for the original story are well documented. Hamlet, however, is a very different case; we know a great deal less about who Hamlet really was (if he existed at all) and about the period in which he was supposed to have lived. Shakespeare probably was not too certain about these facts himself. Still, if we desire to be "historically correct," we must at least attempt to obtain as much information as possible from examination of the internal evidence of the play before starting our search for external material. In other words, what did Shakespeare himself know and how much has he told us in the play?

E. W. Godwin (the father of Gordon Craig) published an article in the British journal the *Architect*, called "The Architecture and Costume of Shakespeare's Plays." In this essay he attempts to determine the historically correct period in which this play, Hamlet, should be set; the date around which he centers his research is about 1012. How did he arrive at this explicit time? He uses as his prime clue a reference made by Claudius in act 3, scene 1, to the "neglected tribute" that England owes the then more powerful Denmark. Following his research, Godwin notes that the last time England was under such an obligation to Denmark was about the first decade of the eleventh century. He believes, therefore, that this is the right and proper time to set the action of the play, the scenery and costumes to be designed accordingly. Having once made this decision, he then proceeds to provide a highly detailed analysis of the locales needed, descriptions of the architectural features of the period (along with information concerning building materials and finishing techniques), and most specific of all, a minutely detailed account of the dress of the time. The primary source for his findings was, according to him, a manuscript now in the Bodleian Library, that contained many illuminations showing contemporary scenes. It is difficult to quarrel with the facts as Godwin presents them; his research is thorough and carefully documented. But does this settle the question of when and how the play would be set if one wants to be completely "accurate"? For a number of reasons the answer must be no.

If one assumes that Shakespeare must have known something of the past history of England and Denmark in order to include such a fact as "neglected tribute," why not then accept the contention that what he said is what he meant, that he wanted the play to be considered as taking place in the time period to which the reference alludes? And if we do give Shakespeare the benefit of the doubt for knowing what he is writing about, there seems to be no reason for not accepting Godwin's research as not only historically correct but also right and, consequently, the way the play should be set. Yet in the same play that gave this information there are other remarks that shed doubt on the correctness of this decision. In the second scene of the first act, this passage occurs:

KING: For your intent In going back to school in Wittenberg, It is most retrograde to our desire: And we beseech you, bend you to remain Here, in the cheer and comfort of our eye, Our chiefest courtier, cousin, and our son.

QUEEN: Let not they mother lose her prayers, Hamlet; I pray thee, stay with us; go not to Wittenberg.

Surely Godwin read this passage. And it could also be assumed that he must have been aware of the fact—since his reasoning for the chosen time of the play's action was based on a much more obscure piece of knowledge—that the action could also be dated, using this reference as proof, no earlier than 1502, the year Wittenberg University was founded. Nor would it be reasonable to assume that Shakespeare thought that that university had been in existence for five hundred years.

What do these contradictory "facts" tell us? Karl Elze, the nineteenth-century German critic thinks that Shakespeare's reason for using Wittenberg as Hamlet's school was that "Shakespeare had to send the *Dane* Hamlet to some northern university, and probably none other was so well known to him or to his audience as Wittenberg." In other words, the decision to use this particular school was more an expedient measure than anything else, not a deeply considered point of reference; certainly it does, however, indicate to us that Shakespeare considered Hamlet a Renaissance figure rather than a medieval one. The play fits much more the sixteenth century than it does the eleventh in spite of the fact that the legend has its roots in the latter. Godwin probably was aware of the possibilities but chose to ignore them in order to satisfy his desire to be "historically accurate." This same problem will face the scenographer of today many times during his career.

In the cinema version of Camelot, all those involved in the production knew that they were working with a legend that supposedly took place before the sixth century C.E. Nevertheless, *they consciously used design elements that spanned a time period of more than nine hundred years.* One complete scene, for instance (the "Lusty Month of May" song and dance sequence), took its entire visual motivation—setting, costume, atmosphere from Botticelli *Primavera,* a painting created in or around 1477. The scenographer often uses an anachronistic detail (or as in this case, a whole series of details) not through ignorance but from the need to reinforce a theme or bridge a gap in understanding that may be caused by differences in time.

Interpretation of a play is rarely in the hands of the scenographer alone, nor are even all the visual aspects of the production. While he has the prime responsibility for the way it appears to an audience, his decisions are almost always the product of more than one mind, more than the reflection of a single artistic sensibility. Jan Kott sums up the problem that interpretation precipitates when the members of a production ask themselves the question, "How are we going to set this play, in what style and period?"

Hamlet cannot be played simply. This may be the reason why it is so tempting to producers and actors. Many generations have seen their own reflections in the play. The genius of Hamlet consists, perhaps, in the fact that the play can serve as a mirror. An ideal Hamlet would be one most true to Shakespeare and most modern at the same time. Is this possible? I do not know. But we can only appraise any Shakespearean production by asking how much there is of Shakespeare in it, and how much of us.

What I have in mind is not a forced topicality, a Hamlet that would be set in a cellar of young existentialists. Hamlet has been performed, for that matter, in evening dress and in circus tights; in medieval armour and in Renaissance costume. Costumes do not matter. What matters is that through Shakespeare's text we ought to get at our modern experience, anxiety and sensibility.

There are many subjects in Hamlet. There is politics, force opposed to morality; there is discussion of the divergence between theory and practice, of the ultimate purpose of life; there is tragedy of love, as well as family drama; political, eschatological and metaphysical problems are considered. There is everything you want, including deep psychological analysis, a bloody story, a duel, and general slaughter. One can select at will. But one must know what one selects, and why.

But one must know what one selects, and why. This could very well become the touchstone of the scenographer's philosophy of interpretation.

The past cannot be re-created, only evoked. If there is one thing to be learned from the Belasco experiments that finally made visual authenticity the only standard in scenography, it is that following this practice although few do today-almost always produces the opposite effect desired; the minuteness of detail, out of context as it must always be in the theater, puts the attention of the audience in the wrong place—on the setting, not the performer seen within it. What is more, it provokes the audience into a situation detrimental to the total production: the more "real" the setting, the more intense the desire on the part of this audience to discover its secret, that is, seek out the unreality they know is there. Given time they will; this cannot be done, however, except at the expense of the actor and the play.

It is important in our definition of research that we do not make the limits too narrow; it is possible that not everything needed for a design will be found in a library (or at least not always where one would think to look). Attitudes toward interpretation are constantly changing and with those changes come changing production demands. The ability to conduct patterns of research that will reveal significant features of other cultures or other ages is an important skill for the scenographer to perfect; but it is not the only kind of research that will be expected in the modern theater. Many scenographers, often at the request of a director, find themselves exploring images, objects, and materials for plays that cannot be located in a precise culture, assigned to an exact historical period, or, for that matter, be found in any place except on the stage of a theater. All of Samuel Becketts' plays, for instance, evade traditional approaches to research; and it is an integral part of most of his plays that they exist in a time frame that has no relationship to that which exists outside the theater. Just where does one begin to research Endgame or Krapp's Last Tape or Waiting for Godot? This is clearly one of the thorniest problems any scenographer ever has to face, since plays like Beckett's are not the only ones to raise this question.

One of the most significant reforms in theater production during the last century was the abolishment of the unauthenticated approach to design of setting and costume; with the advent of the Duke of Saxe-Meiningen company and the establishment of Wagner's Bayreuth Festival Playhouse, theater artists were enjoined to become more accurate in their presentation of historical detail on the stage. And while the results of their work look quaintly unnatural to our eyes today, there was a noticeable improvement when a more unified approach to production was adopted. Star performers no longer went unchallenged when they wore selections that they fancied from their own wardrobes, but which were often inappropriate to the style or atmosphere of the text or the conceptions of the producers; current modes of dress, often mixed with inaccurately crude approximations of authentic costume styles, were no longer the standard practice as it had been in the earlier part of the nineteenth century and during the whole of the eighteenth. This was also true for settings and properties; and while the traditional painted wing-and-drop setting remained the standard mode of practice in some forms of theater — opera and ballet in particular — until well into the present century, there was a steady movement from the middle of the nineteenth century on toward three-dimensional form rather than painted simulation.

The insistence on historical accuracy became, in time, as deadly as its disregard had been earlier; the cavalierly romantic attitudes toward exactitude of historical detail became by equally moribund philosophy. But the reason is easier to see in retrospect than at the time; the primary mistake the scenographers of the late nineteenth century made was to omit from their thinking two very important qualifying elements. First, they copied exact detail with little regard for understanding the period from which these details were taken (their only objective being to copy the detail without attempting to understand the culture from which they were extracted). And second, there was no real link between the desire to be historically exact and the individual qualities of a particular text; if, for instance, the period of *Macbeth* was difficult to determine (as it still is), merely find some approximately plausible period in which it can be set and then duplicate the details from that time. Any other text whose action was set in roughly the same time frame, it was accepted, could use the same costumes and scenery. There was little thought given to unique atmospheric qualities that each text possessed *independent* of its historical period.

The vision of those who would be historically correct and *only* historically correct was, in a word, too *narrow*. No matter how exact a copy is placed on the stage, not to have an understanding of its particular place in the context of the singular text is to preclude its assimilation into a unique total work.

Historical accuracy still has a usefulness in the modern theater; there are many instances when a strictly historical approach to a production is essentially the correct one. But there has been a growing understanding during the past fifty years that a text of a theatrical work has subjective requirements that cannot be satisfied by simple reproduction of period detail; verisimilitude is not dependent on literal copying of source materials alone. The evocation of the past depends more on the sensitive use of the selective eye than on simple photographic copying of details from the past. Conscious anachronism is most often employed in a production to give a sharper edge to a director's or scenographer's vision as to what is presently important in a text whose past meanings have been blunted through time. Further, it often helps a modernday audience form a more understandable link with the past than do slavishly accurate copies of it. This is the crux of creative research. As Lawrence Kubie points out: "By the creative process we mean the capacity to find new and unexpected connections, to voyage freely over the seas, to happen on America as we seek new routes to India, to find new relationships in time and space, and thus new meanings."

The theater, while it can bring to us an accurate vision of past times, is not simply an institution that seeks to give animation to museum exhibitions. Although it is not possible to predict attitudes of the future or to state just how materials of the past will be used in future productions, what undoubtedly will be part of any attitude is the scenographer's increasing use of hybrid forms of research. This is not as difficult to understand as it might first appear. Let me explain by way of a few striking examples I have seen during the past three decades (although these are by far not the only examples which could be cited).

Tyrone Guthrie Theater season, two of the plays presented were Congreve's Way of the World and Shakespeare Richard the Third. The scenographer of the Congreve play designed the production strictly in period: not only were the costumes faultlessly correct in cut, material, color, and detail, they were also constructed in the same manner as they would had they been sewn in the time of the play's writing. No convenience was allowed the actor who had to make a speedy costume change; every button had to be undone—no Velcro, not a zipper on any costume. Richard the Third, on the other hand, gave the impression of historical accuracy but was conceived with a totally different concept in mind. Asked what this concept was, the scenographer replied, "Bugs. Bugs, beetles, scurrying, iridescent, shiney, hardshelled insects." As a concomitant feature of this concept, the director had seen the particular atmosphere of this play as that which one might find in a highly volatile police state: where power shifted from moment to moment, and where no one was untainted by the poisonous politics of the time. The two concepts worked well together: the world of this Richard the Third was a dangerous place, and its inhabitants had the worst features of the insect world. In order to best create this world it was decided to use materials from our own modern world: vinyls, materials that changed color as they shifted in the light, iridescent taffetas, plastics, metallic finishes-none of which existed during Richard the Third's period.

Much of the scenographer's work, as even the most cursory glance will reveal, depends upon using existing images or elements from existing images; many scenographic designs are "lifted" in part or totally from sources complete in themselves. But even when the source material is rich in suggestion, the scenographer often experiences an inability to choose what seems to be the right image or element to use. In most instances this impasse (or block, to use a more current word) is broken by the need to make a decision, and the result of this selection is that it is often arbitrary. In my own experience, I have found that decisions are easier to make when confronted with myriad possibilities, if I have formed in my mind a clear view of how the characters of the text look. That is, I cannot easily visualize an environment empty of people, and I cannot visualize people simply as store-window mannequins. They must have an actuality to their appearance and actions. (I have discussed this problem with many directors who also voice something of the same concern: they tell me that it is not possible to we an action or series of actions without having a particular person with specific characteristics in their mind's eye; not a few directors have confessed that in the earliest stages of studying a text they "cast" the play with strong well-known personalities and not always from the performing arts. I find this practice helpful to my own work and often make the "casting" of the text part of the research problem.)

Now, this may seem, on the face of it, a needless chore for the scenographer to undertake; after all, he is not concerned with the selection of the performers who will enact the roles, nor in most instances, will he be given the task of designing the costumes those performers will wear. But the practice I am suggesting here is primarily concerned not with individual actors, makeup, or costume but with a better understanding of the total production and, perhaps more important than that, a more complete, exact image albeit an imaginary one of the playwright's world, and that is the work of the scenographer. How those characters appear, and more importantly, how they use what he creates are very much germain to his function. The ability to see the characters who will inhabit that yetto-be production often aids in the determination of that world; when visual possibilities are numerous it makes the selection process less arbitrary. In some instances, I have found it necessary to go a step further than just imagining how a character looks; there have been occasions when it became necessary to make this information visible. Let me cite an example as to how this principle works.

While working on a production of Krapp's Last Tape, I found myself unable to "see" the place where he lived. (Beckett does not, after all, give much help; clues as to the physical appearance of Krapp's room are few; and the usual pattern of external research just does not work for his plays. Simple though the requirements of this play are, it is precisely this kind of simplicity that often gives the scenographer the most difficulty: there is no leeway for error.) It seemed to me that the best way to address my problem was to become better acquainted with the single character living in the place I needed to design. To this end, I began a series of small, quickly drawn character sketches—in much the same way a novelist might seek out a fuller knowledge of a character by seeking to understand his physical background. Part of the purpose of this activity was to let the pen "have its own way," as Toulouse-Lautrec once described his own style of drawing, and in so doing bring into my search the blocked levels of my mind. Out of many attempts, the figure of Krapp began to emerge. Finally, I had before me an image of the person I was seeking. Having this physical image directly before me provided a sharper focus. I now found it easier not only to imagine the person of Krapp but to visualize the actions he performed as required by the text. As I watched his actions I also began to find it less difficult to visualize the space he moved through and the objects he touched as he spoke the random words and snatches of thought that Beckett sparingly supplied him. What had formerly been a hazy and formless impression began to take on the sharpness of an actual objective image. The physical qualities of Krapp himself began to inform those things he lived with and used. And I began to "know" what colors, forms, and textures were necessary to Beckett's vision. Most important of all, I found that it became easier to discuss my views of Krapp's world with a sharpness and clarity that had been totally missing from my earlier conferences. But, this did not greatly surprise me because I now *knew* Krapp, the man, better, and not merely knew *about* him. He was a recognizable figure to me; I was able to say to myself, "Knowing this person has also told me something about the place where he would live."

The process I have been describing may seem to be the singularly idiosyncratic method of an individual scenographer. But I believe it to be a more widespread means of approaching early stages of research than might at first appear. To cite another example that indicates that this practice forms at least part of other scenographer's working methods, let me quote the answer of the cinema designer Harry Homer to this question:

Question: What are your first steps as a production designer on a film?

Horner: I find that the first things that I become interested in are the characters and the relationship of the characters. Now the characters, naturally, are tied to a period – a Victorian group of people will act differently toward each other than a group of people who live in our own century. I study the script, and sometimes it takes a terribly long time, with frequent readings, because nothing happens – one has no vision. It is interesting that when you familiarize yourself with a world very thoroughly, you find yourself ultimately not copying the research, but inventing, becoming a person of that period. Many designers fall into a trap of going to the research department and asking, "What might a Gothic window in a restaurant look like?" They take the window from one book and the door from another book, put them together, and they think it looks Victorian. But when you are really familiar with a world, you suddenly find that you don't need any more to copy because you become a period person.

Some scenographers take this approach to even greater lengths; Andre Acquart, the noted French scenographer, says this concerning those crucial first encounters with a text: "In my work, I let myself be guided above all by intuition. *I try to imagine the acting of all the players, all their movements*. I create a setting which is intended to be an ideal acting machine, a sculpture of the scenic space, and I try to bring the setting to life".

I would not suggest that the process I have been discussing – and have demonstrated in the specific case of Krapp's Last Tape – is one which could always be followed to the extent given here; there is simply not enough time to undertake such a detailed portrait study of every character in every text. (Nor does every character or every text deserve such treatment.) But the kind of thinking underlying this demonstration is important to grasp. This is especially true during the formative stages of a scenographer's education. Even when actual sketches of characters are not attempted, there should be a strong endeavor to visualize their physical characteristics along with their actions. The process is not unlike the development of directorial skills: it is imperative that students of directing master the techniques of preblocking action on paper, making their movement intentions clear by diagrams charting that movement. This is a necessary discipline that makes the young director aware of the uses and patterns of movement required by the interpretation of a text; it is entirely beside the point that many directors subsequently arrive at a time in their careers when they no longer preblock productions on paper but approach their work directly in the rehearsal period without first writing out their thoughts. The jettisoning of previous activities is natural in the growth of the professional artist; this same kind of growth could be discovered in that of the scenographer: he too might very well cease to make actual drawings of images that occur to him in the manner that we have been discussing. But it is very important to understand that this advanced stage cannot be reached *without having done the physical work* during an earlier period. The point that must be understood is that only by a thoughtful recording of actions can the director come to the point where he need not preblock, and only through a similar period of time can the scenographer abandon the laborious activity suggested here. The apprenticeship of all artists requires disciplines and practices that, when the art is mastered can be altered or discontinued. A pianist spends untold hours practicing scales; but no one would attend a performance that only included the playing of scales, no matter how expertly played. Preblocking action on paper is, as it were, a form of playing scales for the director; visualization of a text's characters in sketches, I would also suggest, is also a form of playing scales for the scenographer—and a valuable one at that. Practically all artistic education consists of mastering exercises which, when mastery is attained, are no longer necessary except in the imagination.

One last point concerning the visualization of the characters in a text: it would be a grave mistake to limit ourselves to those images that are obtained only from our own imaginations, which are products of our own drawing skills. Our searches should also include the work of other artists. There have been many instances in the past when my own imagined vision of a character was both sharpened and extended by what I found, not by what I drew. One last brief example should illustrate this point.

In Peter Weiss Persecution and Assassination of Marat under the Direction of the Marquis de Sade, there is a demented abbot who at one point in the play must act out the passion of Christ. The character in the play is not a major role; his "scene" — like that of the apothecary's in Romeo and Juliet — is a short one. Nevertheless, brief though his appearance is, the impact of that appearance must be strong and immediate. This character is not explained so much as he is allowed to be seen; his physical appearance must carry with it the information the audience needs to know about him. Moreover, this information must be instantaneously projected to an audience. As the scenographer in charge of all elements of this production — setting, costume, lighting, makeup — my main problem was to make each of the characters in this production a self-contained piece of information. (While this might be true for most productions, in works such as Marat/Sade, the problem is more critical: in most texts characters are either explained or prepared for by other characters, or the character has the opportunity to reveal himself more slowly to an audience; for example, by the time a reading of Hamlet is finished, an extremely dear picture of Hamlet emerges.) The problem presented itself in this way: *How can I show a man suffering from a particular form of insanity, in this case a messianic delusion, without resorting to the stereotyped images of insanity so often seen on the stage?* The power of this play greatly depends on performers who do not "act crazy"; and the particular requirements of this text demanded that almost all of the characters in it are disturbed by recognizable forms of insanity. During the rehearsal period of the Royal Shakespeare Company's production of Marat/Sade, Peter Brook-the director — took members of the play's cast to English asylums for the insane to observe the effects of specific mental illnesses on those who suffered from them. While this form of research is necessary, it may not provide all the information needed to produce the play. Let me give an example from my own experience with this play to illustrate my point.

It is an action photograph taken during the first act of Marat/Sade. In this image we see the moment when the torment of the bishop is greatest; his face is not, however, the beneficent one we are accustomed to seeing in romantic representations of Christ's suffering. What we see here is a vision of a man driven to desperation by his madness. While the creation of this face may seem a task for the performer alone, in this instance his work was aided by the research of the scenographer.

This is, of course, a singular example which cuts across many lines--makeup, costume, acting, direction, not to mention art history. What this instance clearly points out to us, however, is that scenographic research rarely stops at some arbitrary point or is bounded by strict categorical lines; the research we must do in the theater often pervades a whole spectrum of needs and possibilities.

These examples, admittedly, may seem far afield of the usual methods and materials of scenographic research. But there must always be in our investigations the allowance for pursuit of information that does not conform to strict lines of inquiry; creative research must be an activity that is sufficiently open enough to explore the unusual, to capitalize on the unforeseen. Nor should we ever be ashamed to give full credit to the accidental insight that changes (and also charges) our conscious mind and stimulates our imagination. New directions are very often begun when the prepared mind of the artist clashes with unsought materials; the use of Ensor's work in Marat/Sade began with just such an accidental encounter. To progress in any aspect of theatrical art we must allow curiosity a high place in our working procedure and chance a proper respect. Albert Einstein states the case well when he tells us that "the most beautiful experience we can have is the mysterious. It is the fundamental emotion that stands at the cradle of true art and true science." Creative research should always retain, in the bustle of the practical working theater, an element of the mysterious.

This may seem a highly speculative task for the scenographer whose workaday world depends on meeting deadlines and delivering predictable results; but he must come to realize that a significant part of his profession lies specifically in those areas that must be approached intuitively as well as understood objectively. Inanimate objects no longer used, representations of life long since vanished, people dead for perhaps thousands of years, must not only be sought out from the cases of museums and from pages of historical account, they must, in the mind of the scenographer, be restored to a form of life; for much of the past can only speak to us if it is seen in the context in which it existed. This is not as difficult or mystical a task as it might at first sound. There is a kind of understanding that could be best called *time vision* and that can be summoned up by the inquisitive and intuitive mind. The type of information we speak of here, and which must be part of the scenographer's working methods, is a direct result of a certain attitude toward research of the past. Time vision is not only a possibility that the scenographic artist must seek out but is a responsibility that he cannot evade. It is, moreover, very much a part of that practical world of production.

The world scenographers seek to find through their research must never be a dead or sterile piece; as on Robinson Crusoe's island beach, of all the things found there, the greatest interest lies in the human footprint we finally detect. Let us leave this subject with the observations of the present-day critic Donal Henahan whose firm grasp on the issues just studied are evident.

During the reign of Louis XIV, about two centuries before Wagner proclaimed his doctrine of Gesamtkunstwerk, the blending of the arts into a united experience was already an esthetic ideal, honored in daily practice. It was not only an attractive theory but a way of life for composers, choreographers and designers. What is less commonly appreciated is that even playwrights followed the gleam, none more successfully than Molière.

In Paris last month I attended the premiere of An Arts Florissants production of Molière last play, "Le Malade Imaginaire," that was a revelation in many ways. For one thing, it was strange to attend a Molière comedy in the company of a Parisian audience that seemed intent on muffling its laughter. Possibly no one wished to have anyone else think they were hearing the classic lines for the first time.

Still, I came away not only delighted but impressed by as ambitious and successful a staging of an old work as I have ever experienced. Although it is generally understood nowadays that French Baroque operas were mounted as grand spectacles in which musk, words, dance, costumes, scenery and lighting were meant to function in close partnership, until recent years only a few university or dilettante groups have attempted to produce Molière's plays in a historically proper style. But William Christle, the American scholar who directs Les Arts Florissants, staged "Le Malade Imaginaire" at the elegant Châtelet theater as the lavish comedie-ballet that is was intended to be, in the original version of 1673.

The play, by contrast, made do with the few props suggested by Molière. The actors, led by Jean Dautremay as the miserable hypochondriac Argan, needed little help to make the play's sharply witty points, but there prose was occasionally augmented-by a raucous commedia dell'arte interlude.

Perhaps the most remarkable thing about the evening was the air of vitality it radiated. *Missing, though not at all missed, was the faint odor of formaldehyde that arises from many supposedly authentic but in fact merely dead quaint productions of old works. Here, one had the feeling of encountering a living work, not a well-preserved corpse.* There was, too, the appeal of a poignant subtext, impossible to ignore in any performance of "Le Malade Imaginaire": Molière, who was himself snidely rumored to be a hypochondriac by his enemies, died shortly after the first performance, in which he took the role of Argan.

Scenographer's Personal Research Sources

Most scenographers are or soon become-avid collectors of books, images, and printed materials. This is understandable since the mature scenographer uses these materials daily as factual verification as well as sources of inspiration. Imagination an indisputable part of any art—has a voracious appetite. It needs constant feeding. As a result, many scenographers develop early a craving to collect visual materials, building over time large personal collections.

An argument can be made for using large public collections of visual materials. Many larger cities have libraries that house these collections. In many instances such a resource proves necessary to the scenographer, since few can compete with the scope or size of collections found there. The personal library, however, is more than privately owned works. Items personally collected over time—images, lists of materials, photographic slides, technical specifications, etc., in addition to books become an extension of the individual artist's personal vision. In many ways a personal collection determines the direction of a career. Such collections invariably reveal clues to ingrained thoughts and emotions of the artist; they function as a sort or exterior manifestation of the individual artist's subconscious mind. The propensity to collect certain kinds of works is a specific way by which the artist can chart inner directions. One of the twentieth century's most practical politicians—Winston Churchill—gives us a practical reason for a personal library:

> *"What shall I do with all my books?" was the question; and the answer, "Read them." But if you cannot read them, at any rate handle them and, as it were, fondle them. Peer into them. Let them fall open where they will. Read on from the first sentence that arrests the eye. Then turn to another. Make a voyage of discovery, taking soundings of uncharted seas. Set them back on their shelves with your own hands. Arrange them on your own plan, so that if you do not know what is in them you at least know where they are. If they cannot be your friends, let them at any rate be your acquaintances. If they cannot enter the circle of your life, do not deny them at least a nod of recognition.*

Make a voyage of discovery, taking soundings of uncharted seas. No better advice, no better reason exists for the active making of a personal library. Moreover, the scenographer today is more fortunate than those who started even twenty years ago. The printing of low and medium-priced paperback art books has grown tremendously during this time. Concurrently, a phenomenal interest in printing high-quality visual materials has taken place. Pictorial records of private and public buildings, detailed studies of architecture, furniture, and the like, are being brought to a wider public in a diversity unparalled in printing history. A helpful development—especially to the scenographer—is the inclusion of images that elucidate the social and economic reasons underlying the time frames of a certain historical period or style. Books such as *Private Life in the Fifteenth Century* (a collection of letters and documents of a specific family living during the period) has numerous illustrations interwoven with verbal commentary of the text. These books *show* history as well as explain it words. Such works demonstrate clearly how different countries in different ages reacted to, or produced variations on, prevalent styles of art and architecture. Many of these books are expensive. Still, the scenographer should consider them wise investments. While the acquisition of books—even the reasonably priced ones—is always expensive, the practice of buying books on a regular basis is ultimately the least costly way to acquire a working library. (If the scenographer buys a resource work to use in a specific project, that expense, as with other art supplies, is tax deductible.) Personal libraries are positive means by which artists continue to grow in imagination and productivity.

An important part of a scenographer's personal research materials is photographic images. These materials provide several functions for the artist/researcher: not only do they provide verification of facts, they often serve as inspirational points of departure for the imagination Since Jacques Mande Daguerre in 1839, the principal inventor of photography, gave us the ability to capture exact likeness by mechanical means, access to a wide variety of visual material has expanded. As Naomi Rosenblum remarks: "By the time it was announced in 1839, Western industrialized society was ready for photography. The camera's images appeared and remained viable because they filled cultural and sociological needs that were not being met by pictures created by hand. The photograph was the ultimate response to a social and cultural appetite for a more accurate and real-looking representation of reality, a need that had its origins in the Renaissance. When the idealized representation of the spiritual universe that inspired the medieval mind no longer served the purposes of increasing secular societies, their places were taken by paintings and graphic works that portrayed actuality with greater verisimilitude."

While the photograph is now the principal means by which we record productions, it is also among the most valuable resources we have in assembling visual materials during preliminary stages of our research. With the advent of an increasingly sophisticated computer technology, scenographers are now able to scan into computer graphics photographic research images that can be modified into working drawings. Use of computer programs also means that the gap between photographic technique and freehand drawing skill is rapidly diminishing.

The photograph is also of value in training scenographic artists; photographers teach us much even though their work is static, while ours deals primarily with images seen in time (a similarity that we share with the cinema, which Peter Brook pointed out previously). Behind these different basic approaches to seeing the world, there exists profound similarities, concerns and attitudes that the scenographer should attempt to understand and take advantage of.

Shortly before her death, Diane Arbus said this about her work: "I do feel I have some slight corner on something about the quality of things. I mean it's very subtle and a little embarrassing to me, but I really believe there are things which nobody would see unless I photographed them."

The photographer is frequently able to reveal things that would remain virtually hidden from us despite our visual training and sensitivity to imagery. The role of photography is an important one for the scenographer. Sadly, many students do not take advantage of important photographic documents their university or city libraries hold. Most professional scenographers realize that the photographer's work is an invaluable aid to their own. As Samuel Wagstaff, the noted collector of photography points out, "the most interesting thing in looking at photographs is not their art qualities but the ways they open us to all other aspects of life. Photography whets one's eye enormously." Let us direct our attention to a few examples that demonstrate how photographic materials can be useful in the theater research process.

Dickens Oliver Twist has had a long life in both the cinema and on the stage; there have been a number of versions done in both mediums. Dickens himself gives many evocative descriptions of the London where much of the action takes place, a city with which he was intimately familiar. Peter Ackroyd calls especial attention to that relationship when he reflects that "London created Dickens, just as Dickens created London. London entered his soul; it terrified him and it entranced him. It became the material for his fantasy and the arena for his polemic. And in the end, it was truly Dickens' London."

But what was the London Dickens actually saw? Little is left of that city to which he came as a small boy. Nor is there much left of the London he knew as the mature reigning novelist of his age; many of the buildings he knew have since been demolished; many of the buildings that now form London were not yet built. But many visual records still exist of that world, and many of them are in photographic form. These have played a significant part in the research done for those many versions of Oliver Twist. This is not to say that drawing has not also played its part in that research process; there have been some extremely valuable documents left to us from artists of the time, and they too have aided in understanding the visual aspects of Dickens's world. In point of fact, the drawings have actually helped us to better access the photographic records we have. One of the most helpful of those documents is large book printed in 1874 by Gustave Dore and Blanchard Jerrold, *London: A Pilgrimage.* This one book has probably been used as the visual record of Dickens's London by more directors and scenographers than any other single source. Although actually drawn some thirty to forty years after the time Dickens set his novels, we have come to regard the Dote-Blanchard view of London as the last word as to what the city looked like during that earlier period. Not only did David Lean base his 1949 cinematic version of Oliver Twist on the materials of this book, but so have many filmmakers since: the production designer John Box of the more recent musical version, Oliver! made extensive use of these same drawings. And what is even more surprising to find is that the settings for the German film The Threepenny Opera are veritable three-dimensional replicas of some of the plates from the book. Nor is it doubtful that directors and scenographers in the future will soon abandon this unique source of visual information. These different images not only cause us to consider carefully the distinct elements of each image but force us to consider any differences. It is obvious that the viewpoint is roughly similar in both images. It is equally obvious that Dore made changes in what he saw. What is valuable to notice here are the common features of both views. It is clear in both pictures that this area of London—just below St. Paul's Cathedral is a busy place; Ludgate Hill was at this time (and still is) a great intersections of London's various kinds of traffic. Although maps of the area provide us with an accurate location of the place, if we want to *see* what the place was like—to better understand how it *felt* to be on that particular London street during the middle of the nineteenth century.

It might be well to mention at this point the curious relationship that has grown up between the photograph and graphic work in general since the inception of photography and to show briefly how the subject matter of graphic art has developed during that period of time. Even as long ago as 1855 artists were sometimes using photographs rather than firsthand observations as a basis for drawings and paintings. Eugène Durieu took a number of photographs in 1854, which Eugène Delacroix then used the following year. Some years later Toulouse-Lautrec made numerous on-the-spot visual observations of the night haunts of *fin-de-siècle* Paris, recording the people he saw there as well as their actions. Many of these drawings were used as inspirations for later paintings. Doubtless many of his works were based on these sketches; but what few have realized is the extent to which he also used photographs in his work. It is a curious irony, therefore, to find that images of Toulouse-Lautrec have been used by directors to re-create the original things he saw: in *An American in Paris,* director and choreographer Gene Kelly used Lautrec's drawings and paintings — as well as the images of other painters of the period — as the basis for a series of dances. But directors on the stage also find that they can use these drawings as clues to explaining actions to performers. *In your dance what I want is a swoon such as that called for in the tango you have to perform. But I also want your physical attitude to project the same mocking character as I perceive in this Toulouse-Lautrec drawing.* It is a further curious result of showing this image to performers that the actual results on the stage reproduced a natural effect that the director did not consciously plan: while the performer playing Madame Rosepettle did not consciously hold her hands in a set position, the natural result is similar to the observation Toulouse-Lautrec recorded, which to some extent validates the precision of his vision.

The use of the photographic image can be of great value to those who work for the stage. While it will always aid us in verifying details of places and things we cannot easily reach or see, it can also — as in the example just cited — serve as a triggering device for our imaginations. As Van Deren Coke points out in his study *The Painter and the Photograph:* "in the nineteenth century the photograph was most frequently used as a crutch. Only a few artists expanded the potential of their work by using camera vision. In the twentieth century, due to the veritable tidal wave of photographs that appeared in magazines and family albums, the vision of the camera became unavoidable and was absorbed by the artist and the public. *This potent force became more and more recognized as a conceptual agency*".

It is not only to the painter or graphic artist to which these last words apply. Photography can act as a potent conceptual agency that triggers ideas in other artists as well: the writer being a prime example. Although there have been numerous instances where writers have indicated that their original inspirations came from graphic images — Michel de Ghelderode use of a Bruegel painting for his play Three Blind Men is a good example — some writers during the last hundred years have had their work directly influenced by subject matter that they encountered through the photographic work of their contemporaries. It can be demonstrated that the photographers and writers living at the same time and in the same place often shared, as it were, identical subject matter. (The playwright Jean Giraudoux and the photographer Brassaï had similar encounters that resulted in different outcomes. Both lived in Paris during the first half of this century, and both shared many of the same personal relationships and observed many of the same sights.

A good principle to follow when researching the visual background of the works of twentiethcentury playwrights who have written plays set in their own time is to seek out those photographers who also lived in or documented these same places during that same period of time.

Students of scenography should keep in mind from the very beginning of their training that their relationship to photographic images is not only a valuable part of their education but an important factor in their professional practice. Furthermore, their investigations of photographic images should remain a constant activity throughout their lives and not merely applied intermittently to isolated projects. As Robert Hughes said of the painter Wilhem de Kooning, "He is a fierce looker." So should all scenographers aspire to be: *fierce lookers*.

Along with photographs, other collections of loose material—clippings from magazine, brochures, and the like—are used in the research process. Most scenographers, in addition to their libraries, also maintain extensive file collections. These files are as important to their officient operation and production as is the dictionary or encyclopedia to research scholars. Since scenographers cannot purchase these collections readyassembled, as they might a set of books, these must be assembled item by item over time. Most scenographers have extensive collections of materials accumulated over many years. An additional problem to building a good system of files is that much of the materials needed has a shortlived general exposure. Magazine articles and newspaper items are here today and gone today. The explosion of transitory visual materials means that the working scenographer must possess a quick eye as well as a pair of scissors always near to hand.

A file system is the best method of keeping track of the vast amount of information that constantly presents itself. How directly these transitory visual materials are used changes greatly from production to production, from scenographer to scenographer. Individual scenographers vary widely as to how much or how little original sources are used; some are eclectic incorporating into their designs many "quotes," while others rely on a single found image. An example of a design derived from a single-source image is Susanne Lalique's setting for *Le Bourgeois Gentilhomme*. Although the structure of the room is simplified and the feeling of the room has been lightened, the resulting design owes much to an actual room in Danzig, Germany, built in the middle of the seventeenth century. Another example of a scenographic design that owes much to a particular historical resource image is the setting for the premier production of Peter Weiss's Marat/Sade. Given below is a suggested list of file folder headings. The categories should be sufficient for the beginning scenographer, although it should be expected that these categories over time will be subdivided as well as refined. Do not forget that a good file system-like a good personal library conscientiously kept and periodically revamped, will save the scenographer many hours of research away from the studio. Even the fact that the scenographer has a file system causes an increased alertness to new visual materials.Many scenographers, in addition to general files, also begin a separate file for each new production. If a file is created at the start of a project, all the information collected during the designing of the production can be kept in one place. This becomes a valuable resource for later productions of the same shows. In this file, one might expect to keep not only initial ideas, sources, and working drawing, but photos of the finished production, notes and communications with the director, reviews, and so on.

❑❑❑

4

Lighting Costumes and Costuming a Pageant

Introduction

In order to bring out the color of costumes as planned, it is necessary to include in the lighting scheme the colors which will emphasize the color scheme of the costumes. This must be done without changing the value of the light which lights the scene itself. It can be done if the footlights and overhead borders carry the three primary colors, red, yellow and blue, or orange, violet and green. The result of this use of light will be a natural light which if properly focused will not confuse the general lighting which is planned from correct sources, but will bring out each costume in its proper color value. For instance, a scene may be lighted from a window through which is introduced a flood of amber light to give the effect of sunlight. If the costumes of the players happen to be complementary colors of amber and red, the amber flood will accentuate and enhance the colors. But if the costumes should be blues, greens or violets, the entire value of their colors will be lost under the amber flood, unless somewhere there is introduced some blue or green light. This is usually done by using some footlights simply to give color or overhead lights used directly inside the proscenium frame.

If, on the other hand, the scene is lighted from within by table lamps or wall brackets, so that the predominant light will be the rose of interior illumination, it is equally necessary to use blue somewhere in the scheme in order to preserve the color of blue costumes. By the use of baby spot lights from the footlights, or from the wings, certain costumes can be still more emphasized by flooding them with their own color.

When a scene is largely lighted by pale green usually employed to simulate moonlight, the costumes should be carefully planned from colors which will not be dulled or too much changed by the green light. Blues, violets, yellows, turkey red, may be safely used. Turkey red is such a brilliant color that it will keep its value and intensity under almost any lighting. Blues are very easily affected and become gray under amber, or if there is sufficient yellow in them, they will become a greenish yellow. Violets are easily affected and are completely destroyed by an amber light, becoming an ugly brown. When a costume is made of materials which combine several colors blended in the way a gray is obtained by using the three primary colors one on top of the other, it becomes exceedingly beautiful under light combining the three primary colors, because each color brings out its own color. If a costume is colored by dyeing with graduated dyes, so that peacock green, for instance, is more blue at one end of the garment and more green at the other, it is necessary to light such a costume with two colored lights.

The usual equipment of a modern theater supplies all that is necessary to light scenes and give color to draperies. Footlights and overhead borders are usually supplied in blue, amber and white. The best theaters have borders of small spot lamps in addition to the ordinary bulb. This enables light to be focused and angled in different directions. The color of light is obtained by using gelatine in metal frames which fit in front of the lens lights, which is a technical name for spot lights. All colors can be obtained in gelatine which comes in large pieces and costs from 20 to 60 cents a sheet. In addition to footlights and borders, what is known as the portable equipment is used. This consists of open-box flood lights on stands, spot or lens lights on stands placed wherever it is desired to introduce extra lights. It is very important that all colored material for costumes be tested under the colored lights planned for a scene before actually making them up. It is impossible for the best designer to imagine accurately just how his color scheme is going to visualize until he sees it under light. The color will vary in value and intensity according to the degree of light used, the angle of the lamp and the number of lamps used in a scene. It is suggested that all colored materials for costumes be tried for effect under flood lights through the medium of every color in a spectrum. In this way, the mistakes and disappointments will be avoided.

Costuming a Pageant

Costuming a pageant is a problem all its own and in considering this problem there are three aspects. A pageant may be given indoors. It may be given out of doors, either at night under artificial lights or in the day under strong sunlight. The time and the conditions of light will influence the color and to a lesser degree the line of the costumes.

In pageantry the color should be intensified and the massing of color increased as much as possible. The color and shape of the costume is of much greater importance than the texture or any amount of detail which may be added. Costumes which consist of one or two colors are more effective than those which are made of expensive materials with many elaborate details. At a distance, the detail is lost and two or three colors in textile design, unless it is very bold in color and design, are likely to be lost. A bold stencil design on dyed muslin of the right color is more effective in most instances than a very costly brocade, and at a distance will have the effect of a brocade.

A pageant by its nature is a spectacle and is made up of massed groups rather than individual units. It is played in large auditoriums, the largest theater or out of doors where the audience is comparatively far away from the performers. Costume, therefore, must be regarded according to the viewpoint of what will carry to an audience at a distance. Line is the first point. All line must be correct, but it must be exaggerated and the silhouette must be emphasized. Detail of decoration is unnecessary but form and color are most vital. Simplicity is the most powerful way of giving variety to costuming in pageantry. The problem of giving unity and yet variety to large groups of people, costumed in the same period, presents itself as a grave difficulty on account of the danger of the scene becoming monotonous in value and color. This must be carefully considered.

Take, for example, a group of Orientals in the market place of ancient Samaria at the time of the Assyrian domination. The colors used in those days were limited to the primitive blues, reds and yellows, crudely brilliant with little variation. The line of the garment was universally flowing as to under-robe, over-robe and headdress. A large group can be made uninteresting and monotonous if the designer is not watchful. It will not do to give too much individual variety. If this is done, the value of masses is immediately lost. It is possible, however, to keep unity by carrying a basic color scheme through the entire mass, varying the decoration and the color of headdresses. The monotony of line may be broken by making a difference in the manner of draping the mantles and veils of the women and the turbans of the men.

It is valuable in costuming masses where the color scheme is not limited by historical differences to use one color in different tones throughout a group. This is especially true of symbolical pageants. Again it is often tremendously impressive to costume a great mass of people in one or two colors carrying the same type or line throughout.

In planning outstanding figures, especially of symbolical characters, the designer can scarcely overemphasize line or color, particularly if the spectacle is given out of doors where space is so immense as compared with the human figure. The color scheme for a pageant must be planned very differently according to whether the performance is to be indoors or out of doors at night or out of doors in the day. Under artificial light a color scheme can be more subtle and varied depending on the color of the lighting effects. This is true whether indoors or out of doors. If the pageant is produced out of doors in the day, the color scheme must be planned with regard to the fact that the costumes will be shown against a green background. Greens and blues must necessarily be sparingly used, and if used at all, shades should be selected which are either much darker or much lighter than the green of the grass and the trees. No pastel shades such as are used under artificial light will carry at a distance out of doors in the sunlight. Pale blue, pale pink, pale green, orchid or any delicate tint of this kind will look almost white and quite without character under strong daylight. The effect of a pastel group may be obtained by using quite strong tones of these colors. The best effects in outdoor pageantry by daylight are obtained by using very strong, crude colors.

5

Pageants and Triumphs

Introduction

The medieval and Renaissance monarchs were by no means as static as their successors have become. It was their custom, partly for reasons wraf economics and hygiene and partly in order to impress the realm with their greatness, to be almost continually 'on progress,' and all the chief towns vied with one another in an attempt to make the royal *Entree* as magnificent as possible. During the medieval period the emphasis, quite naturally, was on the religious aspects of the kingly office. The king entered the town with his vassals in the full pomp of heraldry and proceeded with them to Mass in the cathedral. The celebrations nearly always included a banquet and a tournament, and the tournament, modified into a harmless game, persisted for many centuries. But even the early *Entrees* were not without certain theatrical elements. For the procession of Queen Isabel of Bavaria in Paris in 1389, a series of stages was, as we have already noted, contrived along the route, each with its symbolical living picture. For the *Entree* of Charles VII in 1437 there was a mime of the Resurrection, and a combat of the Seven Deadly Sins and the Seven Cardinal Virtues.

By the beginning of the sixteenth century, however, a notable change is to be observed. The Renaissance mind, avid of all things which reminded it of antiquity, seized upon the similarity between the *Entree* and the Roman Triumph, and henceforward the old religious element becomes less and less apparent, giving place to an attempt to relate the monarch, whoever he might be, to Cæsar and the scene of his glory to ancient Rome.

It has been suggested that the transition from the old to the new was facilitated by the popularity of the legend of the Nine Worthies, with its jumble of Joshua, David, Hector, Alexander, Cæsar, Charlemagne and Godfrey of Boulogne. Traces of this legend, with the list of Biblical, classical and medieval heroes already complete, is to be found as early as the beginning of the fourteenth century. Gradually the classical element predominated, until only one hero remained, and he, of course, was Cæsar.

This was in line with the whole sentiment of the Italian Renaissance, with the Idea of the Hero gradually replacing the Idea of the Saint, and the movement was powerfully reinforced by the vogue of Petrarch, who has been well called 'the first modern man.' The *virtu* which he celebrated was very different from the theological notion of virtue. He was preoccupied with fame and that survival in the memories of men which was beginning to take the place of the Christian hope of eternal life in another world. Petrarch's *Trionfi* was probably the most popular book of the fifteenth century, and the triumphal cars which he described exercised a powerful influence on all the Renaissance pageants.

Another extremely popular book, and one of the first triumphs of the printer's art, was the anonymous *Dream of Poliphilo*. This was most beautifully illustrated and inaugurated the taste for classical mime which was to play an important part not only in the tableaux and *arcs-de-triomphe* of royal *Entrees,* but in the whole of the arts up to the middle of the seventeenth century.

It was natural that these impulses should first be felt in Italy or in places which had already experienced the impact of Italian ideas. The *Entree* of Charles VIII of France into Paris in 1482 had been entirely in the medieval tradition; it was in the direct line of descent from the ceremony which in 1437 had welcomed Charles VII with a mime of the Resurrection of Jesus and His appearance to Mary Magdalene. Louis XII also was received in Paris in 1509 in the traditional manner, but two years earlier when he made his *Entree* into Milan his victorious procession had been preceded by the car of Mars.

France was not slow to adopt the new enthusiasms. The *Entree* of Anne of Brittany into Paris in 1504 was the last to contain a preponderance of religious motifs. Henceforward the thread on which such festivities were strung was the frank glorification of the monarch as hero. Lyons in 1548 offered to Henry II a river pageant after the Italian pattern with triumphal arches and festival chariots, all the participants being dressed as ancient Romans. It is instructive to note that this was essentially an undertaking of the Italian colony and the commemorative volume was published in the Italian language. The Triumph indeed was one of the means by which the Italian Renaissance made itself felt in the more northern countries of Europe.

By a fortunate chance, some designs by Primaticcio are preserved in the National Museum at Stockholm. Primaticcio was called to France by Francis I and worked there during the three following reigns. In 1560 he arranged for Francis II a pageant to celebrate his *Entree* into the newly purchased château of Chenonceaux, and although it is not certain that the surviving designs are for this fête they none the less serve to show the kind of work he did. The theme of the Stockholm drawings is, as always, the glorification of the monarch, and to this end gods and goddesses, satyrs and sphinxes, Fate and Fame are pressed into service, but there is a relic of medievalism in the Knight of the Swan (the entire figure is a kind of hobbyhorse, but the knight is dressed in Roman costume) and certain Biblical figures.

Primaticcio's drawings are for costume only, but we know from literary descriptions that, at Chenonceaux, special *arcs-de-triomphe* were erected through which the procession passed. The influence which such *arcs-de-triomphe* exercised upon the development of theatrical art has, perhaps, hardly been sufficiently realized. 'It is not astonishing,' says M. Chartrou, 'that the theme of the Triumph arch, triumphal car, equestrian statue which upset the whole of religious iconography, modified architecture both civil and funerary, and created new decorative motifs, should have influenced the ceremonial of royal *Entrees*.' We can trace the emergence of all these elements in the French pageants of the early sixteenth century: the equestrian statue appeared at Rouen in 1517, the triumphal car in the same town, and at Caen, in 1532; the first mention of the *arc-de-triomphe* occurs in the account of the *Entree* of Francis I into Lyons in 1515. The arch undoubtedly gave an impetus to the construction of those magnificent architectural backgrounds *à l'antique* which for so long dominated the whole idea of theatrical scenery.

The Holy Roman Empire, with perhaps more justification than France, seized eagerly upon the idea of the Triumph and identified first Maximilian and then Charles V with Cæsar. There is a Flemish miniature in the Vienna Library (Codex 2591) representing *'La tryumphante et solennelle entree faicte sur le joyeux advenement de Treshault et Trespuissante prince Monsieur Charles'* into Bruges in 1515, while the 'Triumph of Maximilian,' if it never actually took place, has left a splendid record of its intended magnificence in a series of woodcuts, some of which were designed by Hans Burgkmair and the blocks for which are still in existence in Vienna. In the Albertina also is the splendid drawing by Dürer of the Emperor's triumphal car.

As the royal Triumph was essentially an instrument of propaganda, early attempts were made, as we have seen, to expand and perpetuate its effect by issuing illustrated accounts of the ceremony. These became quite frequent towards the end of the sixteenth century and during the seventeenth it was almost taken for granted that a royal *Entree* should be followed by a commemorative volume. It is to such volumes that we owe the greater part of our knowledge of these celebrations. The *Entree* of the Archduke Ernest into Antwerp in 1594 and that of Albert and Isabella into the same city in 1602 both resulted in the production of a series of engravings from which a very clear notion can be gained both of the procession itself and of the *tableaux vivants* that greeted the royal personages at intervals during the route.

London is fortunate in possessing a portion at least of an even more splendid record in the three paintings by Denis van Alsloot now preserved in the Victoria and Albert Museum. The paintings depict the *Ommeganck,* or procession, in honour of the Archduchess Isabella which passed through the main streets of Brussels in 1615, and its most interesting part shows a series of highly decorated cars representing a curious blend of religious subjects and mythological tableaux. The car of Apollo is followed by one representing the Stem of Jesse; the Annunciation precedes Diana and her Nymphs. We are able to watch, as it were, the medieval stage breaking up into a series of episodic tableaux, before the elements of drama were brought together again in that stage picture with its proscenium arch and perspective scenery which is the essence of the Baroque theatre.

In Germany it was the early seventeenth century which saw the greatest number of *Entrees*. Until the Thirty Years' War put an end to them, for a generation there was a perfect orgy of *Entrees:* at Heidelberg (to celebrate the reception of the Garter by Frederick of the Palatinate), at Stuttgart (in honour of John Frederick of Württemberg) and at Tübingen (for the birth of a son to John Frederick of Brandenburg).

This last may be taken as typical of the early seventeenth-century court fete. It lasted from the twelfth to the twentieth July, 1618. On the first day there was a preliminary parade of the participants; on the second the baptism; on the third a *Schaw-Essen,* or great banquet; on the fourth and fifth a procession with jousting; on the sixth a ballet and a banquet; on the seventh a tournament of the Four Elements; on the eighth a hunt; and on the ninth, Sunday, a church service.

Excellent engraved records exist (examples are to be seen in the Victoria and Albert Museum) of the two splendid festivities organized by the House of Württemberg in 1609 and 1616; and the same Museum possesses an illuminated drawing on vellum representing a triumphal car attended by nymphs, the work of Hans Jörg Hochenmauer, later 'Hof-Contrafecter' to the Emperor Ferdinand II. When the latter entered Brussels in 1635 the decorations of the city were designed by no less a person than Rubens, and were afterwards engraved by Theodor van Thulden.

The devastation of Germany between 1618 and 1648 caused the lead to pass once more to France. Louis XIII entered Avignon through a series of Roman- Baroque triumphal archways, and in 1623 a commemorative volume was published with the curious and significant title *La Voye de Laict, ou le Chemin des Heros*. In the following year Galoup de Chasteuil published a *Discours sur les arcs triomphaux dresses en la ville d' Aix à l'heureuse arrivee de Louys XIII*. But it was reserved for the son of Louis XIII, the Grand Monarque himself, to fuse all the elements of the old *Entree* together into one magnificent spectacle which served the double purpose of amusing his courtiers and impressing the world with his glory. The famous 'Carrousel of

Louis XIV' was staged in Paris in 1662 in the Place which still bears its name, and was commemorated eight years later by a superb volume (*Courses de Testes et de Bagues*) which is perhaps the highwater mark of all such publications. Louis appeared, inevitably, as a Roman Emperor with attendant warriors, and the three other parts of the 'quadrille' represented Turks, Persians and Americans, over whom the 'Romans' were destined to be victorious in the feats of skill which were to follow.

Such a challenge could hardly be ignored, and in 1667 a magnificent fe'te was arranged in Vienna, a *'gran balletto al Cavallo'* with festival carriages and elaborate decorations, to show that the Emperor also had some claims to be regarded as the most splendid monarch of Europe. But the engraved records are vastly inferior to those of the French carrousel.

Another sovereign who sought to outshine Louis XIV was Augustus II of Saxony. Tournaments had been very popular at Dresden in the sixteenth century, but by the end of the seventeenth they had become stylized, as all over Europe, into *'courses de testes et de bagues,'* the nearest modern equivalent of which is tent-pegging. A whole succession of fêtes was staged, culminating in the masquerade of 1709 in honour of the visit of the King of Denmark. The entertainment consisted of a contest between the Seven Planets and the monarch Nimrod, followed by an opera-ballet in which the Planets took part, a *course de bague* (running at the ring) for ladies, a carrousel of the Four Quarters of the World, and other festivities. It is interesting to note that ten years later it was thought necessary to include French comedies alternating with Italian comedies and opera.

Before, however, this development had gone so far, the learned Jesuit Claude François Menestrier tried to resume. the principles of such royal entertainment in his *Traite des Tournois Joustes et Carrousels, et autres Spectacles Publics,* published at Lyons in 1669. He had been entrusted with organizing the fêtes which had welcomed Louis XIV to that city in 1658, and, in spite of the pedantry and pomposity of his book, it has much of value to tell us.

'Two things,' he remarks, 'are in use for Carrousels, the Decoration for the Lists and the Machines *pour la Pompe.'* By this he means the procession which, of course, from the theatrical point of view is of much more importance than the actual mock-combat of the 'quadrilles.' These 'quadrilles' had considerable influence on the development of stage costume, serving to popularize the supposed garb of Africans, Americans, Turks and Romans; but the *'Pompe,'* that is, the festival cars which brought up the rear of the procession, have a close connection with theatrical scenery also.

At the reception of Catherine of Austria at Nice in 1585, Menestrier tells us, one of the cars represented the town of Tunis, with its towers and mosques, 'followed by another machine representing twelve elephants with their tails together, each crowned with a castle containing archers.' For a carrousel of Louis XIII there was prepared a chariot forty feet long drawn by four lions, and 'the driver was Terror, represented by an armed man with a dragon's head and a naked sword in his hand.' Another car figured a great rock 'moved by the sound of Apollo's lyre' but really by eight horses. In fifteen grottoes were players of hautbois, and at the summit a great tree hung with trophies.

The festivities on this occasion included an elaborate water-pageant, the description of which by Menestrier may be taken as typical of such entertainments. The royal galley in which the princess sat was surrounded by 'twelve small galleys in each of which were twenty-four gentlemen clad in white satin embroidered with gold. These galleys were followed by three marine monsters, one of which was a hundred and sixty feet long and was full of eyes made of mirrors. His scales were of silver and he carried on his back a vessel full of plants and branches of coral. He had two great wings which covered the oars, the strokes of which were regulated by the beating of these wings. Approaching the royal galley he retracted his neck as a mark of respect and then stretched it out more than twenty feet in length to the astonishment of everybody. A troupe of nymphs was seated in the shell, one of which, clad in gold brocade, adorned with strings of pearls and branches of coral, presented the keys of the town in a basin and recited Italian verses to the Princess. At the top of the rock was Virtuous Love holding fishes in one hand and flowers in the other. Faith, Perseverance, Liberality and Concord were seated on the same rock and two Tritons blew their horns on the wings of the monster.

'The second monster was conducted by Neptune, half-naked. He stood on a group of four marine monsters and, holding a great silver bridle, made the monster open and shut its mouth. The third monster, which was remarkable for the variety of its colours, carried on its back a chair formed by three Sirens painted like nature, on which was seated Thetis clothed in gold brocade sewn with pearls. A nymph conducted this monster and Thetis presented to the Princess a shell full of pearls and precious stones. The Princess having passed from her galley to the town over a bridge a hundred and twenty-five feet long, all the divinities and gentlemen landed from their monsters and their galleys and followed her.'

Such water-pageants were a natural development of the triumphal procession and are of importance because it was possible to build larger and more elaborate scenes on boats than it would have been possible to construct on cars or wagons. The good Menestrier does not fail to give innumerable details of these festivals, even of those earlier ones at which he could not possibly have assisted himself. 'On October 10th, 1581,' he tells us, at the wedding of the Duc de Joycuse and Marguerite of Lorraine, sister-in-law of Henri III, the Cardinal de Bourbon, having prepared a splendid feast for the whole Court at his Abbey of St. Germaindes-Prez, provided at the same time a splendid apparatus consisting of a barge arranged as a triumphal car on which the King, the Princes, the Princesses and the newly married couple were to take their stand to pass with solemn pomp from the Louvre to the Pre aux Clercs. This triumphal car was to be towed by other barges in the form of sea-horses, while others in the shape of tritons, whales, sirens, dolphins, tortoises and marine monsters, to the number of twentyfour, were to carry the rest of the Court, with trumpets, horns, hautbois, violins and a few fireworks.

'At the Court of Savoy were given ballets of sirens and of tritons, half in the water and with their feigned tails making many agreeable motions in the middle of a river. In 1608 the Duke Charles Emanuel, after the marriage of two of his daughters to the Dukes of Modena and Mantua invited them to Millefors. He conducted the company to a part of the wood near a great round pond at the edge of which he had built a Theatre of rocks and turf and shells mingled with mirrors which made a marvellous effect. As soon as the Princes were seated on chairs placed under the great trees, there appeared on the water Arion on the dolphin's back, who gave a wonderful performance with harp and voice. This was the overture to the Ballet of the Tritons and the Sirens.'

Plainly it is impossible to draw a hard and fast line between such festivities and the theatre proper. Coming nearer to his own time, Menestrier describes the famous fetes at Versailles in 1664, the water-pageant of which took place in the enormous Rondeau, or round-pond. 'There appeared on this Rondeau, which was of extraordinary size and shape, a rock situated in the middle of an island covered with various animals who seemed to defend it. Two other islands appeared beside the first and all three, as well as the borders of the lake, were so well lit that the lights made a new day amid the obscurity of night. In a moment one of these islands was filled with violin players richly dressed; the other island was filled with trumpeters and cymbalists not less splendid. But what surprised most was to see Alcine appear from behind the rock carried by a marine monster of prodigious size. Two of the nymphs of her suite, called Celie and Dirce, appeared at the same time and, placing themselves beside her mounted on whales, approached the edge of the take where Alcine began the verses to which her companions replied and which were in praise of the Queen-Mother.'

From the history of Pageants and Triumphs it is impossible to dissociate the theme of triumphal arches, as these had a considerable influence on the actual question of stage decoration. When one considers that stage scenes during the seventeenth century, at least, were almost purely architectural, and that triumphal arches were sometimes furnished with platforms from which congratulatory speeches were delivered, it will be seen that the connection between the two is necessarily close. In the very interesting *Entree* of Albert and Isabella of Austria into Antwerp in 1602 they were welcomed by every variety of triumphal device, including platforms, with living symbolic figures, arches adorned with sculpture, colossal statues and, most striking of all, a revolving stage, on one side of which sat figures representing the horrors of war and on the other representing the blessings of peace. This is probably the earliest example of a revolving stage known, although a similar circular construction (which, however, apparently did not revolve) was seen at the *Entee* of Archduke Ernest into Antwerp in 1594.

As the whole object of the triumphal arch was to glorify the prince, it was frequently engraved in some kind of memorial publication, so that the material for its study is considerable. The plates engraved by Willem Kip after Stephen Harrison show the triumphal arches erected in honour of the entrance of James I into London in 1603. Similar arches were erected for Charles II and for William of Orange. Rubens designed triumphal arches at Antwerp in honour of the Archduke Ferdinand, and the progresses of Louis XIV were everywhere celebrated by the erection of arches, often from the design of Charles Le Brun.

An almost equally important element in that forcing house of theatrical ingenuity the Triumph was the pyrotechnic display. Fireworks hardly form a part of modern theatrical design, but in a less specialized age they undoubtedly did so. Their connection with triumphal arches is also very close, for frequently the elaborate structures erected in the streets of a city for the passage of a monarch were stuffed with fireworks, which were discharged as a final effect. The science of pyrotechnics was in a somewhat crude condition until the nineteenth century, so that the main interest of a discharge of fireworks lay in its architectural setting, an architectural setting which bore the closest relationship to stage scenery. So close, indeed, was the connection with the theatre and so foreign to earlier ideas were the sharp differentiations of the modern world that Bernardo Buontalenti, the Florentine designer of the first operatic scenery, bore the title 'delle Girandole,' that is to say 'of the Fireworks.'

No seventeenth-century festival was complete without a discharge of fireworks. Even ecclesiastical ceremonies were concluded with a pyrotechnic display, and royalty itself seized upon the opportunity of impressing the public and offering a welcome amusement at one and the same time.

Although it is probable that this art came from Italy, it reached its most elaborate development at the court of France, where it was seen at its best under Louis XIII. In 1612 a magnificent fête was given in Paris to celebrate the projected marriages of Louis to Anne of Austria and of his sister to the Prince of the Asturias. One of the main attractions was an immense Palace of Felicity erected in the Place Royale (now the Place des Vosges), and this palace was nothing but the framework for a prodigious display of fireworks. The enchanted castle (borrowed from Spanish romances such as *Amadis de Gaule*) was a frequently recurring motif in early seventeenth-century pyrotechnics. When Louis XIII passed through Bordeaux in 1615 the artillery engineer Jumeau erected on the bank of the Garonne a *'chasteau couvert d'une couronne flamboyante,'* from which a luminous dragon issued vomiting fire.

As the century progressed, however, the mythological element began to overshadow subjects taken from the romance of chivalry. In 1628 the taking of La Rochelle was celebrated in Paris by a firework display representing Louis XIII as Perseus rescuing Andromeda from the dragon of Protestantism. Such a scene must have involved a considerable amount of machinery; in the words of M. Magne: *'De mêe qu'à cette epoque le machinisine envahit l'art theâitral, il envahit l'art pyrotechnique.'* The firework drama was capable of many modifications. In 1618 Jumeau arranged in Paris a complicated battle of gods, and in 1614 Morel a battle of heroes on the Île Louviers in the Seine.

As the century advanced still further the art became overlaid with allegory, the birth of Louis XIV in 1638 being celebrated by the erection in the Seine of an artificial rock at the summit of which appeared the sun. At the foot of the rock stood figures representing France, Prudence, Peace, Abundance, Science and Harmony. From 1650 onwards pyrotechnics showed evidence of the tendency in all the arts towards the solemn and the grandiloquent. Movable machines were abandoned in favour of solid architectural constructions of the antique style favoured by the Academy. The engineer submitted more and more to the dictation of architects and even. of literary men with their love of emblems and abstruse allegories. Of literary men the most notable was once again the Jesuit Menestrier, whose *Advis necessaire pour la Conduite des Feux d'Artifice* shows a perverse ingenuity in making fireworks serve the purpose of moral instruction and political propaganda.

In 1654, and again in 1699, to celebrate the erection of a statue to Louis XIV, a magnificent Temple of Honour was erected in Paris. On both occasions the temple was an immobile framework for fireworks. Even the Ship of the Argonauts on the Seine in honour of Louis and Maria Theresa was not a machine in the earlier sense, for it did not move but exploded its fireworks in situ.

The provincial towns of France vied with Paris in their loyal pyrotechnic demonstrations. Menestrier illustrates some of these in his *Les Rejouissances de la Paix clans la Ville de Lyons* (1660). Valenciennes in 1680, on the occasion of a royal visit, produced an allegory of *Hercule soutenant te Ciel.*

The political element was sometimes strongly stressed, as when the end of the Fronde was signalized by Perseus cutting off the head of Medusa, and in 1685 when a series of illuminated tableaux illustrated the Revocation of the Edict of Nantes. In 1678 the conquest of Franche-Comte was celebrated by a performance of Racine's *"Iphigenie"*d and a firework display.

It was in conservative Rome that fireworks discharged from an elaborate semi-architectural, semi-theatrical structure as a necessary part of a solemn celebration persisted longest, indeed until almost the end of the eighteenth century. It so happens, also, that the Roman documentation is particularly complete especially with reference to the so-called Festa della Chinea. The phrase requires some little explanation.

The Kingdom of the Two Sicilies had acknowledged the temporal dominion of the Papacy from the tenth century, and was accustomed to send every year, in lieu of homage, the present of a horse, which was paraded through the streets of Rome on the vigil of SS. Peter and Paul (the evening of June 29). The word *chinea* is supposed to be a corruption of *asturcones*- i.e. a horse of the Asturias -but in the course of time a mule was substituted for a horse, probably as being a more suitable present to an ecclesiastic.

At the beginning of the eighteenth century Spain and Austria.were contending for Naples and were both anxious for papal support. In 1722, Pope Innocent XIII bestowed the investitute on Charles VI of Austria with the proviso that the yearly acknowledgment of the Chinea should be made with all solemnity. From 1723, therefore, it became the custom, in addition to the procession, to hold firework displays on two successive evenings outside the Palazza Colonna, one member of that family being always Ambassador Extraordinary of Naples at the Papal court. The fashion of the time required a firework display to consist of elaborate architectural erections. Two structures were needed each year for the Chinea festival, and their design was entrusted to the architect of the Casa Colonna. These designs were afterwards engraved as mementoes of the ceremony, and a series of two for each year from 1723 to 1763 is in existence. From these it is possible to trace the development of architectural design throughout a great portion of the eighteenth century, a development reflecting the prevailing currents of taste even more completely than more public and permanent buildings, for in designing temporary structures to be destroyed by fire almost as soon as they were built the architect naturaliy felt more free to follow his fantasy.

Numerous artists were employed by the House of Colonna, some of whom designed the Chinea festival for many years in succession. Alessandro Specchi, whose name occurs first on the engraving of 1724, was followed in 1728 by Gabrielle Valvassori, and he in turn in 1730 by two artists, Bartolomeo Poli and Michelangelo Specchi. In 1745 the structure for one day of the festival was designed by a Frenchman, Louis Joseph Le Lorrain, and the same artist reappears in 1747. The Spaniard Francesco Preziado was employed in 1746, and again in 1748 and 1750, sharing the work with Michelangelo Specchi. In 1751 appears Paolo Posi (born in Siena in 1708, died in Rome in 1776), and his design for one of the 'machines' for the Festa della Chinea of 1761 (Plate 105) is of particular interest, for it seems to be a kind of combination of firework platform and open-air stage — a late reminder of the intimate connection which had once existed between these two forms of entertainment.

In 1776 Posi was succeeded by Palazzi, who continued to design the structures for the Chinea festival at least until 1785 and probably until 1788, in which year the Government of the Two Sicilies decided to cease the presentation of the Chinea. The protest of the Papacy was unavailing, and the general European conflagration of the next few years diverted even the Roman populace from their passion for fireworks.

Throughout the rest of Europe firework displays and even theatrical performances had long ceased to be regarded as a part of the homage due to a monarch. Indeed, from the outbreak of the War of the Austrian Succession, public fêtes fall out of use, or rather they become more popular and are confined to the carnival without any attempt of the monarch to take an official part in them. In fact, it may be said that by the middle of the eighteenth century, or even earlier, the subsidiary amusements with which the *Entree* had been decorated and expanded had overbalanced the whole structure; or, to use another metaphor, the beads had become too heavy for the thread. The thread, which was essentially the Royal Procession, broke, the beads fell apart.

The elements which made tip the Baroque pageant are now dispersed. Its tournament aspect lingers in the modern 'Tattoo'; its mythological aspect has been absorbed and discarded by the theatre; the festival car has been relegated to the carnival or, in England, to the Lord Mayor's Show; its wild animals are banished to the circus, its 'savage' men to Colonial Exhibitions. But all these disparate elements once combined to produce a magnificent series of spectacles which were of the utmost cultural and political importance, fostered the theatrical spirit and played an important part in the costume and decor of drama.

❒❒❒

6

Costume Designing in Shakespearean and Other Platform Stages

Introduction

We have dealt with what might be called the moving elements of Pageants and Triumphs. Attention has recently been directed to the fixed elements, the triumphal arches and the *tableaux vivants* which diversified the route the pageant followed: Mr. George R. Kernodle has set himself to answer the question why there is so little traceable continuity between the theatrical activity of the Middle Ages and the Renaissance theatre in all its forms. To say that the whole attitude to the theatre and to life was different is merely to say that there was such a thing as the Renaissance. If diversity had been the characteristic of the medieval period, unity was the watchword of the new age. The men of the Renaissance were 'done with narrative and ready for drama. They were done with the sprawling sequence of little religious plays that might last for days, and they were ready for a single play that had size and proportion. In their new theatres they were done with the time art of the medieval narratives and processions and ready for the space art of the Elizabethan stage or the perspective setting.' The later Greek and Roman drama had been played before a fixed architectural background; the medieval drama moved about all round a marketplace, or even all round the town. Its 'houses' did not form a unified picture; indeed, even when they were assembled on a single stage with Hell-mouth at one side, Heaven at the other and the Garden of Gethsemane and Pilate's palace in between, no attempt was made to build them up into a unified stage-picture. They remained as arbitrary and separate symbols.

Most previous authors have been content to point to this peculiarity and to stress the fact that the break-up of the Roman traditions of theatrical presentation made it inevitable. The novelty of Mr. Kernodle's approach lies in the fact that while he accepts this break in continuity in the theatre, he does not accept it in art. He claims that the artists did keep some of the elements of background developed in the classical theatre and handed them on in an unbroken tradition. The pictorial arts were in advance of the theatre at least so far as the organization of space was concerned, and, therefore, when the drama felt the need to unify its picture it had dozens of examples before it.

Earlier, of course, the debt had been reversed. It was the artists who had adopted from the theatre the conventionalized architectural background and also the curious manner of treating interior scenes *in front* of such an exterior background, or else, as it were, as seen through holes knocked in it for the purpose. Perhaps this matter goes further even than Mr. Kernodle has chosen to pursue it. It is sometimes forgotten that, until quite recent times, men did not feel at home inside a room. They spent most of their lives in the open air and retired indoors only for shelter or sleep. The idea of a life passed almost entirely within four walls, like the lives of most people today, was entirely foreign to them. The theatre, in Greek and Roman times, was *in the open air,* and the convention long persisted even when dramatic representations began to take place in the halls of kings' palaces and in closed auditoriums. Architects until yesterday 'persisted in treating the whole auditorium as an exterior: they built little roofs above the boxes and painted the ceilings with clouds and stars.'

The problem of the medieval artist was to maintain his exterior view (which he could not help doing) and yet to show interior scenes. His most pregnant device was a kind of baldacchino under which the most important personage could sit or the most important action take place. After all, a baldacchino is nothing but a room with the walls taken away and a column at each corner supporting a roof. And such a baldacclino becomes, in the new theory, the element from which developed the central structure of the Elizabethan stage.

A complication arises from the frequent use in art of another device — the arcade screen. This screen has a long history both in art and in the theatre. It has, for example, the closest possible relationship with the architectural façade of the Teatro Olimpico, but for the moment we are concerned with its influence on the Elizabethan stage, which is essentially a combination of the screen and the baldacchino, or, as Mr. Kernodle calls it, the centre pavilion.

He draws attention to yet a third element in painting which had a profound effect upon theatrical presentation both in the medieval and Renaissance periods. This was the castle, which for several hundred years was the most important background device in art and became the most frequent scene in the *tableaux vivants*. When the castle, instead of being a property wheeled about the streets, is fixed in the centre of a stage, and when it has a doorway in it large enough to admit the passage of the characters, it is ready to blend with that other element devised from the theme of the Triumph, namely the triumphal arch.

Gentile da Fabriani's *Presentation in the Temple*, painted in 1423 and now in the Louvre, shows a centre pavilion, an arcade screen as background and side houses. Here are all the elements which were later to divide and give us, on the one hand, the Elizabethan stage and, on the other, the street of houses receding in perspective of the Italian illusionistic setting. In the end it was the second of these methods of staging which was everywhere victorious and which dominated the theatre until the beginning of the twentieth century; but the battle might easily have gone the other way, and, if it had, students would find it much easier to understand the methods of staging practised by Shakespeare and his contemporaries. The problem of the Elizabethans would have been much less intractable than it has proved to be for so long.

Mr. Kernodle insists, as no one has insisted before him, on the importance of the *tableaux vivants*, those set pieces which enabled the king and his followers to pause in their procession to feast their eyes upon some fine piece of static display. The pleasure of the eyes must have been somewhat counterbalanced by the necessity of listening to long speeches from one or more of the characters represented. Whether or no the kings were wearied by these speeches (they were, after all, entirely in their praise), the historians of the theatre have been universally bored by them and, finding little of literary interest, have passed on without considering their importance, not indeed in the history of literature, but in the history of staging. Mr. Kernodle declares roundly that 'the Flemish and Elizabethan stage façades can be traced directly to the street tableaux vivants built for royal entries.'

The *tableaux vivants* form the link between such sculptured scenes and the theatre as it was to develop in England and in Flanders. At times some of the figures were still sculptured, while some were impersonated by actors. Mention is made by contemporaries of the wonderful way in which these living *figurantes* held themselves motionless, but this naïve pleasure was soon succeeded by the satisfaction of seeing them move, and even expand the theme of the tableau in dumb show. The play scene in 'Hamlet' must have been no novelty to the majority of Shakespeare's audience. They or their forbears had seen scenes from the Bible and from secular legend in the streets of London. If there were any Flemings among them they might have seen such a tableau as that offered to William of Orange in Brussels in 1577, where the scene represented an allegory of delivery from the yoke of Rome.

In the tableaux representing historical events reminders to the prince of the glories of his ancestors and of the city which was receiving him we may see the germ of the historical drama. Philip of. Spain was welcomed in both the Netherlands and in England by all the famous Philips of history. In 1554 in England two genealogical trees were shown, springing from Edward III and united at the top with figures of Mary and Philip.

Some of the tableaux were really indistinguishable from little plays. The words, apart from the words of the introducer of the scene, himself a symbolic character, were at first inscribed on painted scrolls which were revealed at the appropriate moment. There was only a step to take to transform the whole thing into a dramatic performance.

The number of street theatres built to accommodate the *tableaux vivants* was far greater than has been supposed hitherto. London alone, as Mr. Kemodle points out, had spectacular street theatres erected for royal *Entrees* in 1501, 1520, 1522, 1533, 1546, 1553, 1554 and 1558. The next were not built until 1603, but Elizabeth's innumerable progresses round the country gave plenty of opportunity for provincial shows. What this means is that all the mature members of the audience at Shakespeare's plays had seen such stages and it was the most natural thing in the world that the scenes shown on them should be expanded into plays. George Peele had already shown what possibilities of drama were to be found in the comparatively simple Lord Mayors' Shows. Jonson, Middleton, Dekker and Heywood also wrote for the tableaux vivants.

The kind of *scenery* used in the *tableaux vivants* may help us to understand some of the conventions of the Elizabethan stage. Scenic *illusion,* of course, did not exist. There was no unified perspective picture. A single tree represented an arbour or a forest, a few palings a garden. A small painted mound figuring a mountain was another favourite device. Indeed, the scene of Pyramus and Thisbe in "A Midsummer Night's Dream" must have seemed amusing to its first audience from the antics of the players, rather than ridiculous in its conventions as it seems to us. Such conventions were perfectly familiar to them and had been so to their ancestors in the Middle Ages.

Even the architectural façades which were beginning to be imported from Italy were treated at first, in the north, rather as *properties* than as set scenes. The amphitheatre itself was used, not to accommodate the audience, but to mount the show. In Antwerp in 1594 there was such an amphitheatre (Plate 41) filled with rows of beautiful girls holding symbolic devices, and in the same city in 1600 it was built on a turn-table. Inigo Jones used the amphitheatre for a similar purpose in the masque ' Albion's Triumph' as late as 1632.

The unifying element was the architectural façade, which soon dominated the public theatres more completely than it had ever done in the tableaux vivants. It is at this point that the two different kinds of stage presentation which we find simultaneously in existence at the beginning of the seventeenth century divide. 'Because some theatres carried this architectural symbolism to its full development and others carried the desire for illusion to full realization, there was possible the wide divergence we find between the Elizabethan stage and the Italian perspective setting both of which derive from the traditions of the visual arts.'

If it is accepted that the Elizabethan stage developed from the street theatres of the *tableaux vivants,* it is interesting to find a stage which forms, as it were, a half-way house between the two. This is the Rederyker stage of the Netherlands. That it has been so long ignored and, indeed, forgotten is due to the fact that it created no great literary drama. The little 'theme' plays which were performed upon it were contrived by the societies of rhetoric which had grown up in the early Renaissance in the Netherlands and Northern France. Their period of greatest activity stretches from the late fifteenth century to the War of Liberation at the end of the sixteenth, and their great delight was to promote a *landjuweel,* or drama festival: competitions in allegory between different towns and different guilds. Protestantism provided a useful stimulus, for many of the plays had a religious and propaganda intention.

The stage used, sometimes indoors but more frequently in a market-square, consisted of an open platform backed by an architectural façade, and the exact arrangement is plain enough from the illustrations which have, fortunately, survived. The stage setting at Ghent in 1539 (Plate 30) consisted of a central pavilion with two columns supporting a gallery; above that is a formal decorative feature adorned with statues. The central pavilion is flanked by two towers, each of two storeys, the lower one forming part of a formal arcade with five doorways. A more advanced form is shown in the stage façade for the *landjuweel* at Antwerp in 1561 (Plate 31). There were only three openings in both storeys, and the centre ones are shown with curtains. The curtained openings could be used for interior scenes when required, although many actions supposed to take place indoors were played in front of the façade without any sense of incongruity.

The Ghent performance had a religious theme; that at Brussels was concerned with the question: 'What can best awaken man to the arts?' Both used a curious combination of static tableau (and even of painted picture) and drama. 'Some of the Antwerp *figuren*' (says Mr. Kernodle) 'were tableaux without movement, some moved in pantomime, some were little dramas with speech or dialogue within the picture, and some had characters who spoke to the main characters, Mankind and his spiritual advisers. One was an elaborate painting, or possibly a model of a ship. In the pantomime scenes, such as that of the sleeping Hercules being awakened by Virtuous Desire, the characters are usually described to Mankind as in movement. While the upper stage was used for goddesses, muses, and allegorical nymphs, the lower inner stage served for a number of interior scenes of sleeping figures; for Man's adviser usually pulled aside the curtain himself to show them.' And he is surely justified in claiming that 'when we cross the Channel from Antwerp to London, we shall find a more varied use of the façade; but we shall almost think we are seeing just a further development of the Flemish shows.' This view is, of course, in complete contrast to that of such older writers as Sir William Chambers, who claimed for the Elizabethan stage a much higher degree of scenic realism.

While admitting that the transition from the *tableaux vivants* of the street theatres was by no means so direct in England as it was in Flanders, Mr. Kernodle finds a connecting link in the settings at the Inns of Court. The tragedies of "Gorboduc" (1561), "Jocasta" (1566) and "The Misfortunes of Arthur" (1587), produced for the entertainment of Queen Elizabeth, were played before a classical arcade which yet retained elements of the street theatres. This classical, or rather Renaissance, arcade Mr. Kernodle believes to have played a larger part in the Shakespearean stage picture than has hitherto been supposed. Most previous reconstructions show a preference for the half-timber effect of the domestic architecture of the period. Yet 'most of the new buildings erected in England in the latter half of the sixteenth century were of the newer Renaissance architecture, with its classic orders of columns and arches and its marble and gold. The De Witt drawing of the Swan shows two ornate Renaissance columns supporting the heavens. The Fortune contract called for columns carved with satyrs.' In short they resembled the Renaissance columns and canopies which we know from contemporary engravings to have been erected for the *tableaux vivants* in Antwerp and Brussels.

However true it may be to derive the Elizabethan playhouse from the *tableaux vivants,* we must not forget that the latter were occasional performances. The essence of their presentation was that they were regarded as special occasions, for which considerable expense was justified in the provision of properties and the erection of special 'street theatres.' The Elizabethan theatre, although it never attained the regularity of modern performances, was a permanent institution playing in houses built for the purpose and employing professional actors. How did this change itself come about?

The maintaining of small groups of entertainers in the service of the great nobles was of long date: the practice goes back to the singers of epics and the jesters of the early medieval period. But the more elaborate the entertainment provided the less suitable it became for constant repetition in the house of one man. So in the early Tudor period we find groups of actors in the service of great men being lent or hired out. Cardinal Wolsey's men, for example, were called in to perform in Sir Thomas More's house in 1529. As the practice extended such a group of actors would become less and less a mere body of retainers, and more and more a professional travelling company, still retaining the patronage, and the name, of the great lord who originally employed them. With the growth of London under the Tudors it became possible to envisage a permanent settlement in the capital.

From playing in private houses on invitation it was but a step to playing in public, pieferably in an inn-yard which, with its galleries, provided readymade boxes for those of the audience who could afford to pay for such accommodation. The groundlings could be accommodated in the inn-yard itself at one end of which a platform had been erected for the actors.

Perhaps too much has been made of this derivation of the Elizabethan theatre from the inn-yard: Mr. Kernodle's work is, to some extent, a protest against the exclusiveness of this theory so long held by Shakespearean scholars. But certainly the inns played some part in the development of the play-house.

The inns utilized tended, owing to the Puritan hostility of the City Fathers, to be located in the suburbs. Among the earliest we find mentioned the Saracen's Head in Islington, the Boar's Head and the Red Lion in Whitechapel, the Tabard in Southwark. Some, notably the Bell, the Bull, the Cross Keys and the Bel Savage, were found in the City itself. The usual procedure was for the travelling company of actors to make some arrangement with the landlord by which he received a proportion of the takings, and incidentally benefited by what would nowadays be known as the 'bar concession'.

The next step, where the public was sufficiently numerous to justify it, was to take over the inn entirely. John Brayne, the partner of James Burbage, chased the George Inn in Whitechapel in 1578, but was not allowed to use it as a theatre. In 1576 he had financed the erection of a theatre in Shoreditch, and it is hard to think that it can have differed in essentials from the inn-yard, since two years later he was still contemplating using an existing inn-yard as a theatre.

The success of Burbage and Brayne in Shoreditch soon led to the erection of other theatres: the Curtain close by, the Fortune just outside Cripplegate, the Rose, the Swan and the Globe in Southwark. All these were built before the end of the century, and the Hope in Southwark and the Red Bull in Clerkenwell soon afterwards. Shakespeare, as we know, had a hand in building the Globe, the company to which he belonged moving there from the theatre in Shoreditch in 1598. The circular shape was probably suggested by the bull-baiting ring. It is an important departure from the simple rectangular form of the inn-yard.

Shakespeare's company, however, had from 1608 onwards another theatre of a different kind. This was the theatre at Blackfriars, formerly used by the boy actors, the Children of the Chapel. This was an indoor theatre, with some inevitable differences in the manner of presenting plays. It is a pity that we do not know precisely what these differences were. As late as 1606 we find Marston writing of 'the fashion of the private stage,' the Blackfriars theatre being considered as a 'private' stage, in spite of the fact that it was open to the public. No doubt some elements of the new staging were imported from the masque, but there is no question of anything in the nature of 'the theatre of scenic illusion.' The principal action still took place on the apron stage, as indeed it continued to do even in the Restoration period and long afterwards. Hogarth's engraving of a performance of 'The Beggar's Opera' is sufficient evidence of this.

The other platform stages which must be considered are those of Spain and Germany and those of the Jesuit schools. The characteristic of the Spanish and German stages was a back curtain, deriving from the outdoor stage of the medieval mountebank as well as from the simpler kinds of *tableaux vivants,* and Spain retained this system even when other countries had abandoned it in favour of an elaborate architectural fac.

The school plays had made use of the arcade screen ever since the revival of what was supposed to be the ancient manner of presenting plays took place in Rome in the closing years of the fifteenth century. The contemporary manuscripts of Terence provided illustrations which could be copied in actual productions. The result was a row of 'houses,' not arranged, as they would have been later, as part of a perspective picture, but as doorways in a façade which is sometimes flat and sometimes pushed forward in the centre like a medieval pavilion. When the curtains in the arches were drawn there were glimpses of inner stages. This remained the school tradition until the early seventeenth century.

The Jesuit stage was more elaborate. Its development, long neglected by historians of the theatre, has been studied by two German scholars, Müller, who has concentrated upon its literary themes, and Flemming, who has dealt with its methods of presentation. The performance might be described as a dramatized sermon with little illustrative tableaux, each tableau being followed by a spoken play expounding and expanding the theme. This was managed by having a group of inner stages forming a façade, and these inner stages sometimes had painted backgrounds and sometimes were provided with 'properties.' In the performance of 'Hester' in Munich in 1577, which Flemming has described in detail, there was a large central compartment. Mr. Kernodle has pointed out the resemblance between this arrangement and the façade of the Teatro Olimpico at Vicenza, the main difference being that the Jesuit inner stages generally represented interior scenes, while the arches of the Teatro Olimpico revealed vistas of perspective streets. The Jesuits also had separate curtains for each compartment. This arrangement continued with minor variations until the seventeenth century, and as that century progressed the central compartment or arch tended to grow larger and to be filled with some form of perspective scenery, in accordance with the prevailing tendency; yet the formal screen background with spaces for several scenes can be found as late as the middle of the eighteenth century. A notable example is the stage setting of the college at Rennes, here reproduced. The only extant relic of Jesuit staging is provided by the Passion Play at Oberammergau. The history of staging from 1650 to 1800 is the history of the advance of the perspective setting at the expense of any kind of platform stage.

VII The English Court Masques

By a series of fortunate chances there has survived a very considerable amount of information concerning the scenery and costumes of the Court entertainments in England during the first half of the seventeenth century. Indeed, the documentation is more ample than it is for many later periods. Not only have we Ben Jonson's descriptions, but a very large number of drawings by Inigo Jones, preserved in the splendid collections at Chatsworth.

Inigo Jones introduced something entirely new into the history of the English theatre, something for which there is no precedent in either the medieval drama or the Shakespearean stage. It has long been a commonplace that he derived his inspiration from Italy, and the only question is from which Italian master he borrowed most, his own designs being, none the less, original works of the highest merit.

Inigo was responsible for the masques and other entertainments at the English Court from 1605 to 1640. He visited Italy between the years 1596 and 1604 and must have spent a considerable portion of his time in Florence. The Italian artists to whom he was most indebted seem to have been Giulio and Alfonso Parigi, who in turn based themselves upon the work of Buontalenti, as we have already seen.

Most of the scenery designs by Jones are for masques, but a few are for plays, as is shown by the absence of steps from the stage to the dancing floor, on which a considerable part of the action of a masque took place. This is indicated quite plainly in the well-known etching by Callot of a similar entertainment in progress at the Court of Tuscany, reproduced in the plate opposite. The play scenes are particularly interesting, as the printed texts of the period seldom contain any indications of a change of scene. The ' Shepherd's Paradise' contains only two such references and one of these has to be deduced from the dialogue. Yet the numbers on identified sketches at Chatsworth imply many different scenes, and we can only conclude with Mr. C. F. Bell 'that it must have been the custom to make incessant changes, confined no doubt to the "back shutter" of the stage, during the course of a drama.' The 'back shutter' is what we should call the 'backcloth,' but apparently it was not yet lowered from the flies. It is still called a 'shutter' a hundred years later, and drawings of the early eighteenth century show that it still consisted of two pieces.

With the masque designs we are on somewhat firmer ground, and much work has been done by scholars in endeavouring to place them in chronological order and in identifying the subjects. The earliest for which we have any data is entitled 'The Quceucs Masque of Blacknesse'; it was written by Ben Jonson and performed on January 6, 1605. For this and for 'Hymenæi,' performed exactly a year later, only costume designs have survived, but for 'The Masque of Queenes celebrated from the House of Fame,' of three years later, we have a design or two for scenery. One of these represents (to use Ben Jonson's words) a 'glorious and magnificent Building, figuring *the House of Fame,* in the top of which, were discovered the twelve *Masquers,* sitting upon a Throne triumphall, erected in forme of a *Pyramide,* and circled with all store of light.' The lighting effects seem particularly to have impressed the poet, for he goes on to speak of 'the Freezes, both below, and above . . . filled with several-color'd lights, blue *Emeralds, Rubies, Saphyres, Carbuncles, &c.* the reflexe of which, with other lights, placed in the Concave, upon the *Masquers* habits, was full of glory.'

As the masques, unlike the Shakespearean plays, were performed indoors and at night, lighting assumed a new importance in theatrical production. Imigo probably used candles inside coloured glass globes, and he seems also to have made use of screens of oiled paper. That lights were not used merely for illumination is plain from Jonson's description; they were employed from the first for their decorative effect. Another motive is hinted at in the description of the masque entitled 'Tethys' Festival,' of which we are told: 'First at the opening of the heavens appeared 3 circles of lights and glasses, one within another, and came down in a straight motion five foote, and then began to move circularly; which lights and motion so occupied the eyes of the spectators that the manner of altering the Scene was scarcely discerned, for in a moment the whole face of it was changed.'

This brings us to the device known as the *machina versatalis.* It is first mentioned in the text of 'Hymenæi' (that is, in 1606), in which a great gilded globe turned to discover the masquers. It is interesting to note that, according to a contemporary eye-witness, Ben Jonson himself 'turned the globe of the earth standing behind the altar' at the actual performance. This primitive form of revolving stage was therefore operated by hand.

The 'Masque of Beauty' had *two* revolving stages, one above the other, both being mounted on a platform moving on wheels and figuring a floating island. The 'Throne of Beauty' had a circular motion of its own, 'imitating that which we call *Motum mundi,* from the *East* to the *West,* or the right to the left side.... The steps, whereon the Cupids sate, had a motion contrary ... *ad motum Planetarum,* from the *West* to the *East:* both which turned with their several! lights. And with these three varied *Motions* at once, the whole Scene shot it selfe to the land.' It is plain that revolving stages and sliding stages were no invention of the twentieth century, whatever mechanical improvements can be claimed in their methods of operation.

Jones indeed — or his Italian masters — was a real innovator in stage technique. Shakespeare had had little enough in the way of stage scenery, and nothing in the nature of a curtain. Complicated scenery needed a curtain to make it effective, and it is interesting to trace Jones's experiments in trying to devise a satisfactory form of something which the modern theatre takes for granted. At first he seems to have used a *falling* curtain like those employed in the Roman theatre in its later development. In the 'Masque of Blacknesse' 'First, for the Scene, was drawne a Landtschap, consisting of small woods, and here and there a void place fill'd with huntings; which falling, an artificial sea was seene to shoote forth.' This painted drop, as we should call it, is described in a manuscript in the British Museum as 'drawne upon a doune right cloth, strayned for the scene,' but the same manuscript describes it not as falling, but as opening 'in manner of a curtine.' We hear of the curtain being drawn in various other masques, but in 'Cœlum Britannicum,' performed in 1634, the opening scene was disclosed by the curtain 'flying up on a sudden'; so that towards the end of Jones's career the 'drop' had assumed its modern form.

The proscenium arch was another important innovation. At first it was merely a kind of ornamental border erected, as were nearly all such English proscenium arches until the Restoration, specially for each production. Inigo Jones himself has described one of the earliest of these special arches, constructed for 'Tethys' Festival' in 1611:

> *'First on eyther side stood a great statue of twelve foot high representing Neptune and Nereus. . . . These Sea-gods stood on pedestals and were al of gold. Behinde them were two pillasters, on which hung compartments with other devises; and these bore up a rich Freeze wherein were figures of tenne foote long, of Clouds and Nymphes, with a number of naked children dallying with a draperie, which they seemed to holde up, that the Scene might be seene, and the ends thereof fell downe in foldes by the pillasters. In the midst was a compartment, with this inscription,* Tethyos Epinicia, *Tethys' feasts of triumph. This was supported with two winged boyes and all the work was done with that force and boldnesse on the gold and silver, as the figures seemed round and not painted.'*

It is obvious that when the permanent proscenium arch came into existence it followed very much the same pattern, except that instead of the central 'compartment' of the arch carrying the name of the play it bore the arms of the monarch or the prince.

An important part of the Chatsworth collection consists of Inigo's designs for costumes. As might be expected, most of these follow, with modifications, the costumes of antiquity, as was indeed natural enough in view of the classical themes of most of the masques. But the great artist brought to his designs a real ingenuity and eloquence which saves them from being mere copies. Many of the men wear a modification of the Roman warrior's tunic; the women wear the dress of their time, suitably fantasticated and sometimes with a degree of *decolletage* which the modern mind associates more readily with the Folies Bergère than with a Court entertainment. Some of the dresses, especially those worn by the gentlemen and fine ladies of the Court, were extremely rich, and must have cost their wearers considerable sums of money. The costumes of those who took part in the humorous interludes gave more scope for fancy, and here we find Inigo making use of Elizabethan and even of medieval costumes, as well as of animal disguises. In one of the antimasques we find all 'Indian Man' with a bow slung at his back and a crown of upstanding plumes. Another design is for 'a Pagode,' and shows a pagoda-shaped headdress and finger-nails extremely long. This figure, although described as worshipped by 'Indians,' must be one of the first examples of pseudo-Chinese costume in theatrical history. Merlin, in 'Britannia Triumphans' performed in 1638, wears a slashed and beplumed turban. We also find a 'Persian,' an 'Arab' and a 'Dwarf in Dress.'

Some of the antimasques gave an opportunity to introduce the costumes of the lower classes — 'Porter,' 'Vintner's Boy' and 'Kitchenmaid'; and in the description of some of the comic characters in 'Britannia Triumphans' is an entry that must not be overlooked:

> *'In the bottom row on the left is a Mountebanke's man or Zany . . . Cap, with two feathers and long peak, drawn over his brow; loose blouse with hanging sleeves and baggy trousers. Next to him is a Harlequin. . . . He has beard and moustaches. Flat cap; long loose jacket, with sleeves covering hands; and trousers. Inscribed, "*harlekin.*" On the right is a Clown with moustaches and peaked beard. Close round cap or hood, loose jacket with large round buttons and belt, and trousers. Inscribed, "John Farino." '* [1]

Thus we see the Cornmedia dell'Arte suddenly appearing in the Whitehall masques, for Gian Farino was a character in the old Italian comedy, and Harlequin and Zany need no comment.

In 'Salmacida Spolia,' performed in 1660, we find a 'Doctor Tartaglia and a Pedant of Francolin.' The second figure is described as 'a tall, thin man. . . . Long nose and pointed chin. Close cap with upturned brim. Tight-fitting doublet with large round buttons. Short trunk-hose, slashed and pulled, and tights. Long cloake falling to knees.' What is this but the familiar 'Il Dottore'?

'The Queene of Arragon' is the last masque of which we have any record of scenes and costumes. The troubles of the Civil War put an end to this form of courtly entertainment, the interest of which is that its scenery and costumes were so much in advance of those in use in the public theatres.

The English public theatres did not last much longer, for they were suppressed during the Commonwealth; and, although there were certain private entertainments in the houses of the great nobles during the closing years of Cromwell's Protectorate, the general public had to wait for the Restoration before it was permitted to see drama again. But the Restoration theatres were quite different from the stage of Shakespeare; they made use of the scenic devices which we have noted in the Caroline masques, but which were quite absent from the Elizabethan stage.

In one sense this was natural enough, yet an awkward gap existed in our knowledge of the transition period, even in the minds of specialist students. This gap has now been largely filled, owing to the indefatigable Professor Nicoll. One of his former students, Dr.

Clifford Leech, drew his attention to two designs forming part of a manuscript in the Henry E. Huntingdon Library. The manuscript contains a play entitled ' Candy Restored,' written by Mildmay Fane, Earl of Westmorland, and presented by amateurs at Apethorpe on February 12, 1640 (Old Style). The designs show the ground plan and a side view of the wings and are of great importance, for without them the page of explanatory text would be obscure indeed. It reads as follows:

The Scene

A picture of Diana with a Cressant/ vnder which in a scroule written in greate

Candy Restored

Vnder which in perspectiuc a goodly fabrick/ or Cittie the Emblem of Concord/ Vnitie and peace.

Vnder which A Landskipp representing the springe/ for the fresh greermcsse of itt and those innocent/ and vsefall delights of hunting both yt Iland hath/ been famous for, and that season fitted/ the temperature of the ayer too, wch wthout/ a settled recouery of peace and tranquillity/ the greene had withered, and the pleasure been/ dead or layd a sleepe.

On either side the stage a treble entry ouer/ which Heroes men of armes in armes/ and Battles Painted to paint out/ the horrid shape of discord/ which without a miletary word/ turne silently faces about/ at the chang in states fortune/ and are backt wth nothing but/ fresh greenes & faire garden/ Landskips wch consent in/ Vniformity wth ye scene/ it selfe ye trauerse/ being drawne.

As Professor Nicoll interprets it, this means that in ' Candy Restored,' the stage, as at Shakespeare's Globe, was divided into two portions — an outer stage and an inner stage, the latter being concealed by a 'traverse' or 'curtayne.' In the text this inner stage is called 'ye scene it selfe' and (in his own words) 'looking at the plan, we realize that just such an arrangement of wings would have served to transform the bare stage-place into a regular set. Not that the artist has placed the wings correctly; in no conceivable theatre could their angles have provided the appearance obviously desired. In interpreting the plan we have to presume that the three flat wings on each side were placed in position either in a straight line running diagonally back from the front comers of the platform to the edges of the traverse, or else in a slightly overlapping arrangement between the double lines marked out by the draughtsman.'

Professor Nicoll's knowledge of the whole corpus of known theatrical material enabled him to bring forward at this point an engraving from Commenius' *Orbis sensualium pictus,* which shows a scene with an inner stage hidden by a curtain precisely as in the Globe, but with side-wings curiously similar to those shown in the Huntingdon Library plan. These wings are neither the twosided wings described by Serlio, nor the flat wing parallel with the front of the stage and sliding in and out as required in grooves on the stage floor. It is plain that they revolved like the Greek *periaktoi,* but, unlike them, were not prisms but flat frames. And that this system was not peculiar to this particular performance at Apethorpe is proved by a reference in Dubreuil's *Perspective pratique,* published in 1642: 'The scene (he says) may be made to change further by the use of simple frames. In the middle of the frames are put axles or simply two points of iron that rest in pivots — so that when one turns the frames thus mounted they show first one face and then another.'

This then would seem to be the link for which scholars have been looking between the theatre of Shakespeare and the theatre of Dryden, a true transitional form possessing some of the characteristics of both.

❐❐❐

7

Russian Fashion in Costume Designing

Introduction

The Russian art that influenced Western culture and fashion in the first two decades of the twentieth century can be divided into two main categories: native Russian, or Slavic, forms and colors; and themes or motifs that were not Russian in origin, but which were taken up by artists. Diaghilev's Ballets Russes, which popularized themes from the East and antiquity, fell into the latter category. Fin-de-siècle Europe, with its friability of social standards and the gradual changes in the institution of the family as a result of female emancipation, was fertile ground for the new fashionable styles introduced by Diaghilev.

The Russian influence on culture and fashion in Paris began during the period when Art Nouveau, called Art Moderne in Russia, was at its height. This movement, which flourished all over Europe, appeared as a reaction against the industrial revolution with its mechanical production and against Victorian art with its retrospective and eclectic approach. Art Nouveau was a collective child of European artists during this marvelous era when fluid lines were still valued in art and strict rules of composition and balanced relationships of color still existed. Attempting to achieve a unified aesthetic of both arts and crafts, the creators of Art Nouveau rehabilitated folk art in many countries, including Russia. Fin-de-siècle artists, interested in creating new technologies in applied arts while also resurrecting old ones, tried to do everything to unite the natural and artificial in metal, glass, and wood. Art Nouveau works are characterized by organic forms, fluid, pastel colors, and a contrasting variety of surfaces and textures combined with melancholy and mysterious subjects and images.

National romanticism was one aspect of Art Nouveau. The search for the original sources of folk art led many Russian artists deep into their country's traditions and history, creating a heightened interest in folk epics, called *byliny*, and legends and sagas.

National romanticism existed in architecture, painting, applied art, and, naturally, fashion. In the first decade of the century, national romanticism was widespread throughout Europe and was highly developed in the art of Scandinavia and the Baltic countries. In Russia it led to what became known as the neoRussian style, which adopted the forms of Art Moderne. It was this fin-de-siècle neo-Russian style that influenced European fashion.

The neo-Russian style was elevated to semiofficial art in Russia, where the spread of Art Nouveau was undoubtedly aided by the Empress Alexandra Feodorovna, wife of Tsar Nicholas II. Nee Alice, Princess of Hesse, the empress was raised in Darmstadt, Germany, later one of the major centers of European Moderne, and famed for its artistic colony and regular art exhibits. The empress liked *Jugendstil*, the German variety of Moderne, and, naturally, supported the development of analogous forms in Russia. The ball at the Winter Palace with costumes designed by the artist Sergei Solomko is one of the most vivid examples of the court's acceptance of the neo-Russian style.

The studios in the artists' colonies of Abramtsevo, the estate outside Moscow belonging to Savva Mamontov, the owner of a private opera company, and Talashkino, the estate in Smolensk belonging to Princess Tenisheva, were the best-known and most significant centers of neo-Russian arts-and-crafts production.

Diaghilev magazine, *World of Art (Mir iskusstva)*, often published reproductions of works in the neo-Russian style. With the rise of interest in crafts, this style moved into fashion, not changing the fashionable silhouette popular in Russia, but influencing the ornamentation. Thanks to the successful work in Tenisheva's workshops in Smolensk and Polenova's in Abramtsevo, as well as a series of crafts exhibits in the capital and the outlying regions, fashionable outfits included elements of "folk" costumes. Russian lace, more severe than Belgian or French, became more fashionable than the imports. The ruffles and detailing of unbleached linen lace went wonderfully well with the summer dresses worn at the dacha, Russians' country home, during the Chekhovian period of the turn of the century.

Lace makers from Vologda and Eletsk finally achieved national recognition and their handiwork was highly valued in the fashionable circles of St. Petersburg and Moscow. Stylized Ukrainian and Russian cross-stitching embroidery also appeared in fashionable stores in the cities. Embroidery was used not only on everyday summer blouses, but on dressier outfits, such as dresses for walking and receiving guests. But however popular these neo-Russian styles may have been in Russia, they were not what became part of the arsenal of the fin-de-siècle Parisian fashion plates.

The first items borrowed from Russia by Parisian trendsetters were Siberian furs, sable in particular. The visit by Tsar Nicholas II to Paris in 1897 gave rise to French interest in the Russian empire, and fur trim and linings "*à la Russe*" became very prestigious. The celebrated fashion houses of Worth, Doucet, and Drecoll used fur to trim their models.

The patriotically inclined Maria Tenisheva organized an exhibit in Paris of crafts from Talashkino. She hired a hall in the Societe des artistes modernes on rue Caumartin, decorating it with paintings by artists Nikolai Roerich and Ivan Bilibin and with drawings of churches built by Roerich and Pokrovsky, a background that set off brilliantly the embroidery by the peasant women of Talashkino. The princess's own account of the influence of Russian crafts on Paris fashion is important: "Both my Paris shows had a strong effect

On fashion and accessories for women. A year later I noticed a clear influence of our embroidery, our Russian dresses, *sarafans* [peasant women's dresses], shirts, tea dresses, *zipuns* (homespun peasant coats), in fact the term 'blouse russe' appeared, and so on. Jewelry was also affected by our Russian artistry, which pleased me and was a reward for all my efforts and expense. It was clear that everything they saw had a powerful effect on French artists and tailors."

Tenisheva took part in creating the costumes for the opera Snow Maiden (*Snegurochka*) by Rimsky-Korsakov at the Paris Opera Comique. She wrote in her memoirs: "I was given unlimited credit. Since it was impossible to get the right fabrics for the costumes, I made all the *sarafans* embroidered from top to bottom, and that, naturally, was not cheap. The *kokosbniki* [women's headdresses], necklaces, *shugai*, and men's costumes—all passed through my hands, and I made the crown of Tsar Berendei personally in my studio, since the one made by the theater's jeweler was unsatisfactory."

Princess Tenisheva's activity undoubtedly helped Russian style enter western Europe. She wrote: "I am happy and proud that it befell me to introduce the West to our antiquity, our art, to show them that our past had been touching and marvelous."

However, the most significant Russian influence on European fashion came through the genius Sergei Pavlovich Diaghilev. Paris first came to know Diaghilev at the Autumn Salon, when he opened the exhibit of Russian visual art, which spanned the period from Vladimir Borovikovsky, a painter of the late eighteenth century, to Mikhail Vrubel, one of the founders of the Russian Art Moderne. At the festive opening ceremonies a special section was devoted to Russian icons. The show's success is described in the biography *Diaghilev* by Serge Lifar, a loyal friend of the great impresario: "The exhibit of paintings was a brilliant success, Russian artists were understood and appreciated, and many former associates of *Mir iskusstva* were invited to join the Autumn Salon.

They wanted to give Diaghilev the Legion of Honor but he declined it in favor of Bakst could the manifestation of yet another Russian art unknown to Paris be as successful Russian music?"

At the time, France was very friendly with Russia, and Diaghilev's events were supported by society. One of the most elegant ladies of the Belle Epoque, Comtesse de Greffulhe, helped organize the financial support for Diaghilev's projects. The brilliant performances of Felia Litvin and Feodor Chaliapin, Diaghilev gave spoiled Paris the masterpieces of Russian classical and opera music.

Diaghilev's role in attracting European interest in Russian art served different goals, much greater in scope, than the work of Princess Tenisheva, who was a passionate devotee of the neo-Russian style. In the early twentieth century there existed two currents of Russian influence on the West: one, according to Lifar, introduced Paris to "faux Berendeys and Stenka Razins," and the other gave freedom to artistic experimentation of unsurpassed magnificence, by the name of the Ballets Russes, which went on to become a milestone in twentieth-century culture.

Diaghilev had prepared this production for a long time: he wanted to show the authentic Russia of the late sixteenth and early seventeenth centuries, and to that purpose he scoured Russian villages collecting real Russian peasant dresses and Russian pearls and embroidery of the period.

The result of the scrupulous preparation of costumes and scenery, based on the sketches of Bilibin, Konstantin Yuon, and Alexander Benois, executed at the Hermitage Theater in St. Petersburg, was stunning. The magnificent Russian prePetrine garments overwhelmed the Parisians. The critic Arnold Haskell wrote about it in his book *Diaghileff: His Artistic and Private Life*: "This operatic realism was entirely new to the French, and that, together with the beauty of the choral singing and Chaliapin's double triumph, subsequently occupied the chief attention of the press."

The three seasons determined the future success of Diaghilev's Ballet Russes, which lasted until the impresario's death. Thanks to their artistic influence on the social and cultural life of Paris, Russian artists and performers were embraced with delight, and the world of fashion was quite interested in the new Russian colors and forms.

With the help of people close to him—PrincessPolignac, Misia Sert, Prince Argutinsky-Dolgoruky, and, certainly, his faithful colleagues Benois and Bakst—Diaghilev presented the first season of the Ballets Russes in Paris. He managed to bring to Parisa troupe of talented artists headed by the innovative choreographer Mikhail Fokine, and on the memorable day of May 19, the Ballets Russes opened with Fokine's ballet *Le Pavillion d'Armide*, featuring sets by Benois. The troupe performed at the old Paris Chatelet theatre, which Diaghilev remodeled. Among the performers were the incomparable Anna Pavlova, the beautiful Vera Karalli, the "Moscow Hercules"

Mikhail Mordkin, the talented Adolf Bolm, the adorable Tamara Karsavina, and the genius Vaslav Nijinsky. That same evening two other ballets were presented as well—Polovtsian Dances from the Alexander Borodin opera *Prince Igor* and *Le Festin*, a suite consisting of individual duets and dances, including *lezghinkas*, czardas, *hopaks*, mazurkas, *trepaks*, and other Hungarian dances.

The second program of the first ballet season, presented on June 2 at the same theater, included two other productions by Fokine, Les Sylphides and Cleopatra, in which the rare gifts of Fokine's student Ida Rubinstein were seen for the first time in Paris. Diaghilev's first ballet season was a smashing success. Lifar wrote down Diaghilev's assessment: "Success? Triumph? These words mean nothing and cannot convey the enthusiasm, that sacred fire and sacred madness that engulfed the entire audience."

The most popular ballets of the first season were Polovtsian Dances and Cleopatra, which had not only Fokine's innovative choreography in common, but also exotic oriental subjects. The Polovtsian Dances enchanted with their steppe wildness, while the appearance of Ida Rubinstein as Cleopatra was very impressive in the setting created by, Bakst—she was carried out by six enormous slaves.

European fashion was under the influence of the neo-classical style: a silhouette with elevated waist featuring straight lines. Wide-brimmed hats were in vogue and the most fashionable pattern was stripes. It was only during the second season of the Russians' siege of Paris that the fashion world gave in to the pressure of Fokine's and Bakst's Oriental exotica. The Paris season of Diaghilev's Ballets Russes opened on June 4 at the Grand Opera with Fokine's one-act ballet, Carnival, to Schumann's music. This production had been seen before in February of that year in St. Petersburg and in May at the Berlin Westens Theater. Overshadowed by the triumphant success of Fokine *Scheherazade*, Carnival is often overlooked by fashion historians. Yet the costumes for this ballet were harbingers of women's fashion during World War I. The sketches created by Bakst showed the silhouette that became popular, with shorter skirts and Spanish ruffles and a predilection for polka dots and whites.

The Fokine- Bakst *Scheherazade* played another unexpected role it anticipated many artistic forms that later became component parts of Art Deco. *Scheherazade* showed sophisticated Western audiences

Bakst's version of Persian, which consisted of Ottoman costumes and interiors. Arnold Haskell wrote, "*Scheherazade* set the tone in fashion, shedding bright colors into store windows and women's dresses, illuminating the tones of all subsequent theater sets. It moved to the stage of revues and music halls, until Diaghilev himself had to hide from it."

Yes, this production, whose bloody and erotic plot was also invented by Bakst, was for many years the symbol of Russian ballet abroad. The passionate love of Sultaness Zobeide, danced by Ida Rubinstein, for her ebony slave, Vaslav Nijinsky, excited the feelings of the delighted Parisian women. The sheer harem pants of the odalisques, the colorful garments of the eunuchs, the turbans of Sultan Sharir and his beloved but unfaithful Zobeide, the drapes of Oriental palaces, carpets and brocade pillows, lampshades, egrets, and strings of pearls astonished the audience. The characteristic Parisian desire to possess the latest and most unusual came to the fore, and the exotic Oriental winds blew into the ateliers of the Parisian creators of fashion and design.

Beyond fashion, the plot of *Scheherazade* influenced the morals and mores of the period. The sensual delights of semiclad harem girls with half-naked, black, muscular slaves on the palace's pillows was simultaneously shocking and attractive. Fokine was the first choreographer to bring an element of pure sexuality onto the stage, thereby emancipating the views of men and women in the sphere of the theater. The violation of this taboo brought on the wrath of moralizing critics. Bakst was called an erotomaniac and Diaghilev's Ballets Russes a degenerate enterprise. *Scheherazade*'s notoriety only added to its success, and audiences demanded tickets. Everyone expected to see indescribable harem orgies on stage.

The colors and combinations of the costumes and sets created by Bakst had an enormous influence on twentiethcentury fashion. Seemingly incompatible colors combined on stage: purple and blue, yellow and red, green and orange. These types of contrasts were contrary to the concepts of beauty that had long been inculcated in the civilized world by Art Nouveau artists. Only combinations of pale pink with delicate lilac, watery blue or pistachio green were considered in good taste. The vivid colors of Diaghilev's Ballets Russes forced people to look at the world through a prism of bright sensations, to come to love color in its original form. For instance, the combination of orange and green, offered by Bakst, was accepted with delight and lasted a long time. Moving from the stage to the world of fashion and interior decoration.

Other productions by the Diaghilev troupe from the season Giselle with Nijinsky and Karsavina, The Firebird with music by Stravinsky, and the divertissement Orientalia drew mixed reactions. The romantic Giselle was considered old-fashioned by many, but *The Firebird*, with sets by Alexander Golovin and costumes by Bakst, delighted them. In any case, after two triumphant seasons Russian ballet became a permanent fixture of Parisian artistic life.

The productions of subsequent years—Petrotichka, *Le Spectre de la Rose*, Narcissus, *Le Dieu Bleu*, Swan Lake, Thamar, and *L'Après-midi d'un Faun*—were milestones in the history of European culture. Expressing the opinion of many contemporaries, the French writer Louis Fillet remarked, "This was an event, unexpected, a storm, a kind of shock, Scheherazade, Prince Igor, The Firebird, Swan Lake, *Le Spectre de la Rose*. In other words, I can say without exaggeration that my life is divided into two parts: before and after the Russian ballets. All our ideas, our perceptions were transformed. The scales fell from our eyes."

One of the first to succumb to the charms of the Ballets Russes was the fashion setter of the period, Paul Poiret. The great reformer of women's clothing was seven years younger than Diaghilev and belonged to the same generation of people born in the 1870s. In 1898 he began working for the famous fashion house Raudnitz & Cie, directed by Madame Cheruit. The next year he joined one of the most talented creators of fashion of the Art Nouveau era, Jacques Doucet moved to the oldest and most prestigious Paris fashion house, Worth. It was there that Poiret first encountered Russian taste and a few Russian clients. Worth, founded by the Englishman Charles Frederick Worth in 1857, dressed all the brilliant courts of Europe in the era of the Second Empire. Numerous Russian aristocrats who ordered the fabulously expensive gowns from Worth are captured in their finery by the brush of the brilliant Franqois Xavier Winterhalter. During the reign of Nicholas II, the house of Worth which, after the death of its founder, was now being run by his sons, Jean-Philippe and Gaston-Lucien-dressed Empress Alexandra Feodorovna and some of the ladies at her court.

In his memoirs, *En habillant l'epoque* [Dressing an Era], Poiret, who had worked for Worth while Worth was still alive, gives a lively description of a titled Russian client, Princess Bariatinsky: "Once Mr. Worth was looking out the window at the lively rue de la Paix. He liked watching the bustle of the carriages bringing celebrities from around the world to his house. Suddenly he turned quickly and cried out, 'Ladies, ladies, it's Princess Bariatinsky!' I thought his heart was beating harder. All the saleswomen jumped up simultaneously and in the blink of an eye they had set up chairs along the walls, preparing for a show. They turned to the elevator doors. Hearing the noise, the servants came. Mr. Worth himself during this was trying to clamp shut the mouth of his little dog, also excited by the general turmoil.

"I stood at the end of this animated line impatiently awaiting a glimpse of the beautiful princess, the cause of this excitement. When the cab finally reached our floor, I was astonished to see in it a lady in black, resembling a fat priest with a red face, leaning on two canes and smoking a large cigar. All the staff gave her a servile, low bow. Worth himself bent in two. Princess Boryatinskaya announced, with a marked Russian accent, ' Worth, show me your latest,' using the familiar tu with him. The princess wished him to start with coats. Worth suggested that the princess take several chairs. The mannequins scurried, and I had the honor of showing a coat we had just completed, an innovation. Now it would be considered banal, even old-fashioned, but back then nothing like it existed. It was a black wool kimono, trimmed with black satin. The sleeves reached almost to the ground, ending in embroidered stripes, resembling the garments of the Chinese mandarins. I don't know whether the princess did not like the Chinese in general or whether she recalled the siege of Port Arthur or something else. But she shouted: 'How horrible! It looks like a sack!' I was terribly upset, embarrassed, and worried that I would never be able to please Russian princesses."

Poiret opened his first small store on the rue Auber and then expanded the business. His designs, with their unprecedentedly clear lines and simple forms, attracted Parisian women. He was the first couturier to raise the waist in women's dresses, recalling Empire lines and thereby creating an elongated silhouette, like a cue stick. In the model called "Lola Montez," Poiret freed women from corsets, he introduced harem pants and pants-skirts into their wardrobes.

The height of Poiret's creativity coincided with the height of the Ballets Russes.

In museum circles of Paris, the question of whether Poiret was influenced by the Ballets Russes is still discussed. Poiret himself wrote: "Like many other French artists, I was delighted by the Ballets Russes, and I would not be surprised if it had a certain influence on me. But I must stress that my reputation was created much earlier than that of Mr. Bakst." There are definite notes of jealousy in that statement. Bakst and Poiret had never worked together; however, let us note that contacts between Diaghilev and Poiret existed when, several months after the premiere of Scheherazade, Poiret invited Diaghilev and Nijinsky to his salon to show them his latest models.

One thing is indisputable: Poiret's collections are filled with Oriental exotica. He created semisheer harem pants, introduced turbans with egrets, pearl necklaces, and lampshadelike skirts. The colors of his models echoed the fiery tones characteristic of Bakst, with carmine accompanying ultramarine, orange with emerald, and pink with gold. Using "theatrical" trims of fur and fringe and embroidery of beads, jet, and stone, Poiret achieved unusual effects and great commercial success. He could not admit to being an imitator of Bakst, of course, but the influence of the Ballets Russes on Paris fashion was quite obvious to contemporaries.

Prince Peter Lieven in his book, *The Birth of the Ballets-Russes*, wrote: "The influence of this style was felt far beyond the confines of the theatre. The dress designers of Paris incorporated it in their fashions. Poiret and Callot began to model gowns inspired by Bakst's painting. "Ballets-Russes" turbans and cushions came into fashion; dress material, even, began to be manufactured in the same style."

Yielding to the general fascination, some Parisian, and then London and Berlin, fashion houses in prepared collections *à la Ballets Russes*. The most successful in this trend was the famous Callot Soeurs, founded in 1888 by Marie Callot, one of four sisters. It was among the first to introduce saffron yellow in their models, part of Bakst's palette, and to popularize harem skirt-pants.

The house of Paquin, founded in 1891, one of the most respected fashion houses of France, hired Bakst and he created a series of sketches of evening and day dresses for Madame Paquin. The house carried models in the Bakst-Diaghilev manner throughout the seasons. One such exotic outfit of the period is described in detail in the memoirs of the Diaghilev ballerina, Natalya Vladimirovna Truhanova, a Parisian fashion plate and great flirt: "My arsenal I mean my toilette—that evening was outstanding: a dress the color of raspberry geranium with a flower frisson stitched on muslin velvet: the shape of the dress is empire, with a corsage trimmed in pearls and gold embroidery, with short sleeves and a long train that is tossed over the arm. A wide diamond band shone on my head, a diamond necklace on my neck, drop pearl earrings and pearl bracelets. Gold slippers with matching stockings completed the ensemble. The mirror reflected my vision, which even I found astonishing."

Outside France, the Viennese-Berlin house of Christoffe von Drecoll, founded in Vienna and the first-rate Lucile, founded in London by Lady Duff Gordon, were fans of the new forms. After the Diaghilev troupe performed in London, Orientalism filled the salons of British society, and aristocratic women tried to look like harem girls. The London newspaper *Queen* described one such fashion plate: "We noticed a lady in the parterre who must have come straight from the seraglio. Her dress of rich silk with embroidery was shapeless, her head was wrapped in a round turban."

A major triumph for Oriental motifs was the 1002 Nights Ball, given by Poiret in his Paris townhouse on June 24. The occasion, an homage to Russian ballet, was a distinctive quotation from *Scheherazade*. All the guests at the masked ball were dressed as Persian ambassadors, Ottoman eunuchs, Indian *bayadères*, or Arabian odalisques. Poiret in a turban and luxurious caftan was a sultan and his wife, Denise, his favorite harem wife, whose prototype was Zobeide. Most of costumes for the ball had been prepared by Poiret himself, and he had not skimped. Precious Persian rugs were spread right in the courtyard of Poiret's fabulous house, the wine flowed like water, Eastern melodies played all night—the unforgettable theatrical evening was a great success.

After that, Oriental balls became the fashion. Countess Klein Michel held something similar in St. Petersburg, and Countesse de Clermont-Tonnerre in Paris. The primary garment that the fashionable ladies adopted from the endless celebration of Oriental luxury and voluptuousness was the lampshade skirt. Denise Poiret wore one of the first at the 1002 Nights Ball. It consisted of semisheer muslin harem pants and a short skirt with a hoop, like a lampshade. Georges Lepape, the great fashion illustrator, depicted her in it. European women suddenly all wanted to see themselves as slave girls or concubines of a sultan.

Poiret took a group of runway models on a long tour of eastern Europe, visiting Warsaw, Krakow, Moscow, St. Petersburg, Bucharest, Budapest, and Vienna. In Moscow and St. Petersburg he lectured and showed his latest designs and also met with the Russian designer Nadezhda Petrovna Lamanova. In his memoirs, Poiret wrote: " Lamanova was an outstanding seamstress and at that time became my dear friend. It was she who revealed the charms of Moscow, that precious gateway to Asia. Even now I see her against the background of the icons of the Kremlin, the cupolas of St. Basil's Cathedral, and the marvelous collection of modern art belonging to Mr. Shchukin."

Thus, in a roundabout way, Diaghilev's exotica, not without the help of Poiret, reached Russia, thereby closing the circle of the metamorphosis of prewar fashion. It should be noted that Lamanova's exquisite models of those years had an echo of the harem theme. A few of her dresses, from the museum of Baron Stieglitz and the closet of the actress Karakhan, are now in the collections of the State Hermitage Museum in St. Petersburg. The author's collection contains two rare pieces combining the creativity of Lamanova and Bakst: muslin three-quarter-length evening dresses beaded and embroidered at Lamanova's studio after a drawing by Bakst for the Bolshoi Theater ballerina Ekaterina Geltser. She received the sketch from Bakst, when she danced with the Diaghilev troupe.

Among the St. Petersburg fashion houses under the strong influence of Oriental trends were Gindus and Bresac. The first belonged to Anna Grigoryevna Gindus, who studied in Paris at Paquin and then opened her own establishment in St. Petersburg at 45 Mokhovaya Street. The house of the Frenchman Auguste Bresac was on the Moika Canal, number 42, and made elegant designs for St. Petersburg society.

It must be said that all these mindboggling Baghdad toilettes of the season were not taken seriously by Russian high society, the aristocracy, who had more severe, English tastes. In Russia, it was the stars of stage and screen who were the passionate fans of this style. National and provincial actresses including the operetta prima donna Irina Orlova, and the dramatic actresses V. A. Mironova, E. V. Stefanovich, A. P. Milich, E. T. Zhikhareva, B. I. Rutkovskaya, and Maria Verdinskaya had themselves photographed dressed *à la Ballets Russes*.

But the most fertile soil in Russia for Diaghilev's exotic style was in silent film. One striking example is the incomparable film beauty Vera Kholodnaya, the first Russian vamp. Other film stars who liked Oriental fashions were Nathalie Lissenko, Zoya Barantsevich, Lydia Ryndina, and Zoe Karabanova. These stars, most of whom later emigrated to Europe, excited hearts and muddled minds, creating the first images of the femme fatale on the screen. Makeup from the Diaghilev ballets was also introduced to film heavy-lidded, weary eyes, the rustle of long lashes, perfidious lips, and deathly pale skin. The look eventually moved from the screen to fashion, and the femme fatale became the symbol of female beauty.

The Ballets Russes changed tastes in interior decoration, as well. Bright colors and shimmering tones became fashionable, and the tiniest details in bedrooms and living rooms were transformed by the taste for the exotic. Draperies with large Persian patterns became popular; they were used as overhangs on beds, lambrequins, and drapes. Another mania was for carpets and pillows, which created an air of the seraglio. Poiret, who discovered the commercial aspect of this style earlier than the rest, created a decorator's studio called Martine, named after one of his daughters. This salon, which opened on the rue St. Honore, created pillows, wallpaper, fabrics, carpets, and ceramics. Under the direction of Madame Serusier, teenage girls from poor families drew designs for fabrics and embroidery. Thanks to Bakst and Poiret, harem pillows became a fixture for thirty years.

Another element in the Oriental transformation of homes and apartments was the silk, often painted, lampshade with fringe. It was intended to create intimate coziness in the domestic hearth. Additions to the interiors were narrow minaret windows, low, carved Constantinople tables, and soft rugs. The ballerina Natalya Truhanova describes such a fashionable interior: "There was no chandelier. It was replaced by a tall *lampadaire* a lamp on a pole topped by a brilliant alabaster chalice, from which poured a soft and yet bright light. The floor was covered by a multitude of various-sized rugs. Small, low tables with flowers and smoldering scents were everywhere. Simple, woven armchairs covered with gold-embroidered fabrics. Finally, a long and narrow divan-bed, smothered in furs and bright pillows, among which sat our host." The house belonged to Gabrielle D'Annunzio, the famous Italian poet.

Poiret opened his perfume shop Rosine, named after another daughter, at 39 rue de Colisee the first attempt to create a line of perfumes under a fashionable brand name. Other countriers followed suit. Poiret's Oriental flair was obvious in the names for his perfumes and cosmetics: "Maharaja," "Chinese Night," "Forbidden Fruit," and "Golden Chalice." Other perfume firms created spicy scents like "Sacuntala" and "Nirvana." Even the magazine advertisements for the famous German cologne "Troica" began using scenes from *Scheherazade*.

Poiret's rivalry with Bakst did not end his contacts with Russians; they had just begun. Roman Petrovich Tyrtov was the son of Admiral Petr Ivanovich Tyrtov, director of the Naval Engineering School. Poiret hired the young man as an illustrator and designer. They Tyrtov family, of Tatar origin, has served the Russian fleet for over two centuries; but from early childhood, Roman showed no inclination for ships or cannons, and drew instead. This is what he told the author: "I began drawing at three with colored pencils, and at six I drew my first dress design. It was a sketch for an evening dress for my mother, which she gave to her seamstress. The dress was a big success. When Mother saw that I was serious about drawing, she introduced me to the famous Russian painter Ilya Efimovich Repin. He praised the style of my work and gave me my first drawing lesson."

Roman Tyrtov first visited Paris at the age of seven for the World's Fair with his mother and sister. Ever since, memories of Paris gave the child no peace, and he decided to live there no matter what. He studied drawing in St. Petersburg at the studio of the artist Losevsky. Roman Tyrtov told the author in an interview: "When I graduated from high school, Father told me to name my gift, and to his great dissatisfaction, I asked for a passport to travel abroad." But whatever Petr Ivanovich may have felt about his son's request, Russian admirals kept their word and he granted permission for the trip.

Before his departure to Paris, Roman Tyrtov went to the editors of the fashion magazine *Damskii mir [Ladies' World]* and offered his services as Paris correspondent. The artist arrived in magical, tempting Paris at the peak of the Russian influence on the city of muses. The Diaghilev troupe had one triumph after another. Charmed by the Russian ballet, Tyrtov recalled, "I was present at three scandals involving Vaslav Nijinsky. The first, was *Gisèlle* at the Maryinsky Theater in St. Petersburg, and then twice in Paris. First, with *L'Après-midi d'un faun* and then *Le Sacre du printemps.*"

Concern for earning his daily bread forced the artist to work in the small fashion house Caroline. He recalled: "I lived very modestly then in a furnished flat. My first year in Paris was very difficult, and the owner of Caroline did not like my drawings at all, and one fine day she said, 'Young man, do what you like in life, but never try to be a costume designer again, you'll never succeed.' And then she tossed my sketches in the waste basket."

Today, even the most scrupulous historians of fashion do not remember the name Caroline, but our hero became world famous. Pride injured, the young artist pulled his drawings out of the wastebasket, put them in an envelope, and sent them to Paul Poiret. The next morning he received a pneumatic letter with an invitation from Poiret himself.

Once at Poiret, Roman Tyrtov took the pseudonym Erte, based on the initials of his name (R.T.). At Poiret's studio, Erte designed coats, dresses, hats, and hairstyles. In the spring, he designed the play Minaret, with the artist Jose Zamora, at the Renaissance Theater in Paris. During his work on the costumes for Minaret, Erte dealt with the notorious Dutch adventuress Mata Hari, who at the time danced at the Renaissance. It was during his time with Poiret that the artist created his unique style for illustrating fashion.

Drawings signed by Erte were first published in the glossy fashion magazine, *Gazette du bon ton, and his fame grew. His drawing style of languorously elongated silhouettes evinced his closeness to the Diaghilev aesthetic; but, to the end of his days, Erte denied any influence by Bakst on his work, insisting that he found inspiration in Persian miniatures and red-figured Greek vases that he had seen in the Hermitage.*

He is having worked for Poiret for eighteen months, Erte left the house and created his own collection with the help of Poiret's first seamstress. This led to a suit against Erte, which Poiret won, leading to a cooling of relations between the two fashion leaders that lasted up to Poiret's death.

In addition to its influence on fashion, the Ballets Russes gave rise to the adoration of Russian ballerinas. In fashion, the influence of Anna Pavlova and Tamara Karsavina was particularly evident. Pavlova, without question the most famous ballerina of the twentieth century, had no equal as a dancer. Her name was the standard of perfection, which was why so many tried to imitate her manner of dress. Her perfectionist taste was described vividly in a book by her husband Victor Dandre: "In selecting a design of, say, light blue, she found it necessary to repeat it in another color. Naturally, all the trim had to be changed. Then, perhaps, in addition, Pavlova wanted to change the form of a sleeve, the cut of the corsage, until the confused and dispirited tailor shouted: 'But, Madame, what is left of my design?'"

Alice Vronska, a ballerina in Pavlova's troupe, told the author about Pavlova's need to supervise the smallest details of her personal wardrobe and her finickiness in selecting clothing: "Going to fashion houses and stores with Pavlova was torture. She kept trying on and rejecting things, always dissatisfied by something." Her personal wardrobe was impeccable, and her manner of dress created a special trend. Nina Kirsanova, who had danced with Pavlova, told the author: " Pavlova had a special way of wearing things. She particularly liked Manila silk shawls, which she draped in the Spanish manner. They took the place of dresses for her. It became very popular, and many imitated her."

Another soloist in Anna Pavlova's troupe and a former dancer in Sergei Diaghilev's Ballets Russes Valentina Kachouba, celebrated for her grace and beauty shared her reminiscences with the author: "In life Pavlova dressed simply: a modest suit, hat—so that no one recognized her on the street. But she had such individuality, something so utterly special about her face, that people always noticed her, even if they didn't know her. I considered her very beautiful. She always dressed with great taste, usually having her elegant clothes made at Pitoeff. And when she was in evening clothes, it was something marvelous. Pavlova looked like a mannequin."

Her popularity and beauty became the stuff of legend. Naturally, the world of fashion could not let this pass, since it had faith in beauty and obeyed the laws of commerce. There was a brand of cosmetic soap in South America called "Pavlova." Textile manufacturers also used Pavlova's fame: the famous Paris fashion magazine *Art, gout, beaute [Art, Taste, Beauty]* announced a new fabric Pavlova satin, perfect for dishabille. This was a light, semisheer fabric with a satin sheen, its airiness making it suitable only for marvelous undergarments. The Terpsichore of packet boats" in a dress from Drecoll in panne velvet trimmed in sable. The famous French fashion illustrator Georges Barbier wrote of her, "It seems that she has torn away from the earth and like a flower without a stem, flies up, spinning."

❑❑❑

8

Kitmir House of Embroidery for Costume Designing

Introduction

Alexandra Georgievna died at the age of twenty-one at the Ilyinsky estate near Moscow, six days after giving birth to her second child, Grand Duke Dmitrii Pavlovich, Maria Pavlovna's brother. Paul Alexandrovich entered into a morganatic marriage with Olga Valerianovna Pistolkors in Livorno, thereby losing the right to raise his children. Maria and Dmitrii were left virtually orphans and were raised by their uncle Grand Duke Sergei Alexandrovich, the governor-general of Moscow, and his wife, Elizaveta Feodorovna, who was pious and artistically gifted but-according to Maria Pavlovna's description rather cold and unfeeling.

At home Maria and Dmitrii learned English—their governesses were English and French—and Maria Pavlovna spoke Russian badly until the age of six. At the age of seven she traveled in her own personal railway car accompanied by a servant and her loyal governess, Mademoiselle Helène, to visit Germany and France. To be sure, Maria Pavlovna and Dmitrii Pavlovich were brought up exclusively, as befitted their rank. During their walks they were accompanied by servants and footmen, and on Sundays they were allowed to play only with children from aristocratic families. Despite these refinements during her childhood, Maria Pavlovna was able to find the inner strength to live by her own labor as an adult.

Maria Pavlovna's personal life was not a simple, smooth one. The crown prince of Sweden, Duke Wilhelm of Södermanland, visited St. Petersburg and was introduced to the sixteen-yearold Maria Pavlovna. Grand Duchess Elizaveta Feodorovna, her guardian, told her niece that it was her destiny, and Maria Pavlovna agreed to the crown prince's proposal, which soon followed. The wedding was postponed until her eighteenth birthday, and bride and groom were married in St. Petersburg on April 20. The marriage was positive politically and diplomatically for both Russia and Sweden, but unhappy due to the absence of feelings on the part of the newlyweds for each other. On the occasion of his cousin's wedding, the tsar pardoned the bride's father, Grand Duke Paul Alexandrovich, permitting him finally to return to Russia with his new family.

After a honeymoon in Germany, Italy, and France, the newlyweds went to Sweden, where an official ceremonial reception awaited them with the state flags of Russia and Sweden waving all over Stockholm. In Sweden, Maria Pavlovna went hunting, attended horse races, and even played field hockey on Crown Princess Margaret's team. While living in the Oak Hills palace in Stockholm, she decided to study the applied arts. Maria Pavlovna (or the Duchess of Södermanland, which was her title in Sweden) had little interest in her husband, and vice versa.

Maria Pavlovna departed with her husband on a long journey to attend the king of Siam's coronation. The Swedish journalist Staffan Skott, in his recent book, *The Romanovs*, relates how the King and Duke of Montpensier, "a hunter of wild beasts," began to court her. Relations between the couple cooled even more. When they returned to Stockholm, doctors found that Maria Pavlovna had a serious kidney ailment, and it was decided that the duchess of Södermanland be sent to Capri for treatment in the fall and winter.

Returning to Moscow briefly for the celebration of the 300-year anniversary of the Romanov dynasty, Maria Pavlovna then set off for Capri, but got only as far as Berlin, where her brother Grand Duke Dmitrii Pavlovich was waiting for her. Taking leave from her husband at the first opportunity, Maria Pavlovna changed her travel plans and left for Paris with her brother. Commenting on this,

Princess Zinaida Yusupov wrote to her son from Coreiz, in the Crimea: "Maria Pavlovna of Sweden is also a sad example of a disorderly life without any principles or a foundation."

It was obvious to close relatives in both Russia and Sweden that divorce was unavoidable and finally, on March 13, their marriage was officially dissolved, an action then confirmed by an edict issued by Nicholas II on July 15. Unfortunately, Maria Pavlovna's son remained at the Swedish court, and she was unable to see him until she fled Russia.

In Paris Maria Pavlovna studied at a painting school, then traveled in Italy and Greece. A true Russian patriot, she returned to Russia when World War I began and set out for the front as a nurse. For two and a half years, the grand duchess worked as a nurse in Pskov, treating and bandaging wounded soldiers and officers, and even performing simple surgery herself. This difficult labor served Maria Pavlovna well-without this crucial experience her success with the fashion house of Kitmir might not have been possible.

Maria Pavlovna was stunned by the news of Grigory Rasputin's murder in the Yusupov palace in Petrograd in December, in which her brother Dmitrii Pavlovich was directly involved; her cousin Nicholas's abdication from the throne followed soon thereafter. Maria Pavlovna left Pskov for Petrograd. There she made the acquaintance of Prince Sergei Mikhailovich Putyatin, the son of the palace commandant at Tsarskoe Selo, the tsar's country residence. The meeting grew into a happy affair and, in love for the first time, Maria Pavlovna married Putyatin in the Pavlovsk Palace on September 9, two months before the tragic events that forced millions of Russians to abandon their country. As Maria Pavlovna wrote in her memoirs, *A Grand Duchess in Exile*, "Old Russia ceased to exist and will never be restored."

Maria Pavlovna was expecting a second child at the time. Through stormy Moscow and a calmer Kiev, Putyatin, his parents, and Maria Pavlovna made their way to the south of Russia. Maria Pavlovna left everything behind: her father, Grand Duke Paul Alexandrovich, was arrested and killed soon after by the Bolsheviks; the entire Romanov family lost their country, which they had ruled for three centuries.

After reaching Kishinev, Moldavia, Maria Pavlovna and Prince Putyatin received an invitation from the Romanian royal court to stay a while with Queen Marie of Romania, whom Maria Parlorna had not seen since her first wedding. Maria Pavlovna wrote: "Of the royal families remaining on the throne who were in more or less close kinship with us, they were the only ones who met us with real sympathy and compassion. "

Romania, with all its comforts and amenities, surprised her after so many years of military adversity. Russian officers strolled the streets of Bucharest in full regalia. It was at the court of the Romartian queen that Maria Pavlovna made friends with Crown Princess Elizabeth, who later married King George of Greece. The princess had a passion for embroidery, collected Romanian folk embroideries and embroidery with Ottoman motifs, and then copied them on her hoop. Like her mother Queen Marie, she worshiped Romanian folk handicraft. After the breakup of the Austro-Hungarian Empire, the Romanian royal house did everything "to put Romania on the map of the world." The princess's other passions were fashion and perfumes, and it was unquestionably in Bucharest that an interest in such things was stimulated in Maria Pavlovna. Embroidery, fashion, and perfume became the grand duchess's longtime traveling companions.

In the meantime, Grand Duke Dmitrii Pavlovich, exiled by Emperor Nicholas II to the Persian border, wound up in Tehran, where he spent about two years. Thanks to the sympathetic attitude of Sir Charles Marling, the British envoy to Persia, Dmitrii Pavlovich not only found compassion there, but was able to locate his beloved sister, who was also wandering around the world.

Having settled in the Cotroceni palace with Prince Putyatin, Maria Pavlovna finally attended to her poor wardrobe. As she writes in her memoirs: "I had with me only one or two worn dresses, altered from my pre-war outfits, which were four years old, and also unbleached linen underwear. I didn't even have a pair of silk stockings, just the remnants of former luxury in the form of a few handkerchiefs with holes where the monograms had been cut out. While I still lived at the hotel, I sent for a seamstress who brought me several Parisian designs; among them was a brown dress of heavy silk. This dress, I was told, was a design from the house of Chanel. At that time Chanel was the rising star on the Paris fashion horizon. These designs cost much more than I could pay at that time, and I didn't buy anything.

I didn't even know how these clothes were supposed to be worn, because I had lost all touch with the world of fashion. But I remembered that name-Chanel. A young woman with the same name owned a small lingerie shop on rue Cambon before the war. And I thought: was this the same woman?" In the near future both Maria Pavlovna and Dmitrii Pavlovich would link their destinies with Chanel's.

Fortunately, Maria Pavlovna received as a gift from the Romanian queen several dresses that did not fit the queen, but which were immediately altered to fit the grand duchess. Prince Putyatin received several suits from the wardrobe of the king. On ceremonial days, Maria Pavlovna, like all the women of the royal house of Romania, wore Romanian national costumes.

In the meantime, successively more tragic news came from Russia. Maria Pavlovna learned in the British Mission in Bucharest that her aunt, Grand Duchess Elizaveta Feodorovna, and Prince Volodya Paley, her stepbrother, and several other close relatives were savagely murdered in Alapayevsk. She was in despair, and wrote: "None of us Russians believed that our exile would last, we thought that the fall of the Bolsheviks would be a matter of a few months, no more, and that, of course, we would all then return to Russia."

Maria Pavlovna's desire to meet with her brother in Europe at that difficult time was so great that she decided to leave with Putyatin for Paris, then London. Taking leave of the cordial Romanian court, she left her young son in Romania. Maria Pavlovna settled in Passy, and visited her deceased father's palace in Boulogne-sur-Seine, where he had lived in exile from the Russian court for twelve years with his second wife and three children. When he returned to Russia, his sumptuous furniture and rich art collection had been taken to the newly built Paley palace in Tsarskoe Selo.

Paris was the place where Russian emigres met and socialized. Christmas and Easter holidays were especially splendid, and on Sundays crowds of Russian emigres filled the church courtyard and garden. Maria Pavlovna was in deep mourning for her father: she wore a trimmed black crepe dress and a black hat with a crepe veil—this is the way her contemporaries remember her.

In Paris Maria Pavlovna was forced to face everyday problems for the first time in her life. In spite of the fact that she was nearly twenty-eight years old, she did not understand the value of money very well. She recalled: "I had never before carried cash with me, nor had I ever written a check. I knew the approximate price of jewels and dresses, but did not have the vaguest idea how much bread, meat and milk cost."

Maria Pavlovna greeted her brother Dmitrii Pavlovich with great joy when he arrived in London. Having sold his St. Petersburg palace during the revolution, he had some means and lived modestly but comfortably in the Hotel Ritz. However, his move from Tehran to London had entailed enormous suffering. He had set sail for Great Britain on an English military boat via Mesopotamia and Bombay and along the way had contracted typhoid fever; fortunately, he was nursed back to health by his Russian boatman. Dmitrii Pavlovich got to Marseilles by way of Port Said and Cairo, then to Paris, and then getting to London was easy.

In order to conserve their resources, Maria Pavlovna and Putyatin rented a small apartment on Berkeley Street in London and would visit Dmitrii at the Ritz. The British court exhibited extraordinary coldness in those years toward their Romanov relatives. However, in London Maria Pavlovna managed to find the address of her father's widow,

Princess Paley, who was then in Finland with her daughters. Fortunately, the crown prince of Sweden and his wife brought Maria Pavlovna's jewels some of which she had left there for safekeeping even before World War I, and others that she had prudently concealed in inkwells, candles, and paperweights and had sent to Sweden from Russia when they came to London to visit. Maria Pavlovna was advised to sell her entire jewelry collection at Christie's auction house, but the power of the sentimental memories associated with them was too great—many were family jewels of the Romanov House, and besides, Maria Pavlovna still naively believed in the possibility of returning to Russia. Meanwhile, the European jewelry market was saturated with Russian jewelry. Jewelry store displays were bursting with tiaras, diadems, necklaces, bracelets, earrings, and rings. These were difficult times, and demand was low and the supply enormous. The rarest of pieces went for very low prices—the same situation was occurring in Constantinople and Harbin.

Summoning up her courage, Maria Pavlovna went to a jeweler on Bond Street to sell the family's matching ruby set and recalled:

"'You are deeply mistaken if you think that this jewelry is very valuable,' they usually told us everywhere. Our jewels were always either too large or too small, or faceted instead of cabochon or vice versa, and never in an appropriate set. If they knocked the price of the Romanov jewels down so low, what did other families have to face?" The grand duchess was forced to sell all her adornments over the course of the next few years.

Another blow befell Maria Pavlovna in London: in a letter from her motherin-law Princess Putyatina in Bucharest, she learned about the sudden death of her one-year-old infant child. To be closer to his sister in this difficult time, Dmitrii Pavlovich rented a small house in the London suburb of Kensington, where the Romanovs and Putyatins had settled together. Unfortunately, relations between Dmitrii Pavlovich and Prince Putyatin soon soured.

Given the situation, Maria Pavlovna decided to become involved in something in order to earn a living. She had loved to sew, knit, and embroider as a child in St. Petersburg. As a little girl she loved to embroider after lunch, sitting in the grand duke's palace library. How useful her childhood passions turned out to be in her London exile! Knitted sweaters and dresses had just become fashionable in London and Paris at that time. Knitting, a craft that had been practiced since the Renaissance, was lifted to the level of virtue in the Victorian era; during the difficult years of World War I, when many women first experienced a shortage of clothing, especially of warm children's clothes, knitting and crocheting became a necessity of life. Women took to knitting in order to pass the time while riding the underground or waiting in queues for milk or bread. There was still a shortage of good fabrics and thus knitted articles became not only practical, but fashionable.

Maria Pavlovna bought some needles, yarn, and a guide to home knitting. After a botched sweater, with characteristic persistence she started working on a new sweater, but that became one she wore at home because of an error in counting the loops. She recalls: "I found out about a shop where I took my first successful sweater, wrapped in paper and tucked under my arm. The shop owner had no idea who I was, and was very surprised when she learned about the purpose of my visit. I opened the package, held up my work for her careful examination, my heart sinking. She bought the sweater from me for 21 shillings and asked me to bring others."

Maria Pavlovna began knitting sweaters and dresses for the London shop. Every four or five days she would finish up a new sweater; dresses took up to ten days. She knit constantly, from rising early in the morning, at the table at lunchtime, when she read, and on the underground. But no matter how hard she tried, for this work it was impossible to earn more than six pounds sterling a week, which was a drop in the sea of the family budget. Something more substantial had to be devised.

In her closet, Maria Pavlovna had only a few shabby dresses that she had had altered in Bucharest. Life in London and changes in fashion required a new wardrobe, and she made the decision to sew her own. She bought a cutting and sewing magazine and fabric, and made a pattern, then boldly cut her first dress directly on the parquet floor of her home with enormous dressmaker's scissors. Maria Pavlovna had no sewing machine, nor did she know how to use one, so she basted and sewed her first dress by hand, occasionally asking her husband for his opinion. She sewed herself a copy of a dress from the Callot Soeurs fashion house, with a skirt that used a kilometer of tulle. Encouraged by her first success, Maria Pavlovna began sewing dresses for herself and her Russian friends, and designed a fanciful dinner jacket for her husband and a robe for her brother Dmitrii in a fabric with a pattern of a flock of birds scattered across a black field.

A group of Russian emigres in London appealed to Maria Pavlovna with a request that she become the head of a sewing atelier that made military and medical supplies for the Volunteer Army fighting on the Don River in southern Russia. After finding a suitable building, she, together with other Russian emigre women, began sewing for the soldiers. Meanwhile, more groups of Russian refugees kept arriving in London. The dowager Empress Maria Feodorovna arrived in London from the Crimea on board an English military boat with her daughter Grand Duchess Xenia Alexandrovna and her grandchildren. The English Queen Mother Alexandra met her beloved sister, now a tired woman with a lifeless gaze wearing a black traveling suit, a small hat embroidered with sequins, and a short boa, pinned with a brooch at the throat. Europe did not yet know about the tragic death of the tsar and his family, and many people, especially Maria Feodorovna, religiously believed in their miraculous salvation.

Maria Pavlovna went to Paris to meet with the widow of her father, Princess Paley. Marisha, as she was called at home, had changed radically: her suffering due to the execution of her beloved husband and her losses in Russia had completely undermined her health and she had grown thin and aged. The warm-hearted Maria Pavlovna met with her every day and eased her grief. Paris was gradually filling up with Russian refugees, and Maria Pavlovna decided to sell her house in London and settle down in Paris. Her brother Dmitrii followed her to Paris, where their enchanting stepsisters – PrincessesNatalya and Irina-had already settled. Maria Pavlovna rented a small apartment on rue Courcelles and furnished it with the bare essentials of her new life: a table for cutting and a sewing machine.

Maria Pavlovna devoted a great deal of time to philanthropy for the Russian Red Cross, organizing parties and special sales of handicrafts to raise money for Russian refugees. At one of these evenings in the International Circle club, she was noticed by a journalist from *Vogue* magazine in a remarkable dress she had made – a long chemise of raspberry crepe, scattered all over with silver brocade leaves, a belt at hip level and a necklace of large pearls from the collection of the murdered Grand Duchess Elizaveta Feodorovna.

Maria Pavlovna missed her son, who had been left in Sweden, and with help from the Swedish King Gustav, Maria and Dmitrii Pavlovich went off to Denmark, where she finally saw Prince Lennart, who had grown up and matured, and the Dowager Empress Maria Feodorovna, her aunt. After returning to Paris, Dmitrii Pavlovich went to work at a major champagne firm because his financial resources had run out. Destiny brought the grand duke together with the talented fashion designer Gabrielle Chanel. They became completely inseparable, and the affair determined to a large extent Chanel's favorable attitude toward the Russian emigre community. Thus two worlds-that of imperial Russia and that of peasant France – met in Biarritz. Chanel despised titles and once said: "I always feel pity for born, blueblood princes: their trade, when they have one, is the saddest in the world, and when they don't have one – it is doubly sad."

In fact, Dmitrii Pavlovich rather liked older women, and, back in Russia, he had had quite a romance with the splendid countess

Natalia Brasova, the wife of Grand Duke Mikhail Alexandrovich, the tsar's brother.

Maria Pavlovna met Chanel for the first time. Chanel already had a solid reputation and clientele in those years. She was a born businesswoman, but not a born seamstress. However, she was the one who created the image of the new woman. In the new economic situation of the day, Chanel, in defiance of her rival Paul Poiret, democratized fashion and transformed the wardrobe of Parisian women with her designs, which were simple in cut and often copied for the mass market.

Maria Pavlovna decided to try her luck with Chanel and, knowing her rather intimately through her brother, set off for a meeting at her studio, located on the third floor of the House of Chanel on rue Cambon. At the time Chanel was interested in embroidery and even imported colored knit sweaters from the Faeroe Islands in the hopes of transferring their ornamentation to her silk blouses. Just at the point that Maria Pavlovna appeared at the studio, Chanel was bargaining with her permanent embroiderer, Madame Bataille. Chanel, certain of the stability of her reputation, assumed that everyone should consider it an honor to embroider for her house, even for a low price. Madame Bataille was asking 600 francs for an embroidered blouse and, not obtaining it, was withdrawing.

Maria Pavlovna recalled: "I suddenly addressed Chanel and offered to embroider the same blouse for 150 francs less." Chanel gladly agreed, afraid only that Maria Pavlovna was unfamiliar with the methods of machine embroidery. Maria Pavlovna immediately promised Chanel that she would buy an embroidery machine and thus began her first professional experiment in Paris.

Nearly three months later, Maria Pavlovna, happy and proud of her work, appeared at Chanel's carrying her first machine-embroidered silk blouse, for which, as agreed, she was asking 450 francs. This work was the first order of the future Kitmir – the fashion house of embroidery – to which Maria Pavlovna devoted so much of her energy and strength.

The beginning was the most difficult: for all her effort and passion for handicraft, Maria Pavlovna did not, of course, know how to use an embroidery machine. When she bought her first embroidery machine, she asked the proprietor of the shop to teach her how to use it. Trying to hide her too-famous name, Maria Pavlovna enrolled under an assumed name in a course for machine embroidery at a factory, where her first awkward attempts elicited only the ridicule and contempt of the workers. Finally, the work began to go well, and the idea of founding a fashion house of embroidery dawned on her.

The story of how the house got its name is as follows: among Maria Pavlovna's close friends in Paris was a former Russian ambassador to Washington, Bakhmetiev, a monarchist and great lover of animals. The name of one of his three sweet Pekinese dogs was Kitmir — in honor of the legendary dog of Persian mythology. This was the name that Maria Pavlovna chose for her house.

The grand duchess and her motherin-law Princess Putyatina found a place in the back courtyard of a wealthy private residence on fashionable rue Francois 1, not far from the Champs Elysees. She invited two Russian girls to work for her and sent them to take the same embroidery courses that she herself had just completed. They bought two more embroidery machines, and the Kitmir atelier was ready to take orders. As Maria Pavlovna recalled: "Suddenly the machine became the emblem of my new life."

There was very little time left. She instructed Maria Pavlovna to design the embroidery patterns and choose the fabric and threads. Chanel spent hours explaining her ideas to Maria Pavlovna, discussing the sketches of the embroideries and the fabric samples. All of this was completely new for Maria Pavlovna. She had to go to all the suppliers' shops, bargain with them, and solve the many organizational and commercial problems with which she had been unfamiliar until then.

The fabrics were cut at the house of Chanel, brought over to the Kitmir atelier where the embroidery patterns were transferred onto them from tracing paper, and then the Russian artisans got to work. The first set of orders from Chanel consisted of a series of blouses, tunics, and coats. For this series, Maria Pavlovna made several of the same tunics of light gray silk herself, embroidered in the same shade thread with a sprinkling of red motifs. This Kitmir house design, which was created for Chanel, became especially popular. With pride, Maria Pavlovna happened to see her tunic once on a lady who was having lunch at the Ritz.

Chanel and Maria Pavlovna met daily at the time. Chanel dressed very simply, even in everyday style. She loved to work in a warm studio near the fireplace, dressed in a sporty suit, a dark sweater and dark skirt the embodiment of her fashion revolution that changed women's clothing for the twentieth century. According to Maria Pavlovna's recollections, that season Chanel always wore the same clothing, and changed only when she went out to meet people, dressed in a coat of priceless fur.

Chanel worked often in Maria Pavlovna's presence: cutting away, trimming, and pinning. Her word was law for her employees, her will unshakeable, her thinking quick and precise. She made decisions in the blink of an eye, surveying the entire collection at once. Chanel was capable of executing, or saving, any one of her dresses; her concerns were to ensure the harmony of everything she created, its clarity of line, its comfort, and the prestige of her label. When the crucial day finally arrived-the day when designs were to be shown to foreign clients at the house of Chanel on rue Cambon—Maria Pavlovna could hardly hold back her tears when she saw the embroidered work of her brainchild, Kitmir, on the models (some of whom were also Russian). The procession lasted nearly three hours and, when it ended, it was the embroidered articles that clients competed with one another to order from the Chanel saleswomen. Their originality and the freshness seemed completely novel. Maria Pavlovna was ecstatic—it was Kitmir's first triumph.

The success of the Kitmir embroideries surpassed all expectations. Maria Pavlovna literally drowned in orders immediately. At that time there were only three or four embroiderers working at Kitmir, including herself. They worked for weeks without days off, sleeping at their embroidery machines, thinking only about the deadlines for completing their orders. Maria Pavlovna's right hand was, undoubtedly, the loyal Princess Putyatina, who helped her daughter-in-law with everything. Before a fabric with a pattern already transferred onto it was embroidered, it was basted onto rigid, chemically treated mousseline that burned away when it was pressed with a blistering hot iron. Its ashes floated around the room, making it difficult to breathe, but Maria Pavlovna, her hands scorched from working with the iron, kept on embroidering and embroidering Chanel's orders.

Nearby, ladies in garments embroidered by Maria Pavlovna were strolling under the tree canopy in the Bois de Boulogne while the grand duchess herself was climbing the back stairs to her small atelier. Work began early in the morning and the fatigued Maria Pavlovna would often fall asleep after lunch right on the floor of the Kitmir workshop, lying down on her fur coat instead of a mattress.

Kitmir's main problems were always organizational. Soft-hearted Maria Pavlovna kept hiring more and more Russian emigre workers, giving them preference not for practical reasons but from a desire to help her needy compatriots. Many advised her to hire professional embroideresses, but she firmly followed her patriotic convictions. The expanding business required more and more substantial outlays and, in order to cover them, Maria Pavlovna was again forced to sell her jewels. This time a valuable Romanov family matched set of large emeralds was sold, the price of which, in spite of the considerable sum received, was obviously incommensurate with its real price. Financial "advisors" rushed to Prince Putyatin like vultures to carrion when they found out about the major proceeds from the sale of Maria Pavlovna's emeralds. Inexperienced in commercial affairs, the grand duchess agreed to entrust all her money to a Dutch industrial society, which not only did not accrue any interest on the capital she invested in it, but swallowed up the entire sum when it went bankrupt. Kitmir did not get a single franc. In the meantime, Prince Putyatin, who had once worked in a private bank, mastered the subtleties of the profession—thereby surprising even Chanel's meticulous accountant—and began working as Kitmir's accountant.

Kitmir received twice as many orders during its second year of operation and its troubles increased. Despite additional staff, the quantity of orders noticeably surpassed the possibility of fulfillment. The Chanel saleswomen rang Kitmir's phone off the hook, demanding more and more embroidered goods, the fashion for which had reached its apogee.

It should be noted that Chanel wasn't the only house showing embroidered things. Jeanne Lanvin, who showed garments with Romanian and Slavic embroidery, was serious competition. After World War I many houses were experiencing a shortage of elegant fabrics and needed beautiful trim, so Kitmir's production sold like hotcakes. The firm Babani, located on boulevard Hausmann, did a great deal to support this needlework fashion. Its exclusive specialty was embroidered articles with folk art motifs from the outlying areas of the former Ottoman Empire and the Slavic provinces of the former Austro-Hungarian Empire.

In spite of the competition, demand exceeded supply that season, and Kitmir was so besieged with work that it could not keep up with the plethora of orders. Some of Chanel's clients complained and rejected their orders, there by arousing a storm of indignation on the part of Chanel's saleswomen. Maria Pavlovna was afraid even to come to rue Cambon and would sometimes hide in the closet in Chanel's studio just so she wouldn't have to listen to the severe reprimands of angry saleswomen who were losing good clients. In addition, Kitmir did not have the right to copy Chanel's orders. However, it could copy orders in volume if they came from abroad and, thanks to this, Kitmir got some American clients. One of them, Mr. Kurzman, ordered a set of embroidered blouses on condition that he receive them in a completely ready-for-purchase form. All of this was so new that Maria Pavlovna stayed up nights with her English maid, completing the sewing on these blouses herself.

Money soon came from Kurzman in America, along with newspaper clippings of an interview in which he proudly announced that he was the first in the United States to import articles from Kitmir. The advertisement was accompanied by an image of the Russian imperial crown and the initials of the grand duchess, as well as her full title. This type of commercial advertisement was alien to Maria Pavlovna. She earned money with her labor, not her background, and had never mentioned her title before in representing Kitmir. More American clients followed, including the New York fashion designer Francis Klein, who remained loyal to Kitmir's embroidery right up to the day it closed down.

Maria Pavlovna recalled: "I loved the feel of silk, the play of its half-tones, contrasting transitions. In it I saw the fabrics which spoke to me about my past. I once found a piece of yellow cord which reminded me of the thread used in Moscow monasteries. In the past I had learned from the nuns the old method of embroidering saints' faces with silk floss of one shade, on which the play of the light and shadow was achieved merely by the change in the direction of the stitch. I found the same non-tarnishing silver and gold threads which were used to embroider in relief the cotton-stuffed nimbuses and crowns around the saints' faces. Are these kinds ofthings still used?"

Chanel taught the somewhat oldfashioned Maria Pavlovna Parisian practicality. She once told her: "You're harming yourself by dressing like a refugee. Don't think that you can elicit sympathy in this way. On the contrary in the end, people will avoid you. If you want to do business, first and foremost you have to look appropriate, remember this!" Maria Pavlovna, taking the wise advice, began to take care of herself, to dress better, wear a little makeup, and even hired a Swedish masseuse in order to lose a few pounds. Chanel also advised her to cut short the long hair that she wore in a bun all the time, taking a pair of scissors and cutting Maria Pavlovna's hair herself in the rue Cambon studio. Her influence on Maria Pavlovna did not stop there. The tenacious and smart Frenchwoman wanted to help her Russian friend. The grand duchess lacked toughness. Chanel demanded that she completely root out any spirit of "charity," which should not be mixed with commerce.

On Chanel's insistence, Kitmir updated their selection of embroideries each season. Initially it consisted of Maria Pavlovna's designs in a pseudohistorical style. She studied antique ornament and collected a basic library, essential for making sketches, and used ornamental motifs from Oriental carpets, Persian ceramics, Bulgarian and Russian embroideries, and decoration from Coptic fabrics, Chinese porcelain, and the jewels of Indian maharajahs. The most popular embroidery method at Kitmir was the *cornely* stitch (twisted silk thread) and, from the season on, Maria Pavlovna began embroidering not only in silk and gold, but also with seeds, beads, and sequins.

One of the employees of the house of Kitmir, Kira Alexandrovna Sereda (nee Baroness von Medem), recalls: "Having arrived in Paris from Constantinople, my mother and I were hungry and looking for work. We came to Kitmir to Grand Duchess Maria Pavlovna and got an order to embroider evening bags with beads and sequins. Colored purses were very fashionable at that time. The Duchess asked us: 'Do you know how to embroider the *cornely* or Chinese stitch?' We said that we did, and got more orders for embroidered belts, and my mother, Baroness Nina Vladimirovna von Medem, nee Shlitter, got an order to embroider shawls with an elaborate design, like an entire picture. There were many Russian women working there and all were gifted. The Duchess gave us work to take home and paid decently. And we were so poor then, that we were happy to do any work!"

Rostislav Mstislavovich Dobuzhinsky, the son of the remarkable Russian painter Mstislav Dobuzhinsky, gave the author the following account of his wife's work for Kitmir. The young Rostislav had arrived in France by boat with his lovely wife, actress Lydia Kopnyaeva. He recollects: "When my wife came here, of course, for her as an actress, the French theater was out of the question. She had much experience making theater costumes, and she got work as a cutter and draper at Kitmir. She worked there under the name of Dobuzhinskaya with Vera Sudeikina, Stravinsky's future wife. Kitmir, which belonged to Grand Duchess Maria Pavlovna, was a very interesting atelier. Only Russian ladies worked there. They were jacks of all trades. Their specialty was beaded articles, embroidery, different kinds of inlay work which they did for many big houses like Lanvin, Chanel. They sewed an especially large number of "beaded" dresses. Kitmir's manager was Baltic Baron Gerst, a fat, broad-shouldered giant."

In addition to purses, belts, and shawls, Kitmir produced embroidered mules, slippers with motifs from Persian miniatures, which, despite their high price, were very much in demand. The revival of embroidering in chenille should be added to the list of Maria Pavlovna's contributions. This yarn, popular as far back as the end of the eighteenth century, was widely used in needlework in the Victorian era and then half forgotten. Maria Pavlovna undertook the production of hats crocheted in chenille, Chanel started selling them, and many thousands of such hats were worn around the world.

Maria Pavlovna rented an entire private residence at no. 7 rue Montaigne to expand production. The office and showroom were on the first floor; the workshops were on the other two. Professional French embroiderers were added to the staff after several Russian needleworkers left Kitmir, using its production secrets to open ateliers under their own names. More than fifty embroiderers worked for Kitmir, with additional cutters and technical people. The name Kitmir was proudly written in gold letters at the entrance to the courtyard. Maria Pavlovna settled into the spacious office with a mahogany desk, a fireplace with a mirror, two chairs, and a small table on a blue carpet. She bought most of this furniture from the previous tenants of the house; it seemed luxurious compared to the refugee furniture of the old atelier.

Several French fashion houses contacted Kitmir with extremely enticing offers. Among the possible clients was the house of Jean Patou, one of Chanel's main competitors, who became especially famous for his jersey and knit sportswear. Patou's popularity, right up to his death in 1936, was enormous. Many Russians worked in his house not only as models but as stylists as well; in particular, the young artist Dmitrii Dmitrievich Bouchene, who created several designs for Patou.

Afraid to offend her patron Gabrielle Chanel, Maria Pavlovna decided to seek her advice and share her plans for expansion with her. Chanel seemed glad about her plans, but immediately created a list of big houses with which Kitmir was forbidden to work—all of those in competition with her. Not only was Patou on the list, but also other potential clients. This list became the stumbling block between Chanel and Kitmir. An enraged Chanel, accusing Maria Pavlovna of ingratitude, forbade her to come to her studio fearing that the grand duchess would pass on production secrets to competitors. However, she did not limit herself to working exclusively with Kitmir; she took her orders to other houses of embroidery, of which there were a great many by that time.

The loss of the exclusive connection with Chanel was very costly to Kitmir. Having acquired new clients, Maria Pavlovna was obliged to create up to 200 new embroidered designs to suit all tastes by the coming season; due to this, Kitmir lost its unity of style and originality.

Maria Pavlovna had to spend long hours in the salons waiting to meet with Paris's dictators of fashion, listening to their comments and criticism, and continually changing the patterns, shades, and manner of embroidery in order to satisfy the taste of each fashion house. There was such an avalanche of orders that they were dispatched to other ateliers in the provinces. By that time, hundreds of embroiderers across all of France worked for Maria Pavlovna.

Maria Pavlovna rarely left Paris for vacations because she could not live for long away from her beloved creation, Kitmir. The vacation place she and Putyatin chose was Biarritz or Saint-Jeande-Luz. There, on the Atlantic shore, in the company of Princess Paley and her stepsisters Irina and Natalya, she forgot about difficult everyday life in Paris. Biarritz was the fashionable vacation spot for European titled aristocracy and American millionaires and a sizeable colony of Russian emigres settled near it. The proximity of the Spanish royal family further increased the attractiveness of this expensive resort. Grand Duke Dmitrii Pavlovich's affair with Gabrielle Chanel had developed in Biarritz, and after they parted ways, it was there that Dmitrii Pavlovich met the young, attractive American millionairess Audrey Emery, who later converted to the Russian Orthodox faith. A few years later, she married the grand duke and received the title of Princess Ilyinskaya, after the name of the estate owned by Maria's and Dmitrii's father near Moscow.

The family jewels ran out, Kitmir ate up most of the profits, and Maria Pavlovna wound up heavily in debt. A financial disaster was imminent. Maria Pavlovna's family life was also crumbling: her marriage with Putyatin had developed a crack. The grand duchess devoted all her energies to work while Putyatin preferred to spend his time in the company of Russian officers, fastliving squanderers of money and time. His lifestyle did not correspond to Maria Pavlovna's notions of duty, and the family atmosphere became strained. When her patience came to an end, Maria Pavlovna left Putyatin in the company of his friends in Paris and departed for Scotland, then the Netherlands, alone. Handing over the business to the care of her mother-in-law, she was finally able to withdraw from everyday concerns and be alone. Putyatin wrote her tong letters every day.

After four months of voluntary exile, Maria Pavlovna returned to Paris only because the business required it. She decided to send her husband to Vienna without seeing him; the family had financial interests there connected with a failed bank. In Paris, Maria Pavlovna took the management of Kitmir into her hands again and continued to meet daily with her husband's parents, who lived in the same house in which the Kitmir atelier was located. Warm relations with her in-laws made Maria Pavlovna reconsider many times her pending decision to break with Putyatin; but a return to the past was no longer possible.

Serious changes were on the horizon for Kitmir's work. While from the end of World War I through , Russian folklore in all its manifestations was extraordinarily in vogue, now a new trend was replacing it. The archeological excavations in Egypt and the discovery of Tutankhamen's grave by the Englishman Howard Carter gave rise to Egyptomania in the full sense of the word. The gaze of the fashionably dressed of the world turned to Egypt, its burning hot landscape, mysterious graves, and eternal pyramids. The legislators of fashion were attracted to the geometric forms of Egyptian art, the precision of its lines, the balance of its composition, and contrast of its color combinations. Everything Egyptian sharply crowded out everything Russian, which could not but be reflected in what Kitmir produced. Embroidery, however, did not go out of style but merely changed its forms, and Kitmir successfully created numerous geometric patterns on Egyptian themes. Kitmir's style stayed in tune with the times and Maria Pavlovna began appearing in the public eye more. Fashion magazines of the time wrote about her often, and Paris *Vogue* published a large-format photo portrait of her in profile by Havrah.

After her divorce, Maria Pavlovna became close friends with one of Chanel's main competitors, the famous fashion designer Jean Patou, a lover of the fair sex and an inveterate bachelor. Patou was ten years older than the grand duchess, had a large fortune at the time, and surrounded himself with extravagant luxury. Maria Pavlovna began appearing with him at society receptions and even spending time at his private residences in Biarritz, Deauville, and on the Riviera. *Vogue* published a drawing portrait of Maria Pavlovna in a red crepe Chanel dress at a soiree at the Hotel Ritz arranged by Count Cyril de Beaumont, a society lion of Paris, who was well known in the period between the wars. The splendor of Parisian society captivated Maria Pavlovna, and she was its natural and esteemed decoration. The relationship between the grand duchess and Patou, the Parisian prince of fashion, went so far that rumors about a possible marriage spread. The Parisian press even wrote about it; the well-known fashion reporter Elsa Maxwell talks about it in her memoirs. This was the first time Patou's name was ever mentioned in connection with an affair of honorable intentions. We can only speculate why the marriage did not take place. It seems likely that the obstacle was Jean Patou's character, his habit of living as a bachelor; he never did get married. At that time Russian women were in vogue. Picasso, Dali, Leger, Rolland, Maillol, and many other European celebrities succumbed to the charms of Russian beauties.

Kitmir was past its golden years of prosperity. Its finest hour had been, during the Exhibit of Contemporary Decorative and Industrial Arts (l'Art Deco) in Paris. This major international exhibit summed up the work of artists during the post-World War I period. Many countries opened their own pavilions at it, granting complete representation of applied arts of that time. Parisian fashion houses took their places in the main pavilion. An exception was the house of Paul Poiret, the great dictator of prewar fashion. Seeing his business as superior everywhere and in everything, he constructed on the banks of the Seine three barges with the romantic names "Amour," "Delices," and "Orgues," where one could visit the exhibit hall and restaurant and delight in "an orgy of fragrances" at the presentation of the famous perfume from his subsidiary house, Rosine. Initially, the house of Kitmir had not planned to take part in the exhibit, but as soon as Maria Pavlovna found out that there would be a pavilion from Soviet Russia representing Russian art, the blood of the Romanovs boiled up in the grand duchess. She recalls: "I found out that the Soviet Russians were going to have a separate pavilion at the exhibit, and made the decision that we, too, must show our work to the general public. It would be especially fair that everyone know what we refugees, most of whom had never worked before and who comprised the majority of my atelier, were capable of in our exile." Maria Pavlovna succeeded with great difficulty in renting a space in the main exhibit for an extensive showcase of samples of embroidered articles from Kitmir.

The exhibit lasted several months. The USSR pavilion exhibited samples of Soviet textiles: cotton prints with the hammer and sickle, wool challis scarves from Pavlov-Posad, as well as several dresses by Davydova, Lamanova, Pribylskaya, Mukhina, and Makarova. The real professional of Russian fashion among them was Nadezhda Petrovna Lamanova. Born in 1861 in the province of Nizhny Novgorod, Lamanova opened her prominent fashion house in 1885. She began to supply the court with her designs and it is possible that she even dressed ten-year-old Maria Pavlovna. Lamanova's dresses (she worked primarily in the technique of pricking out a pattern) were distinguished by the cleanness of their lines and forms. For many years Lamanova was associated with the Moscow Art Theater, for which she began making costumes.

Remaining in Russia after the revolution, Lamanova survived many troubles and lost a great deal, most significantly her fashion house with its convenient linden-tree cutting tables. She was eventually arrested and sent to Butyrskaya prison. Thanks to Maxim Gorky's help, she was finally freed and continued working on her own, making dresses out of towels and coats out of blankets due to the shortage of fabrics. She wrote articles for fashion journals and maintained continuous authority in the field of fashion. Familiar with the success of the "Russian style" in fashionable Paris from rumors and magazine articles, Lamanova decided to create a series of handcrafted Russian designs for the international exhibit.

As Tatiana Strizhenova, a Soviet specialist on the history of fashion, writes: "Simple homespun fabrics—canvas, linen, cotton linen weave—became the basis for chemise-style dresses. They were trimmed with embroidered inserts of either genuine folk embroidery, which the artists had found, or embroidery which they did according to Vera Mukhina's sketches. She also prepared and showed her own original embroidery as separate art works."

All the designs were shown with the appropriate accessories: shoes, belts, hats and beads made of soft bread paste. Lamanova's design, which completely corresponded to the demands of the day, won the Grand Prix. The artist was awarded, it was written, "for clothing based on folk art." This fact, while a very happy one in and of itself, was presented in the USSR as the triumph of "Soviet fashion," as true Russian folklore conquering Europe. Excessive indulgence in this style later affected fashion in the USSR in a sad way. Naively believing in the permanence of Parisian taste and fashion standards, fashion designers there, encouraged by Lamanova's success, became engaged almost exclusively in decoration and embroidery, copying the "Russian style" that had been elaborately developed. However, for obvious reasons, in the USSR the success of the other Russian participant in the exhibit was passed over in silence.

When the exhibit ended, Maria Pavlovna was invited to take down her showcase in the main pavilion, where her embroidered designs were displayed. Some time later, Kitmir received a letter from the executive committee with a request that the manager of the atelier, Baron Gerst, stop by the board of directors. Maria Pavlovna expected another routine annoyance. How great was her surprise when she found out that Kitmir had been awarded a gold medal and an honorary degree as an exhibit participant, both of which were addressed to Mr. Kitmir: the board had not even suspected who the real owner of Kitmir was.

Success at the Paris Art Deco Exhibit, especially receiving the gold medal, boosted Kitmir's reputation tremendously. Fashion magazines of France—*Jardin des modes, Vogue, L'Art, goût, beaute, and L'Art et la mode – continually published striking drawings advertising the house of Kitmir. It is no wonder that Kitmir responded to the fashion of beadwork on embroidery so easily: beadwork and knitting were widespread in Russia in the nineteenth century. Many Russian ladies who embroidered for Kitmir were familiar with the technique of beading from childhood. Kitmir specialized in producing beaded fringe. Short, straight party dresses of silk crepe georgette or crushed velvet were trimmed with beaded fringe that was especially mobile when the wearer was dancing the Charleston. The preferred color scheme was the black-graywhite spectrum with a sprinkling of other colors.*

Maria Pavlovna devoted a great deal of time to philanthropic and religious activities. Through her efforts, land was bought around an abandoned Protestant chapel on the outskirts of Paris, which was rebuilt into a Russian seventeenthcentury-style church. Maria Pavlovna commissioned the painter Dmitrii Semyonovich Stelletsky, well known at the time, to work on the iconostasis and murals; it took him nearly two years to complete them. To this day the Sergievsky monastery church on the rue Crimee is one of the most significant monuments of emigre creativity.

After her divorce from Putyatin, Maria Pavlovna moved to Boulogne, the southwest suburb of Paris where Russians loved to take up residence. There were several Russian Orthodox churches, Russian restaurants and shops. Life in Boulogne was cheaper, and Maria Pavlovna rented a small three-story summer house on the street where her father Grand Duke Paul Alexandrovich's palace had been; it had been sold by Princess Paley and made into a Catholic school. The proximity of Boulogne to Paris was convenient for Maria Pavlovna for her communication with Kitmir's office, which was located not far from the Champs Elysees. The grand duchess furnished her new dwelling with antique furniture acquired at the flea markets. The dining room was Louis Philippe, with a set of mahogany furniture somewhat reminiscent of the Russian furniture of Tsar Nicholas's time and the salmon-color boudoir was furnished in Empire-style Karelian birch Russian furniture. Maria Pavlovna spent a great deal of time in the garden, resting in her pajamas under the canopy of large trees. The household was managed by the old Russian valet Karp, who served for many years abroad in the families of the Romanov grand dukes. Maria Pavlovna, following good old country estate traditions, surrounded herself with animals. Living with her in Boulogne were a Scots terrier, three Persian cats, rabbits, white doves, nightingales, and a pheasant.

In the meantime, Kitmir began to experience increasing financial difficulties. It often placed advertisements in the leading fashion magazines in order to attract new clients. Articles made from printed fabric, such as shawls, scarves, and fabric borders with large floral patterns were added to the atelier's repertoire. Unfortunately, Maria Pavlovna was unfamiliar with the laws of commerce. She paid too much for embroidery patterns, she allowed herself to be shortchanged, and she sold the finished goods at too much of a reduced price. Her atelier did not have professional managers, which she avoided because she felt so helpless in business matters. Trying to save the failing business, Maria Pavlovna accepted financial assistance from a well-to-do Russian emigre. In order to pay back the debt to her partner, she was forced to sell the last of the remaining Romanov family jewels, including a famous necklace with large pearls that had belonged to her mother.

In about 1928, embroidery began to go out of fashion. People grew less interested in it, showing a preference for smooth printed fabrics. Art Deco was living out its last days on the eve of the Wall Street crash. Maria Pavlovna attempted to revive her dying business up until the day the ruined Kitmir was swallowed up by the experienced old French embroidery firm Fritel and Hurel, who still owns the most extensive collection of Kitmir embroidery samples. Maria Pavlovna obtained the right to use the Kitmir name on articles produced by the firm. Many of the Russian embroiderers who had worked for the grand duchess began working for the new owners.

Having suffered a defeat, but not wishing to surrender, Maria Pavlovna departed for London in the spring in search of a new business. A new passion was sweeping over the Parisian fashion houses at that time perfumes. Both large and small fashion houses followed the infectious example of Paul Poiret, who as early as had established a subsidiary perfume company, and began to create their own fragrances. Many of these fragrances, such as Chanel No. 5 and Jean Patou's Joy are still with us today.

Russian emigres also enthusiastically took up creating new perfumes. Many well-known fragrances were created with the participation of Russian specialists. For example, Ernest Beau, chief perfumer of Moscow's Ralle cosmetics, was one of the creators of Chanel No. 5, which was inspired by an image from Pushkin short story *"The Queen of Spades."* The fragrance was infused with "the fresh scent of Finnish lakes" and the "bouquets of Yalta." The idea of creating her own perfume inspired Maria Pavlovna. The Paris market was saturated, so she decided to try her luck in London. She spent hours searching for the right combination of scents. She called her first perfume "Prince Igor" and she launched it in a small trial series in bottles bearing her name. Clearly lacking in commercial sense and business abilities, Maria Pavlovna did not generate the necessary advertising for it and did not distribute it properly. Failures plagued and pursued her, but she did not lose hope: Europe seemed to be a lost battlefield, so she set her sights on America, which was the promised land to many. One of Maria Pavlovna's American friends invited her to stay with her for a while, and new unexplored opportunities opened up.

Preparations to leave for the United States were cut short by the death of Maria Fedorovna, the widow of Alexander III. She had lived her last years in her native Denmark and was for many the last symbol of the imperial dynasty. Maria Pavlovna returned to Paris via Berlin in December and set sail for America from Le Havre. Grand Duchess Maria Pavlovna Romanova's arrival was greeted by the press with great enthusiasm and curiosity. She was photographed and interviewed a great deal. In America she finally realized the seriousness of the state of her health, which she had constantly neglected in Paris. For many years she had suffered from pain in her ankle and even limped a little: the necessary surgery was performed in New York.

In the United States Maria Pavlovna hoped to find a market for her "Prince Igor" perfume and to publish the memoirs of her life in Russia, which she had been working on for many years. She took the advice of her friends and sent her manuscript to a publisher. How great was her surprise on the eve of her birthday, she received a proposal from the editor to publish the first volume of her memoirs. The book was translated from Russian into English and French and was published in two volumes: the first was entitled *The Education of a Grand Duchess*, and the second was *A Grand Duchess in Exile*. They subsequently became bestsellers in the United States and Europe, which improved Maria Pavlovna's financial situation.

It seemed that a period of success had begun. In May Maria Pavlovna was invited by the New York department store Bergdorf Goodman's to serve as a consultant, purchasing fashionable clothing from France; for example, from the Russian fashion house YTEB. She returned to France with a light heart and got busy selling her house in Boulogne. Bidding farewell to Princess Paley, Maria Pavlovna departed for the Gare de Lyons, where she was seen off by her stepsister Princess Natalya Paley and the latter's husband, the owner of the fashion house Lucien Lelong. She sailed from Marseilles to the United States a second time, bringing along her favorite seven-string guitar, a typewriter, and $300 (all that the grand duchess had, besides, naturally, her large debts).

Maria Pavlovna worked at Bergdorf Goodman's, prepared her memoirs for publication, and gave lectures at universities. Hearst Publishers invited her to write fashion articles and reviews Maria Pavlovna was sent by them to Germany as a photojournalist. This new profession completely engrossed her and she mastered the technique down to its subtleties.

While living in New York, Maria Pavlovna began a new hobby: collecting Russian books. A fortunate incident helped her acquire several volumes from her deceased father's library. By the order of the King of Sweden, who sympathized with the grand duchess, she received a Swedish diplomatic passport to replace her old Nansen passport, which gave her broad freedom of movement. She was frequently published at the time: for instance, *Vogue* ran her enchanting description of Russian Christmas. At Bergdorf Goodman she began to create hat collections. There followed a series of divorces in the family. Her brother Dmitrii Pavlovich divorced his American spouse. Their stepsister, Princess Nathalie Paley, a society beauty and Hollywood actress at the time, divorced Lucien Lelong and moved to New York to become even closer to Maria Pavlovna. The United States entered World War II as an ally of the Soviet Union. America's friendly attitude toward the Communist nation was unendurable for Maria Pavlovna. She could not live in a country that supported the government that had executed her father and most of her relatives. Taking leave of her New York friends—PrincessPaley, the well-known German photographer Horst, Valentina Sanina, founder of the fashion house Valentina, and her husband George Shlee—she moved again, this time to Argentina.

Maria Pavlovna rented a small house with a garden in the Barrio Norte, the best section in Buenos Aires, and devoted her spare time to painting, even managing to sell several of her paintings. Argentine newspapers published her articles about interior design, fashion, and art. The Russian fashion house belonging to Natalya Nevolova opened around this time—this is where Evita Perón, the beautiful wife of the Argentine president, got her clothes.

A large number of Russian emigres took up residence in Argentina. Landless Cossacks from Gallipoli were invited. There was a marvelous Russian church, decorated in majolica, that had been consecrated at the turn of the century. Maria Pavlovna felt peaceful, and became especially close friends with the family of Prince Mestchersky, who had moved there from Paris. Maria Pavlovna's son Prince Lennart came to visit from Germany for several months and for the first time genuinely got to know his Russian mother. Two years later Maria Pavlovna visited Europe where, at the home of her son on a little island called Mainau, in Germany, she met her first husband, Prince Wilhelm of Sweden, for the first time in many years. In spite of the unexpectedness of the meeting and the awkwardness of the situation, they parted good friends.

Maria Pavlovna became the Honorary Patron of the Organization of Young Russian Scouts in Argentina. The last years of her life, Maria Pavlovna often visited Europe, where she would live with her son or with friends. She would unexpectedly appear in Mainau with her camera, easel, and paints. Grand Duchess Maria Pavlovna died from pneumonia on December 13 in Konstantz, Germany. She is buried in a side altar of the Palace Church in Mainau next to her brother Grand.

Foreseeing her coming death, the grand duchess bequeathed the family icon, which was at Prince Mestchersky's home in Buenos Aires, to her son, Prince Lennart. However, Miguel Kireeff, the chief editor of the Russian-Argentine newspaper *Nuestro Pais* told us: "The icon remained at the Mestcherskys when she moved to Europe.

Unfortunately, the icon never did reach her son and is in the possession of Father Vladimir Shlenev, who inherited all the Mestcherskys' personal articles."

Most of Maria Pavlovna's memorabilia, such as her court dress, her portraits, and her photographs, are in Prince Lennart's possession at the family castle at Mainau.

❑❑❑

9

Ardanse House of Fashion for Costume Designing

Introduction

The house of Ardanse turned out to be more solid than the rest. The unusual taste of its owner and the lack of grandiose ambitions helped the house survive in a period when many of its competitors were closing down. Cassandra Nikolayevna opened her business on the Right Bank, in a prestigious neighborhood of Paris. A luxurious mansion, at no. 37 rue Blenfaisance, built by the architect Troncoix in 1877, the house was decorated exquisitely in a single color scheme. "Here everything is violet," wrote a charmed visitor to the house, "and not that boring violet shade, but warm and modest, bringing to mind the color and fragrance of violets de Parme. The armchairs, carpets, showrooms, fitting rooms, even the writing paper, boxes and wrapping paper are all the same violet color, and this color unity creates an indescribable charm. The saleswomen and pretty models who inhabit these magical sets are dressed in violet without exception, harmonizing with the interior. I don't suppose you could find a more soothing tone to show off the wealth of color demonstrated in the designs."

The pale violet was not the only "corporate color" of Ardanse. It was replaced by aquamarine, which was then seen in every detail of the decor. Baroness Accourti personally met every invited client and presented glorious roses, tied with a ribbon of pale blue with an amazing aquamarine tint. The color selection, naturally, was not random. Pale violet and aquamarine were the favorite colors of Empress Alexandra Feodorovna. Baroness Accourti's color talent was noted in the press and the reviews of Ardanse collections included analyses of its evolution. The "aristocratic charm" of Ardanse, which all the fashion magazines described, overcame the initial mistrust of the high aristocracy. Ardanse began dressing the noble ladies of the Russian emigre colony.

The feminine and elegant dresses of Ardanse were created by Baroness Accourti herself. She preferred delicate pastels, washed-out color combinations based on the traditional tastes of the Winter Palace. Judging from a portrait, she had once been a follower of Art Nouveau and liked clothing in those colors. In this portrait Cassandra Nikolayevna is depicted in a dress of light soft fabric in pale colors, contrary to the fashion of the day, which dictated bright contrasting colors in clothing. Her preference for calm, gentle femininity was retained in her own designs. She used the corporate color Ardanse blue in many of her day and evening ensembles, which were "full of charm and brilliance" according to the critics. Noting the beauty of her designs, they were pleased to see that her fashions were suitable for everyday wear as well.

Shows of the Ardanse collection took place in salons elegantly decorated with flowers, on a small stage with fiery orange velvet curtains. One such collection was called "A Day in the life of a Parisian Woman," featuring a woman wearing Ardanse perfume and clothing set off by hats, furs, and jewels from Agnès, Ostertag, and Heim, "serving as excellent frames for the designs."

Every collection from Ardanse was an event in the world of fashion, as can be seen from the regularly published reports in the authoritative and popular Paris magazine *L'Art et la mode [Art and Fashion]*. There were so many magical, enchanting outfits with exotic or romantic names! For instance, "Amourette" from the collection, made of soft draped black silk jersey with a pleated skirt—a contrast to the dress with the flying collar of snowy organdy. "Fabienne" astonished the imagination of fashion plates with lovely billowing sleeves that revealed the shoulders. It was replaced by a dress of tulle the color of pink champagne ("Petit Sax"), which charmed with its saucy youthfulness. At the waist was a wide belt of taffeta in the same shade, tied in a bow. But the pearl of the collection was "The Last Goddess," an evening dress made of snowy jersey, embroidered with sparkling strass, it seemed to flow over the model's body, creating an incomparably feminine line.

Collection was another design that caught the eye of journalists—"Sister Teresa," a dress of black crepe satin with a snow-white collar "flying up at the slightest breeze and enchanting with its sorrowful charm." The silhouette of "Sister Teresa" was clearly built on the memories of the nursing uniform worn by the baroness in Petrograd during World War I, probably not without a hint of coquettishness. The personal experiences of the creator of Ardanse were reflected in many of the house's designs. Following in the footsteps of Jeanne Lanvin, Ardanse had a specialty clothing line for girls and young women. "It is impossible to resist the dresses for young ladies from Ardanse. There is nothing more adorable than 'My First Dance' of foaming champagne tulle, so appropriate for our seventeen-year-olds, to be shown with the design 'My First Doll,' a miracle in miniature of taffeta the color of blue porcelain, modeled by a delightful eight-year-old. Both designs were joyfully received." Ardanse had many orders for these dresses as their wealthy clientele was always looking for sweet presents to give to their daughters.

The house of Ardanse survived the economic collapse and, even during the most difficult post-crisis seasons continued to show designs ornamented with precious stones and lace, reacting only slightly to the new economic reality. The reason for the long life of Ardanse was that it never oriented itself to the American market, as had Irfe, Yteb, Bery, and Ymedy. Ardanse was more oriented to the traditional Paris haute-couture market, and its clients were frequently ladies of wealth and family, of the same age as Baroness Accourti.

An interesting description of an Ardanse collection is dated February: "This young house, which is being spoken about more and more frequently today showed a complete collection of original beach pajamas, distinguished by excellent taste. Ardanse also has very beautiful evening gowns, which resonate with the aristocratic being of its creator. Herself a woman of society, she works primarily for society ladies who are capable of appreciating the subtleties of her taste.

"Among the spring outfits for women, who are used to being distinguished by their elegance, is the 'Trilby' dress with Scottish skirt. The 'Chiberthe' in light blue with dark blue sheen, which we have come to love and which is now called 'Ardanse,' consists of a bolero with a flirtatious lacy trim reminiscent of Madeira embroidery. Since the elegant clients of this select house are not yet feeling a financial pinch, Ardanse practically tosses over its evening designs charming cloaks, pelerines, or wavy boleros of muslin, covering the arms and decollete. We hail these new models of elegance, which allow one to head off straight from tea to dinner or the theater, removing if one wants only the airy, intangible veil through which the whiteness of skin glows tenderly. Ardanse has come up with many innovations, and its sense of total harmony is such that the chosen ones say that they make appointments with the refined mistress of the artistic studio so that she can study their figure and create an absolutely individual look for them."

Let us note that it was rare for there to be such a detailed review in the pages of the respected magazine *L'Art et la mode* of a collection of a fashion house established by Russian emigres. From the descriptions it is clear that Baroness Accourti created first and foremost for herself, that is, she trusted her feminine intuition and knowledge of society. The designs for the collection were more practical than before, which is a vivid demonstration of her sense of the times and of the attention she paid to the shifts in the fashion market. In that sense the work of Baroness Accourti deserves the highest praise. Without yielding to the theatricality and decorativeness typical of Russian creators of fashion, she used only the most noble fabrics and had a clear preference for transparent materials with a lacy effect—lace, tulle, muslin, and organdy. From season to season she created varied and unified collections that sold well in Paris for many years.

However, the work of Russians in fashion was often resented by French couturiers. To quote the famous fashion designer, Jean Patou: "Take the Russians, for instance. Their artists had a strong influence on our theater costumes, especially in color and embroidery, but I can't remember if I've ever heard of a great Russian fashion designer."

Some other Russian houses, but was handled professionally and methodically. Collections were prepared and shown regularly and were widely reviewed in the press. Madame de Mirecour, the reviewer from L'Art et la mode, wrote about the collection shown: "In that luxurious mansion, drowning in extraordinary flowers, it was hard for us to find a free place on the day of the opening, when beautiful, tall and slender girls presented a well-thoughtout collection.

"I particularly liked 'Rendezvous,' a cloak of fumikasha of Mediterranean blue trimmed in gray karakul, and 'For Tomorrow,' a housedress in a pale green mother-of-pearl, with long sleeves of silk lace that are just right for coquettes.

"'Sèvres Biscuit' is made of almost intangible lace through which the whiteness of skin shows through, and seems to be a design of rare perfection.

"Another dress with the promising name 'I Always Smile' seems to be named appropriately. Made of light blue taffeta, it will ornament our eighteen-year-old daughters. Without a doubt, everyone will smile at the sight of the outfit."

Although Russian style, imbued with decorative elements, went out of style, Ardanse carried nostalgic Russian elements in its collections. Of course, the Baroness Accourti did not introduce Russian folk art in her designs, but her high society style with the sparkle of the St. Petersburg pre-revolutionary splendor retained a delighted memory of Russia. Madame de Mericour wrote: "The ornament of the Ardanse collection is 'Neva Ice,' which consists of a waisted jacket and a slightly A-line skirt out of Russian ermine the color of a white lily. What fashionable woman doesn't dream about this inaccessible ensemble? Let us note that most of the formal afternoon and evening dresses were presented with accessories from Weil jewelers, with whom Baroness Accourti collaborates fruitfully."

A definite advantage of Accourti's house was the presence of permanent models from among the Russian emigre community, slender tall women, brilliant not with noble titles but with stature and beauty. At various times the models at Ardanse included young women from Russian families: Kitty Upornikova, Ksyusha Katkova, Thea Bobrikova, and Nina Tverdaya.

Rapponet—the future star of Schiaparelli during the war years—worked at Ardanse. Ardanse hired a finalist of the Miss Russia contest organized by *Illustrirovannaya Rossiya*. Nina Vasilyevna Egorova, married name Tverdaya, was one of the two runners-up, and her photograph was published in the Paris magazine, which was distributed in all the countries of the Russian diaspora, so that the contest finalists were known from Harbin, China, to New York. They received fan letters and were adored.

Nina Egorova was invited by Boris Evelinov, an organizer of fashion shows, to enter the "Elegance" competition for models that took place on the Côte d'Azur. Baroness Accourti saw her there and took her into her fashion house, where she modeled for several seasons. Nina recalled: "The designs of Ardanse were quite varied. There were many silk dresses with lace in pastel tones. I often showed evening gowns, since I was tall." Another model, Thea Bobrikova, also recalled the house's special predilection for lace trim.

L'Art et la mode wrote on February 20: "In the overflowing lovely mansion, where the celebrated fashion designer set up her Penates, at the impressive staircase decorated with garlands of flowers, gathered famous Parisian women in obedient anticipation of a marvelous festival of beauty. This anticipation was the result and everyone knows this now—of the creations of Baroness Accourti being completely devoid of banality. The refinement of her ensembles lies in the fact that they are harmoniously completed with a flower or a precious necklace from Ostertag. And now she has added yet another charming detail—'runless' stockings manufactured for the first time in an American factory. Ardanse has the monopoly on production in Paris. All these details compete among themselves for most refined. The impression is perfect: exquisiteness combined with enchanting chic. In giving the public this magnificence, Baroness Accourti has selected beautiful young women with marvelous deportment, which is not always simple, to model the designs, and the effect has surpassed expectations.

"Among the evening gowns the most marvelous was 'Mirage' of snowy white muslin and airy laces, which was very popular. It is hard to resist 'Opium Smoke' with long muslin sleeves, falling with smooth softness. Exceptionally fine are 'Gloria' and the mysterious 'Fantaisie d'Ardanse' of black tulle stitched in white. Its clinging sleeves are embroidered from elbow to wrist with diamonds, shimmering, and are trimmed with tulle that floats like a cloud resembling the contorted shapes of Japanese trees.

"In conclusion, yet another discovery a dress of violet pink with a veil attached to the hair with a comb with roses in the same shade. This design, marked with great taste, is cleverly called 'My Second Marriage.'"

The unusual decision to make a wedding dress in violet-lilac tones, and a bold name were repeated in the design 'My Third Marriage, which also delighted Madame de Mirecour: "The recently shown designs from Ardanse had a great success thanks to the ideas of Baroness Accourti. The last special show was intended for connoisseurs and ended with a reception that began at 10 P.M. The brilliant fashion designer appeared in a charming lace dress revealing her marvelous shoulders. The pure lines of the dress may be the fashion of the season.

"This reception for the select was given to mark the success of the House of Ardanse. The interior, decorated with rare blooms, the luxurious repast, and the lively social conversation made the fortunate guests completely forget the time.

"Would you like to hear about some of the 'small miracles' shown there? For instance, 'Desire,' a dress of white muslin trimmed with golden 'mordore' lace; 'Hauteur' — a design of black tulle and velvet with a high waistline, decorated with a snow-white camellia. There was also an ensemble of wool in a blue stripe on ochre, called 'End of April,' with a blouse of ocher crepe de chine.

"There was 'Love of Ardanse' in black tulle. The dress was sewn with white lace on the diagonal, and the pattern resembles thin branches. And Ardanse also presented 'My Third Marriage' a dress of fiery carmine red, whose brightness was dimmed by a short cloak of amethyst crepe de chine.

"Among the original dresses that made us fall in love is 'Joy of Life' of golden yellow muslin with inserts of lace in the same shade and a floating shawl. "In conclusion," wrote Madame de Mirecour, "there was 'Tenderness' of black tulle combined with tulle scarves of various shades of gray with a delicate nuancing of tones. This astonishing dress is simultaneously the most Parisian and the most aristocratic in the world and it astonished everyone."

These descriptions by Madame de Mirecour, the faithful admirer of the talent of the Baroness Accourti, show what an important role tulle played in the designs of the house of Ardanse. Working with this airy material allowed the designer to achieve her favorite effect of transparency and weightlessness. The last delighted report from *L'Art et la mode* is declared in August. Here it is in full:

"Ardanse is distinguished by young girls whose function is to elicit applause. They have sophisticated hairdos. The precious fabrics are so becoming to them. At first we saw modest youthful sports ensembles, then a series of evening gowns. It is impossible not to fall in love with them. They created the reputation of this totally unique house. Here is a black dress with a jacket of 'angel skin' the color of white camellia, trimmed with black karakul, that deserved the bravos it elicited. And here is an emerald green satin, enchantingly beautiful. The design 'Boldness' harmoniously combines lace of a delightful cherry color with airy tulle of the same shade.

"Here is 'Fire and Flame,' a design difficult to describe, for it has so many different shades of the most lovely red tones. They all combine in a eye-pleasing silk drapery. The red tones of Ardanse seem to have been created especially for this dress, since one feels flawless taste in the selected scale of colors. And here is yet another unique color in 'Roxana.' The dress is made from Ophelia tulle, the low waistline is underlined with precious ornamentation in the form of a branch, which gives the design a rare wholeness.

"And so many other designs using inserts of lace, more than can be mentioned! I will stop on just one very beautiful dress, consisting of black tulle skirt and corsage of nymph tulle. This refined ensemble is successfully completed with embroidery along the edge. This is the most exquisite embroidering from the house of Batay and is called Souvenir de Malmaison. It depicts slightly faded roses in mother-of-pearl and pale pink tones. The embroidery added to the charm of the ensemble and did not go unnoticed by the connoisseurs.

This detail is enough to understand that Baroness Accourti, a great artist who heads the House of Ardanse, is not afraid to cooperate with other firms if it is for the greater good."

Ardanse's work with other French and American firms helped solidify the house's reputation. The house's exclusive designs, combined with jewelry and embroidery of the highest class from other houses, achieved enviable success. Ardanse's primary Russian competitor in Paris was Nadine Oblonsky's fashion house, which dressed the British nobility. Another competitor was the house of de Nagornoff, which advertised heavily.

In the February collection an unusual design, wittily named "Wedding in an Airplane" by Baroness Accourti, garnered general accolades. The last mention of this interesting Russian fashion house in Paris was in the May issue of Femina, where an Ardanse design — a summer suit with padded shoulders and raglan sleeves is mentioned along with designs from such famous houses of the postwar period as Hermès, Carven, Jacques Griffe, and Germaine Lecomte.

The press illustrates Ardanse's fidelity to its style: "An Ardanse suit of crepe in the shade of blue sax with raised designs in the shape of landscapes and white people. In front the jacket closes with four large buttons of white and gilt wood. The skirt has deep, wide pleats." As you can see, the Baroness Accourti retained her love for porcelain figurines forever.

The direction chosen by the house of Ardanse was highly valued by the picky Parisian arbiters of fashion, and the mistress of the house had their deserved respect. Ardanse enjoyed a wide range of clientele. "Baroness Accourti," they wrote, "has shown designs that charmed the representatives of the knowing elite. In creating wedding dresses and trousseaus for brides, she uses old family lace with tact. To ornament a cloak she uses rare furs that can be appreciated only by Russians. Thus, gradually, her creations in the highest taste found their way from her house for the elite to big foreign clients, who did not care about price and demanded her work."

Admirers of Ardanse in Paris were not only the aristocrats of the salons, but the famous stars of the Paris stage. Mistinguett, the popular singer who sang of love for princes, bought a famous dress called 'The Only One' for two million francs. The corset belt was made of precious stones by Ostertag jewelers. The skirt of gold lace looked like butterfly wings. The dress astonished connoisseurs with its freshness and lovely lines.

❑❑❑

10

Notable Costume Designers

Introduction

The Costume designer is the person whose responsibility is to design costumes for a film or stage production. He or she is considered part of the "production team," alongside the director, scenic and lighting designers. The costume designer might also collaborate with a hair/wig master or a makeup designer, with the latter two operating on a subordinate level. In European theatre the role is somewhat different as the theatre designer will design both costume and scenic elements.

Costume designers will typically seek to enhance a character's persona, within the framework of the director's vision, through the way that character is dressed. At the same time, the designer must ensure that the designs allow the actor to move in a manner consistent with the historical period and enables the actor to execute the director's blocking of the production without damage to the garments. Additional considerations include the durability and washability of garments, particularly in extended runs. The designer must work in consultation with not only the director, but the set and lighting designers to ensure that the overall design of the production works together. The designer needs to possess strong artistic capabilities as well as a thorough knowledge of pattern development, draping, drafting, textiles and costume/fashion history. Professional costume designers generally fall into three types: freelance, residential, and academic.

- A freelance designer is hired for a specific production by a theatre, dance or opera company, and may or may not actually be local to the theater that he or she is designing for. A freelancer is traditionally paid in three installments: Upon hire, on the delivery of final renderings, and opening night of the production. Freelancers are not obligated to any exclusivity in what projects they are working on, and may be designing for several theatres concurrently.
- A residential designer is hired by a specific theatre, dance or opera company for an extended series of productions. This can be as short as a summer stock contract, or may be for many years. A residential designer's contract may limit the amounts of freelance work they are allowed to accept. Unlike the freelancer, a residential designer is consistently "on location" at the theater, and is readily at hand to work with the costume studio and his or her other collaborators. Residential designers tend to be more established than strict freelancers, but this is not always the case.
- An academic designer is one who holds professorship at a school. The designer is primarily an instructor, but may also act as a residential designer to varying degrees. They are often free to freelance, as their schedule allows. In the past, professors of costume design were mostly experienced professionals that may or may not have had formal post-graduate education, but it has now become increasingly common to require a professor to have at least a Master of Fine Arts in order to teach.

Both residential and academic designers are generally also required to act as Shop Master or Mistress of an onsite costume shop, in addition to designing productions. In a resident theatre, there is almost always a shop staff of stichers, drapers, cutters and craft artisans. In an academic environment the shop "staff" is generally comprised of students, who are learning about costume design and construction. Most universities require costume design students to work a specified number of hours in the shop as part of their course work.

USA is the union that represents costume designers. Although most professional designers are union members, USA has relatively few collective bargaining agreements with theatres when compared with other theatrical unions. However, most major US opera companies do have CBAs with USA. The majority of union contract work for designers is on a project by project basis, not as a part of Collective Bargaining Agreements with theatrical establishments. The notable costume designers are given below:

Theoni V. Aldredge

Theoni V. Aldredge (born Theoni Vachlioti on August 22, 1932 in Athens, Greece) is a renowned costume designer for theatre, film, television, opera, and ballet.

Aldredge received her training at the American School in Athens and at the Goodman Theatre in Chicago. Her first Broadway assignment was designing costumes for Geraldine Page in Tennessee Williams' *Sweet Bird of Youth* in 1959; her most recent was the 2006 revival of *A Chorus Line*. Aldredge won the Oscar and a British Academy Award for her work on *The Great Gatsby* in 1974. Her designs for the film were adapted for a clothing line sold exclusively by Bloomingdale's in Manhattan. In 2002, she won the Theatre Development Fund's Irene Sharaff Lifetime Achievement Award. She is the wife of actor Tom Aldredge.

Broadway Awards and Nominations

- 2001 Tony Award Best Costume Design (*Follies*, nominee)
- 1991 Tony Award Best Costume Design (*The Secret Garden*, nominee)
- 1990 Tony Award Best Costume Design (*Gypsy*, nominee)
- 1984 Tony Award Best Costume Design (*La Cage aux Folles*, winner)
- 1984 Drama Desk Award Outstanding Costume Design (*La Cage aux Folles*, winner)
- 1982 Tony Award Best Costume Design (*Dreamgirls*, nominee)
- 1982 Drama Desk Award Outstanding Costume Design (*Dreamgirls*, nominee)
- 1981 Tony Award Best Costume Design (*42nd Street*, nominee)
- 1981 Drama Desk Award Outstanding Costume Design (*42nd Street*, winner)

- 1981 Drama Desk Award Outstanding Costume Design (*Onward Victoria*, nominee)
- 1980 Tony Award Best Costume Design (*Barnum*, winner)
- 1979 Tony Award Best Costume Design (*Ballroom*, nominee)
- 1979 Drama Desk Award Outstanding Costume Design (*Ballroom*, nominee)
- 1977 Tony Award Best Costume Design (*Annie*, winner)
- 1977 Tony Award Best Costume Design (*Threepenny Opera*, nominee)
- 1977 Drama Desk Award Outstanding Costume Design (*Annie*, winner)
- 1976 Tony Award Best Costume Design (*A Chorus Line*, nominee)
- 1976 Drama Desk Award Outstanding Costume Design (*Trelawny of the Wells*, nominee)
- 1974 Tony Award Best Costume Design (*The Au Pair Man*, nominee)
- 1973 Tony Award Best Costume Design (*Much Ado About Nothing*, nominee)
- 1973 Drama Desk Award Outstanding Costume Design (*Much Ado About Nothing*, winner)
- 1972 Tony Award Best Costume Design (*Two Gentlemen of Verona*, nominee)
- 1972 Drama Desk Award Outstanding Costume Design (*Two Gentlemen of Verona*, winner)
- 1970 Drama Desk Award Outstanding Costume Design (*Peer Gynt*, winner)
- 1961 Tony Award Best Costume Design (*The Devil's Advocate*, nominee)

Bob Mackie

Robert Gordon Mackie (b. March 24, 1940 in Monterey Park, California) is an American fashion designer, best known for his costumes for Cher and for *The Carol Burnett Show*.

Mackie is also known for his exclusive designs of dress for high-priced Barbie dolls. Two of Mackie's best-remembered creations had a humorous element. While working on the "The Carol Burnett Show", he designed a "curtain dress" (complete with a curtain rod across the shoulders) that Carol Burnett wore in the *Went with the Wind* parody. Mackie also designed the garish ensemble worn by Cher at the March 1986 Academy Awards: black stretch pants, a bejeweled loincloth, kneehigh boots, a black chainlink top, and a huge feathered Mohawk headdress that was one and a half times taller than her head. Introduced by Jane Fonda with the words, "Wait'll you see what's gonna come out here," Cher was appearing as a presenter after what many considered an Oscar snub (Cher was not nominated for her performance in *Mask*). "As you can see," said Cher, "I did receive my Academy booklet on how to dress like a serious actress."

Mackie is often called *the sultan of sequins*, or *the rajah of rhinestones* known for his sparkling and imaginative costume designs. He has won seven Emmy Awards for his designs and was thrice nominated for an Academy Award. He attended Pasadena City College and Chouinard Art Institute.

Mackie has said *A woman who wears my clothes is not afraid to be noticed.* Some of the many celebrities who have worn Mackie's outfits include:

- Bernadette Peters
- Dottie West
- Carol Burnett
- Raquel Welch
- Cher
- Mitzi Gaynor
- Joan Collins
- Diahann Carroll
- Judy Garland
- Lucille Ball
- Barbra Streisand (in the film *Funny Lady*)
- Madonna (at the 1991 Academy Awards)
- Diana Ross
- Charo
- Elton John

- Marlene Dietrich
- Oprah Winfrey (at the 1986 Academy Awards)
- Bette Midler
- Tina Turner
- RuPaul
- Pia Zadora
- Whoopi Goldberg (at the 1999 Academy Awards)
- Sharon Stone (in the film *Casino*)
- Brooke Shields (in the film *Brenda Starr*)
- Ann-Margret
- Anjelica Huston (on a 1990 cover of Vanity Fair)
- Barbie
- Bart Simpson - In the episode "Burns' Heir"

Julie Taymor

Julie Taymor (born December 15, 1952) is an American director of Broadway theatre and film. Taymor's work has been received many accolades from critics, and she has won several Tony Awards for her work, noted for its visual flair and colorful costuming choices.

Biography

Born in Newton, Massachusetts, United States, Taymor's interest in theatre took root early in her life. At the age of seven, she was already drawing her sister into stagings of children's stories for her parents. By the age of nine, she became entranced with the Boston Children's Theatre and became involved with them. In high school, she became interested in international travel, and made trips to both Sri Lanka and India with the Experiment in International Living. Being the youngest member of theatre groups became common, as she joined Julie Portman's Theatre Workshop of Boston at the age of 15. Yearning for a more in depth approach to her work, Taymor went to Paris to study with L'Ecole de Mime Jacques Lecoq. During her studies there, she became exposed to mime which helped in the development of her physical sensibilities.

Although in 1970 Taymor enrolled in Oberlin College in Ohio, she sought experience with Joseph Chaikin's Open Theatre and other companies and studied through correspondence. Hearing that director Herbert Blau would be moving to Ohio, she returned there and auditioned successfully, becoming, once again, the youngest member of a troupe. In 1973 Taymor attended a summer program of the American Society for Eastern Arts in Seattle. The instructors were performers of Indonesian topeng masked dance-drama and wayang kulit shadow puppetry. This would prove to have a great effect on Taymor in later years. Taymor graduated from Oberlin College, with a major in mythology and folklore, in 1974. After her college years, Taymor went on to study pre-Bunraku puppetry on the island of Awaji, Japan in order to learn more about experimental theatre, puppetry, and visually oriented theatre.

Achievements

Taymor's greatest acclaim as a director for the stage has come from the popular musical *The Lion King*, a 1997 adaptation of the animated film of that name. Taymor received two Tony Awards for her work on *The Lion King*, one for Direction and one for Costume Design, making her the first woman to receive a Tony award for directing a musical.

Taymor has transitioned from stage to screen in recent years, directing the films *Titus* in 1999 (an adaptation of the play *Titus Andronicus* by William Shakespeare) and *Frida* in 2002 (a movie based on the life of artist Frida Kahlo). Both movies received positive reviews for their stylish filming: *Frida* was the more acclaimed of the two, garnering six Academy Award nominations and winning in two of the six categories (Best Makeup and Best Original Score).

In 2006, Taymor completed production of her latest film, a musical set in the 1960s entitled *Across The Universe*, starring Jim Sturgess and Evan Rachel Wood. The premiere date is scheduled for September 2007. For the Metropolitan Opera during the 2005/2006 season, Taymor directed a successful production of *The Magic Flute*. It was revised for the 2006/2007 season and, in addition to full-length performances, was adapted for a 100-minute version over the Holiday season to appeal to children. That version of the opera was the first of a series of NCM Fathom *Live on the Big Screen* presentations of MET operas downloaded via satellite to movie theatres across North America and parts of Europe for the 2006/2007 season.

Also, for the Los Angeles Opera, Taymor directed the opera *Grendel* which was presented on June 1, 2006. The opera was also part of the Summer 2006 Lincoln Center Festival in New York City.

Ann Roth

Ann Roth (born October 30, 1931 in Hanover, Pennsylvania) is a prolific Academy Award-winning American costume designer for films and theater.

She won a Best Costume Oscar for the film *The English Patient* and was nominated for *Places in the Heart, The Talented Mr. Ripley,* and *The Hours.* Her more than one hundred screen credits include *Midnight Cowboy, Klute, The Day of the Locust* (for which she won a BAFTA), *Working Girl, Silkwood, The Unbearable Lightness of Being, The Mambo Kings, The Birdcage, Primary Colors, Cold Mountain, Closer, Freedomland,* and *The Good Shepherd.*

Her dozens of stage credits include *The Odd Couple, The Star-Spangled Girl, Purlie, Seesaw, They're Playing Our Song, The Best Little Whorehouse in Texas , Biloxi Blues,* and *Butley.*

Roth is a two-time Emmy Award nominee for the miniseries *Roanoak* (1986) and *Angels in America.* In 2000, the Theatre Development Fund honored Roth with the Irene Sharaff Award for Lifetime Achievement.

Santo Loquasto

Santo Loquasto, born 26 July 1944 in Wilkes-Barre, Pennsylvania, is a production designer, scenic designer and costume designer for theatre, musical theatre, film and more rarely television, as for *Don Quixote (ballet), Don't Drink the Water, Fosse* (for *Great Performances: Dance in America)* and *TriBeCa.*

Santo Loquasto has been nominated several times for Tony Awards and has so far won three:

- Tony Award for Best Costume Design

  1977: *The Cherry Orchard,* in a tie with Theoni V. Aldredge for *Annie.*

  1990: *Grand Hotel: The Musical.*

- Tony Award for Best Scenic Design

  1989: *Cafe Crown.*

Loquasto has been a production designer for many Woody Allen films. He has a B.A. in English literature from King's College, Pennsylvania.

Ann Curtis

Ann Curtis is an Olympic Gold Medal winner and native San Franciscan. She was coached by Charlie Sava and was a member of the San Francisco Crystal Plunge team. Curtis participated in London's 1948 Olympic Games winning a gold medal in the 400 meter freestyle competition. Her second gold was won as a member of the woman's freestyle relay team when she came from behind to win the event. In addition to her gold medal wins, she also won the silver medal in the 100 meter freestyle. In 1944, at age 18, Curtis received the coveted James E. Sullivan Memorial Award. She was inducted into the Bay Area Sports Hall of Fame in 1983.

William Ivey Long

William Ivey Long is an American 5-time Tony Award-winning costume designer for mainly Broadway plays and musicals including his most notable work on The Producers, Hairspray, Nine, Crazy for You and his newest Tony-winning work on Grey Gardens. He is also currently working on the newest Mel Brooks' musical Young Frankenstein.

Early Life and Education

He was born in 1947 to William Ivey Long, Sr. a Winthrop University professor, and stage director, and his wife Mary, who was a high school theatre teacher, actress and playwright. His father was the founder of the Winthrop University theatre department. William grew up in Rock Hill, South Carolina and has two younger siblings, a brother Robert who is a theatre architect and a sister Laura who is also involved in numerous theatre activities. Upon graduation from high school Long attended the College of William and Mary where he studied history and graduated in 1969. He then attended the University of North Carolina at Chapel Hill to pursue a Ph.D. in art history. While at this university he met visiting professor Betty Smith who suggested he apply to the design program at Yale University. Upon his acceptance to Yale he left the Ph.D. program at UNC and began to study set design at the Yale School of Drama. It was here that he met Sigourney Weaver (his roommate at the time), Wendy Wasserstein, Meryl Streep, Christopher Durang, and Paul Rudnick, who were all also students at the university. While at Yale he studied under designer Ming Cho Lee, whom he has credited with being a major influence on his work.

Professional Career

Upon his graduation from Yale in 1975, he made the move to New York City where he worked for couturier Charles James as an unpaid apprentice until James's death in 1978. After a few months of selling dolls a friend of his from Yale, Karen Schulz, who was the set designer for a revival of Nikolai Gogol's *The Inspector General*, suggested that Long be hired to do costume designs for the show, this was Long's first Broadway production. Since then he has celebrated being the costume designer for over 50 different Broadway shows. *A Streetcar named Desire* marked his landmark 50th. He currently has four shows running on Broadway: *Grey Gardens; Curtains; John Water's* Hairspray; *and* Chicago. *He has been nominated for ten Tony Awards, winning five (for* Nine, Crazy for You, The Producers, Hairspray, *and* Grey Gardens*). He has also won the Drama Desk Award for outstanding costume design for* Hairspray, The Producers, Guys and Dolls, Lend Me a Tenor, *and* Nine.

In 2000 Long was chosen by the National Theatre Conference as its "Person of the Year" and was honored with the "Legend of Fashion" Award by the Art Institute of Chicago in 2003. Most recently he was inducted into the Theater Hall of Fame in January of 2006.

He remains active in many local activities throughout the state of North Carolina including working with Paul Green's The Lost Colony Outdoor Drama in Manteo, North Carolina which he and his family have been a part of since he was a young child.

Works

Broadway

Long has designed for over fifty Broadway productions, including:

- *The Inspector General* - 1978
- *The 1940's Radio Hour* - 1979
- *Passione* - 1980
- *MasS Appeal* - 1981
- *Nine* - 1982
- *The Tap Dance Kid* - 1983

- *Play Memory* - 1984
- *End of the World* - 1984
- *Smile* - 1986
- *Sleight of Hand* - 1987
- *Mail* - 1988
- *EasTern Seaboard* - 1989
- *Lend Me a Tenor* - 1989
- *Welcome to the Club* - 1989
- *Six Degrees of Separation* - 1990
- *The Homecoming* - 1991
- *Crazy for You* - 1992
- *Private Lives* - 1992
- *Guys and Dolls* - 1992
- *Laughter on the 23rd Floor* - 1993
- *Picnic* - 1994
- *Smokey Joe's Cafe* - 1995
- *Company* - 1995
- *Big* - 1996
- *Chicago* - 1996
- *Steel Pier* - 1997
- *King David* - 1997
- *1776* - 1997
- *Cabaret* - 1998
- *Annie Get Your Gun* - 1999
- *The Civil War* - 1999
- *Epic Proportions* - 1999
- *Swing!* - 1999
- *Contact* - 2000
- *The Music Man* - 2000
- *The Man Who Came to Dinner* - 2000
- *Seussical* - 2000
- *The Producers* - 2001
- *Thou Shalt Not* - 2001
- *45 Seconds From Broadway* - 2001

- *Hairspray* - 2002
- *Little Shop of Horrors* - 2003
- *The Boy From Oz* - 2003
- *Never Gonna Dance* - 2003
- *Twentieth Century* - 2004
- *The Frogs* - 2004
- *La Cage aux Folles* - 2004
- *A Streetcar Named Desire* - 2005
- *Sweet Charity* - 2005
- *The Caine Mutiny Court-Martial* - 2006
- *Grey Gardens* - 2006
- *Princesses - 2006*

He has also designed for the following non-Broadway productions

- *Me Jack, You Jill* - 1976
- *Face Value* - 1990

Off-Broadway

- *Two Small Bodies*
- *Conjuring an Event*
- *The Vienna Notes*
- *Mass Appeal*
- *Passione*
- *True West*
- *Hunting Scenes from Lower Bavaria*
- *Sister Mary Ignatius Explains It All for You* and *The Actor's Nightmare*
- *Twelve Dreams*
- *Poor Little Lambs*
- *American Passion*
- *The Lady and the Clarinet*
- *Hey, Ma...Kaye Ballard*
- *After the Fall*
- *The Marriage of Bette and Boo*
- *Hamlet*

- *Principia Scriptoriae*
- *Wenceslas Square*
- *Italian American Reconciliation*
- *Eleemosynary*
- *Assassins*
- *The Food Chain*
- *Splendora*
- *Tovah: Out of Her Mind*
- *The Mystery of Irma Vep*
- *La Terrasse*
- *Contact*
- *Godspell*
- *The Syringa Tree*
- *A Bad Friend*
- *Valhalla*
- *Grey Gardens*

Long has designed for five films, namely:

- *Life with Mikey* - 1993
- *The Cutting Edge* - 1992
- *Curtain Call* - 1999
- *Chop Suey* - 2001
- *The Producers - 2005*

And for television:

- *Ask Me Again* - 1989
- *Crazy for You* - 1999
- *The Man Who Came to Dinner* - 2000

Long has also costumed for Siegfried & Roy at the Mirage Hotel, Leonard Bernstein's operas *A Quiet Place* and *Trouble in Tahiti*, and ballets at the New York City Ballet for Peter Martins, Paul Taylor and Twyla Tharp.

Gregory Gale

Gregory Gale is a New York-based costume designer. Gale is a graduate of the Fashion Institute of Technology and is well known for his character-driven designs. In 2007 Gale won the Lucille Lortel Award for Outstanding Costume Design for his work on *The Voysey Inheritance*. He was also nominated that same year for his work on *The Milliner*.

Works

Gale has designed for numerous Broadway and Off-Broadway productions. Some of the most notable are:

Broadway

- *The Wedding Singer (musical)* - Al Hirschfeld Theater (2006) Drama Desk Nomination
- *Urinetown* - Henry Miller's Theater (2001 - 2004) Lucille Lortel Nomination
- *Band In Berlin* - Helen Hayes Theater (1999)

Off-Broadway

- *The Voysey Inheritance* - Atlantic Theater (2006-2007) Lucille Lortel Award
- *The Milliner* - CSC Theater (2006) Lucille Lortel Nomination
- *Pig Farm* - Roundabout Theater Company, Laura Pels Theater (2006)

Colleen Atwood

Colleen Atwood (born 1948, Quincy, Washington) Upper Education: Cornish College of The Arts, Seattle Washington and then New York University School of Film N.Y, N.Y., is an Academy Award-winning costume designer. Colleen has been nominated for an Academy Award numerous times and won Academy Awards for the movies "Chicago" in 2002 and "Memoirs of a Geisha" in 2006. Colleen has collaborated several times with directors Tim Burton and Jonathan Demme. Beginning her career as a fashion advisor in Washington State in the early 1970's, Colleen eventually ventured into the world of costume design for play's and film initially coming to fame through her work on Sting's *Bring on the Night* World Tour.

Colleen has been partially involved in developing or has been the lead designer for producing the costumes on over 50 films to date. Colleen is also the lead costume designer for all of the new costumes created for Ringling Bros, Barnum Balley Circus in 2005-

2006. She has also recently designed the new uniforms for the band My Chemical Romance. As a designer of costumes that take people off into the imaginary world of film by portraying the visual ideas of the costumes for the time period a particular film represents. Colleen's genius in expressing herself through her art form continuously reveals the multi-talented abilities of one the great costume designers of this era in film.

Cecil Beaton

Sir Cecil Walter Hardy Beaton (January 14, 1904 – January 18, 1980) was an English fashion and portrait photographer and a stage and costume designer for films and the theatre.

Biography

Born in Hampstead to a society family, Beaton was fascinated by the society magazines and the images within. Educated at Harrow, when he was age 11 Beaton's grandmother bought him a Kodak 3A Camera, a popular model which was renowned for being an ideal piece of equipment to learn on. Beaton began to teach himself the basics of photography and would often get his sisters and mother to sit for him. When he was sufficiently proficient, he would send the photos off to London society magazines, often writing under a pen name and 'recommending' the work of Beaton.

Despite having little or no interest in academia, Beaton moved on to St John's College, Cambridge, and studied history, art and architecture. Beaton continued his photography, and through his university contacts managed to get a portrait sitting with the Duchess of Amalfi actually George "Dadie" Rylands, and as Beaton recalled years later: *"It was a slightly out-of-focus snapshot of him as Webster's Duchess of Malfi standing in the sub-aqueous light outside the men's lavatory of the ADC Theatre at Cambridge."* The resulting images gave Beaton his first ever piece of published work when Vogue magazine bought and printed the photos. Beaton left Cambridge without a degree in 1925, but only coped with salaried employment in his father's timber business for eight days.

Photography

Beaton designed book jackets and costumes for charity matinees, learning the professional craft of photography at the studio of Paul Tanqueray, until Vogue took him on regularly in 1927. He also set up his own studio, and one of his earliest clients and, later, best friends was Stephen Tennant; Beaton's photographs of Tennant and his circle are considered some of the best representations of the "Bright Young Things" of the twenties and thirties.

He was already taking photographs for the British edition of Vogue in 1931 when George Hoyningen-Huene, who was a photographer for the French Vogue traveled to England with his new friend Horst. Horst himself would begin to work for French Vogue in November of that year. The exchange and cross pollination of ideas between this collegial circle of artists across the Channel and the Atlantic gave rise to the look of style and sophistication for which the 1930s are known.

Beaton is best known for his fashion photographs and society portraits. He worked as a staff photographer for *Vanity Fair* and *Vogue* in addition to photographing celebrities in Hollywood.

Beaton's first camera was a Kodak 3A folding camera. Over the course of his career, he employed both large format cameras, and smaller Rolleiflex cameras. Beaton was never known as a highly skilled technical photographer, and instead focused on staging a compelling model or scene and looking for the perfect shutter-release moment.

Beaton often photographed the Royal Family for official publication. Queen Elizabeth, the Queen Mother was his favourite Royal sitter, and he once pocketed her scented hankie as a keepsake from a highly successful shoot. Beaton took the famous wedding pictures of the Duke and Duchess of Windsor (wearing an ensemble by the noted fashion designer Mainbocher).

During the Second World War, Beaton was initially posted to the Ministry of Information and given the task of recording images from the home front. During this assignment he captured one of the most enduring images of British suffering during the war, that of three-year-old Blitz victim Eileen Dunne recovering in hospital, clutching her beloved teddy bear. When the image was published, America had not yet officially joined the war but splashed across the press in the USA, images such as Beaton's helped push the American public to put pressure on their Government to help Britain in its hour of need.

Beaton had a major influence on and relationship with two other leading lights in British photography, that of Angus McBean and David Bailey. McBean was arguably the best portrait photographer of his era in the second part of McBeans career (post war) his work is clearly heavily influenced by Beaton, though arguably McBean was technically far more proficient in his execution. Bailey was also enormously influenced by Beaton when they met whilst working for British Vogue in the early 1960s, Bailey's stark use of square format (6x6) images bears clear connections to Beatons own working patterns.

Stage and Film Design

After the war, Beaton tackled the Broadway stage, designing sets, costumes, and lighting for a 1946 revival of *Lady Windermere's Fan*, in which he also acted. His most lauded achievement for the stage was the sets and costumes for Lerner and Loewe's *My Fair Lady* (1956), which led to two Lerner and Loewe film musicals, *Gigi* (1958) and *My Fair Lady* (1964), both of which earned Beaton the Academy Award for Costume Design.

Additional Broadway credits include *The Grass Harp* (1952), *The Chalk Garden* (1955), *Saratoga* (1959), *Tenderloin* (1960), and *Coco* (1969). He is the winner of four Tony Awards.

Later Life

In 1972, he received his knighthood, but suffered a major stroke two years later. It took several months of recovery before he realised one side of his body would be permanently paralysed. Although he learnt to write and draw with his left hand, as well as having all his cameras adapted, Beaton became frustrated by the new limitations the stroke had put upon his work.

As a result of his stroke, Beaton became anxious about financial security for his old age and, in 1976, entered into negotiations with Philippe Garner, expert-in-charge of photographs at Sotheby's. On behalf of the auction house, Garner acquired Beaton's archive excluding all portraits of the Royal Family, and the five decades of prints held by Vogue in London, Paris and New York. Garner, who had almost singlehandedly invented the photographic auction, oversaw the archive's preservation and partial dispersal, so that Beaton's only tangible assets, and what he considered his life's work, would ensure him an annual income. The first of five auctions was held in 1977, the last in 1980. By the end of the 1970s, Beaton's health had faded to that of an old man. In January 1980, he died during the night at his grand home in Broadchalke in Wiltshire.

Personal life

Though primarily homosexual the great love of his life was the wealthy art collector Peter Watson he did have relationships with women, including the actress Greta Garbo and socialite Doris Castlerosse. He claimed that his heterosexual virginity was taken by American socialite Marjorie Oelrichs. Beaton also claimed to have had an affair with the American actor Gary Cooper, who was a close friend of his for many years.

Portfolio of Works

Notable Photographs

- *Elizabeth II's Coronation,* 1953.
- *Audrey Hepburn,* 1964.
- *Bomb Victim,* 1940.
- *Dame Edith Sitwell,* 1956.

Books

- *Ashcombe The Story of a Fifteen-Year Lease,*1949
- *Persona Grata,* 1953.
- *Indian Diary and Album*
- *The glass of fashion*
- *My Bolivian aunt: a memoir*
- *My royal past*
- *Chinese Diary and Album*
- *Japanese*
- *Ballet*
- *Portrait of New York*
- *Self-portrait with friends : the selected diaries of Cecil Beaton 1926-1974.*
- *The wandering years; diaries, 1922-1939.*
- *The years between; diaries 1939-44.*
- *The strenuous years, diaries 1948-55.*
- *The restless years : diaries, 1955-63.*
- *The parting years : diaries, 1963-74.*
- *The Unexpurgated Beaton: The Cecil Beaton Diaries as He Wrote Them, 1970-1980.*
- *Beaton in the Sixties: The Cecil Beaton Diaries as He Wrote Them, 1965-1969*

- *Cecil Beaton's 'Fair Lady'*, (1966) (diary excerpts and costume sketches)
- *The face of the world : an international scrapbook of people and places.*
- *I take great pleasure.*
- *Quail in Aspic: the life story of Count Charles Korsetz*

❑❑❑

BIBLIOGRAPHY

APPELBAUM STANLEY, and CAMNER JAMES. Stars of the American Musical Theatre in Historic Photographs. New York: Dover, 1981.

ASCAP. Hit Songs. New York: ASCAP, 1977. (Year-by-year listings of great songs, 1914- 1976).

BOND FREDERICK W. The Negro and the Drama. Washington, D.C.: Associated Publishers, 1940.

BORDMAN GERALD. American Musical Comedy. New York: Oxford University Press, 1982.

BURRIS-MEYER, HAROLD, and COLE, EDWARD C. Theatres and Auditoriums. 2d ed. New York: Reinhold Publishing Corp., 1964.

CHINDAHL GEORGE L. *A History of the Circus in America*. Caldwell, Idaho: Caxton, 1959.

CHURCHILL ALLEN. *The Great White Way*. New York: E. P. Dutton, 1962. (The story of Broadway.)

CLARK JOHN R., and MORRIS WILLIAM E. "Scherzo, Forte, and Bravura: Satire in American Musical Theatre." *Journal of Popular Culture* 12, no. 3 (Winter 1978): 459-81.

COGSWELL, MARGARET, ed. The Ideal Theatre: Eight Concepts. New York: The American Federation of Arts, 1962.

DE AGNES MILLE. America Dances. New York: Macmillan, 1980.

DEER HARRIET, and DEER IRVING. "Musical Comedy: From Performer to Performance." *Journal of Popular Culture* 12, no. 3 (Winter 1978): 406-42.

EELLS GEORGE. *The Life That Late He Led; a Biography of Cole Porter*. New York: G. P. Putnam's Sons, 1967.

EMERY LYNNE PAULEY. *Black Dance in the United States from 1619 to 1970*. Palo Alto, Calif.: National Press Books, 1972.

ENGEL LEHMAN. The American Musical Theatre. A Consideration. New York: CBS Legacy, 1975.

FARNSWORTH MARJORIE. The Ziegfeld Follies. New York: Bonanza Books, 1956.

FIELD JAMES J. The Book of World Famous Music. New York: Crown, 1966.

FRANKEL AARON. Writing the Broadway Musical. New York: Drama Book Specialists, 1977.

GILBERT DOUGLAS. *American Vaudeville. Its Life & Times*. 1940. Reprint. New York: Dover, 1963.

GOINES MARGARETTA Bodo. "African Retentions in the Dance of the Americas." *Dance Research Monograph One*, 1971- 1972. New York: Committee on Research in Dance, 1972, pp. 207-29.

GORELIK, MORDECAI. New Theatres for Old. New York: Samuel French, 1955.

GOTTFRIED MARTIN. Broadway Musicals. New York: Harry N. Abrams, 1979. (With good illustrations, in color and black-and-white.)

HART DOROTHY. *Thou Swell, Thou Witty: The Life and Lyrics of Lorenz Hart*. New York: Harper & Row, 1976.

HODGES, C. WALTER. The Globe Restored. New York: Coward-McCann, Inc., 1954.

HOWARD JOHN TASKER. *Stephen Foster: America's Troubadour*. New York: Tudor, 1945.

HUBLER RICHARD. *The Cole Porter Story*. New York: World, 1965.

HUGHES LANGSTON, and MELTZER MILTON. *Black Magic!* Englewood Cliffs, N.J.: Prentice-Hall, 1967. (A pictorial history of the Negro in American entertainment.)

JOHNSON JAMES WELDON. *Black Manhattan*. New York: Alfred A. Knopf, 1930.

KATKOV NORMAN. *The Fabulous Fanny*. New York: Knopf, 1953.

KIMBALL ROBERT, and GILL BRENDAN. *Cole*. New York: Holt, Rinehart & Winston, 1971.

LAUFE ABE. *Broadway's Greatest Musicals*. New York: Funk & Wagnalls, 1977. (Focuses on productions that have run over 500 performances.)

LEWINE RICHARD; LEWINE SIMON; and LEWINE ALFRED. *Encyclopedia of Theatre Music*. New York: Random House, 1961.

MCCABE, JOHN. GEORGE M. *Cohan: The Man Who Owned Broadway*. New York: Doubleday, 1973.

MCSPADDEN J. WALKER. *Operas and Musical Comedies*. New York: Thomas Y. Crowell, 1946.

NICOLL, ALLARDYCE. The Development of the Theatre. 5th ed. London: Harrap & Co., Ltd., 1966.

PARKER DEREK, and PARKER JULIA. *The Natural History of the Chorus Girl*. Indianapolis: Bobbs-Merrill, 1975.

PASKMAN DAILEY. "Gentlemen, Be Seated". *A Parade of the American Minstrels*. Rev. ed. New York: Clarkson N. Potter, 1976.

SHAPIRO NAT. *Popular Music*. New York: Adrian, 1964- 1973. (Annual annotated index to music.)

SMITH CECIL, and LITTON GLENN. *Musical Comedy in America*. New York: Theatre Arts Books, 1981.

SOBEL BERNARD. *The New Theatre Handbook and Digest of Plays*. New York: Crown, 1959.

SOUTHERN, RICHARD. The Open Stage. New York: Theatre Arts Books, 1959.

STEARNS MARSHALL, and Stearns Jean. *Jazz Dance: The Story of American Vernacular Dance*. New York: Macmillan, 1968.

STOTT WILIAM, and STOTT JANE. *On Broadway. Dan Danciger Publishing Series*. Austin, Tex.: University of Texas Press, 1978. (Performance photographs by Fred Fehl, arranged chronologically, including previously unpublished interviews with Broadway personalities.)

TAUBMAN HOWARD. *The Making of the American Theatre*. New York: Coward McCann, 1967. (A history from colonial times.)

TAYLOR DEEMS. *Dome Enchanted Evenings*. New York: Harper & Brothers, 1953.

TODD ARTHUR. "Four Centuries of American Dance: Negro American Theatre Dance, 1849-1900." *Dance Magazine,* November 1950, pp. 20-21, 33-34.

TOLL ROBERT C. *Blacking Up: The Minstrel Show in Nineteenth-Century America.* London: Oxford University Press, 1974.

WILDER ALEC, and MAHER JAMES T. American Popular Song. New York: Oxford University Press, 1972. (Analysis of works of the great innovators.)

WILK MAX. *They're Playing Our Song.* New York: Atheneum, 1973. (Interviews with twenty-two composers and songwriters.)

Winter Marian Hannah. "Juba and American Minstrelsy." *Dance Index 6,* no. 2 (February 1947): 28-49.

ZEIDMAN IRVING. *The American Burlesque Show.* New York: Hawthorn, 1967.

ZOLOTOV MAURICE. *No People Like Show People.* New York: Random House, 1951.

INDEX